helping
YOUTH
interpret the
BIBLE

▪ *A TEACHING RESOURCE*

A. Roger Gobbel
Gertrude G. Gobbel
Thomas E. Ridenhour, Sr.

John Knox Press
ATLANTA

Library of Congress Cataloging in Publication Data

Gobbel, A. Roger, 1926–
 Helping youth interpret the Bible.

 Bibliography: p.
 1. Bible—Hermeneutics. 2. Bible—Study.
3. Youth—Religious life. I. Gobbel, Gertrude G.
(Gertrude Gustafson), 1928–   . II. Ridenhour,
Thomas E. (Thomas Eugene), 1937–   . III. Title.
BS476.G63   1984   220.6'01   84-3916
ISBN 0-8042-1580-4

© copyright John Knox Press 1984
10 9 8 7 6 5 4 3 2 1
Printed in the United States of America
John Knox Press
Atlanta, Georgia 30365

To
Karl, Karin, Kristin
and
Tom, Mary Beth, Bill

preface

This book is one response to the frequent complaint, "Our youth will not study the Bible. They do not want anything to do with it." We are convinced, however, that adolescent young people will enter into a serious engagement with the Bible and will join with us in the adventure of interpreting and being interpreted by the Bible.

We have not produced a curriculum for the study of the Bible. Rather, we have set forth a model or an approach for interpreting the Bible with adolescents. As readers utilize this approach with its accompanying expressions, we expect and hope that they will further develop and refine it for use with particular texts in particular situations marked by specific concerns.

We are firm in our conviction that adolescents should have the opportunity to engage biblical texts directly, as they are able. They do not need to hear first what others have to say about a text. They will resist, and rightly so, attempts to impose predetermined interpretations upon them. They need first to encounter directly the biblical witness, to ask questions of it, to pose possible interpretations and test them, and then to be questioned and challenged.

The "as they are able" will be determined by various abilities possessed, by range of experiences, by already held understandings, and by life-content. Thus, not all youth of the same age can engage the task of interpreting the Bible with the same clarity of thought, the same perceptions, and the same abilities. At any given time and with any given text, we can expect a diversity of interpretations. For that diversity we will rejoice and give thanks. If we can but introduce and initiate adolescents into learning a larger task of interpreting than was possible for them as children, we shall have served them well.

When young people engage the Bible, they do not do so in a vacuum. They bring their abilities, experiences, understandings, and life-content—including their present struggles. What they bring to the text not only influences how they engage the task of interpreting but also influences the resulting interpretations themselves. As they move from childhood to adulthood, adolescents experience a number of process changes. They encounter developmental tasks which require the beginning of some resolutions, that demand their time, energy, and attention. An engagement with the Bible which is isolated from those process changes and tasks will not command the attention and interest of maturing youngsters. For adolescents an engagement with the Bible must be a dynamic interaction between life-content and biblical witness. Thus the question: "In what ways might the Bible inform and shape the responses of youth to their life tasks and to the demands of the process changes in their lives?"

We have chosen for consideration in this book six developmental tasks which confront adolescent youth at some point. These tasks can be separated from each other only for the purpose of discussion. In reality, the various life tasks and process changes interact with and influence each other. We have cast the developmental tasks into six questions which adolescent young persons ask. And about each question we have asked: "How might the Bible assist adolescents to move toward adequate, useful, and appropriate responses to those questions?" As we have moved back and forth between the life-content of youth and biblical text, we have endeavored to describe an approach for engaging adolescents in a larger work of interpreting and being interpreted by the Bible. We have endeavored to describe an approach that is an ongoing and dynamic interaction between adolescents and the Bible, between their life-content and the biblical witness, an interaction which has no completion but which calls members of the household of faith to ever new and marvelous understandings of who they are as God's people.

This book is designed to encourage and assist pastors, ministers of education, teachers, and parents working with youth. The exercises and directions suggested here should not be imposed summarily on any group of young persons. The exercises should be regarded as models, though not perfect for all occasions. Thus, they will need to be "translated" for use in any given group, responding to particular situations.

While there are no extensive biblical quotes in this book it should be noted that biblical words and phrases used reflect the Revised Standard Version of the Bible.

To Mary C. Miller we express our gratitude. With patience and haste, she has typed the manuscript through its several versions.

A. Roger Gobbel
Gertrude G. Gobbel
Thomas E. Ridenhour, Sr.
Gettysburg, Pennsylvania

contents

Part Two: *Doing the Task*

PART ONE

understanding the task

·1
Introduction

This book is about helping youth to learn an ongoing task of interpreting the Bible. The period of adolescence affords the church a unique opportunity to introduce, initiate, and aid teenagers in a larger task of interpreting the Bible than was possible for them as children. If we can but *introduce* and *initiate* our Christian youth into that larger work, we shall have served them well.

Our focus here is but one of many legitimate concerns of the church in Christian education with adolescents. A multifaceted youth ministry is affirmed. Our youth must deal with several contents of the faith, including the Bible. However, we claim for the Bible a place of primacy and cruciality. This book describes and sets forth an approach which can aid the church to do its work in a very particular area—that of helping adolescents learning an ongoing task of interpreting the Bible.

Our work as pastors, teachers, and parents is done within the broader context of Christian education. Christian education is for Christians. It is to encourage, assist, and enable them to interpret, order, and construct their lives under the event of Jesus. It assists Christians to be, do, and become who they already are—members of the household of faith.

As Christians we are a pilgrim people ever on the way of becoming who we are. Aid along our pilgrim way comes from a diversity of sources. The Scriptures provide the critical and necessary data for Christians to interpret, order, and construct their lives.

Christian education occurs within the context of human existence and development. In the large arena of human existence all persons participate in a continuing activity of interpreting, ordering, and constructing their lives. They endeavor to make sense of and give meaning to their lives and the world.

At any point in human development, all individuals are subject to both possibilities and limitations in cognitive, affective, motivational, and social realms. They are the recipients of a range of particular experiences. At any point they have already created their own values, commitments, understandings, and meanings. All of these variables interact, working together to influence and to give shape to the continuing activity of interpreting, ordering, and constructing. A task of Christian education is to bring "particular" data and experiences to bear upon the lives of Christian people as they engage in that continuing activity. These data and experiences challenge and enable persons to construct their lives under the event of Jesus.

Our work as pastors, teachers, and parents of youth is difficult and complex. There are no short-cuts. There are no easy, simple methods or materials. If we determine to engage adolescent young persons in learning the ongoing task of interpreting the Bible, we must perceive and accept our work in all its complexity and difficulty. It demands our time, energy, patience, and best thinking. And above all, we enter an exciting, always surprising adventure with young Christians in the household of faith.

What Shall We Do with the Bible?

All Christian traditions, with varying emphases, regard the Bible as a norm for faith and practice. Every Christian tradition expects its members to enter into some engagement with the Bible. But what will that engagement be? Many Christians regard the Bible with vague reverence. They have the sense that those stories from years long past have "something" to do with God. Because it has "something" to do with God, the Bible is to be revered, even if what "that something" has to do with the present remains an unsolved puzzle. Others devoutly learn the contents of the Bible, memorizing large portions of it under the assumption that they have learned the Word of God. They know what God says. Still others turn to the Bible as some authority, searching for passages to justify positions taken and behaviors exercised. These understandings, however inadequate they may be judged, are not to be sneered or ridiculed, for they may be genuine efforts in faithfulness and piety.

Instructors in church schools have devoted much time and energy teaching about things in the Bible. They have been most effective in assisting persons to accumulate vast amounts of discrete bits of information about the Bible. A host of Christians possess collections of disconnected bits of biblical information. But why should anyone know or want to know those things that are in the Bible? And knowing them, what is one to do with them? Until adequate, appropriate responses are offered to these questions, the Bible remains a strange and peculiar book coming from an equally strange and peculiar past.

A variety of things can be and have been done to and with the Bible. The variety itself attests to disagreements, if not confusion, concerning the nature of the Bible and how it is to be interpreted. A large segment of Christian people are uncertain about what to do with the Bible. In this regard, uncertainty is not the particular province of the young.

There is not much difference between children and many adults in their understanding and use of the Bible. Adults have gathered *more* information about the Bible, possess *greater* abilities in quoting the biblical material and have *greater* facility in using biblical language than children. From this perspective, the difference appears great. Yet in reality and practice the difference is primarily quantitative, not qualitative. Many Christian adults do not use or interpret the Bible in ways substantially different from that of children.

Should there be a difference? And if so, how might that difference be described? We are convinced that there should be a "difference" and that it can be described. Moreover, that "difference," residing in a larger task of interpreting, can be learned. Therefore this book is *one* response to the question, "What is it that we can and should do to assist Christian youth to engage in a larger task of interpreting the Bible?"

How Adolescents Respond to the Bible

One of the authors is engaged in a continuing research project designed to discern the perceptions of youth who are participating in catechetical or confirmation instruction. A series of questions in the research instrument explores adolescents' understanding of the Bible. Responses of the young people interviewed in the project illustrate the limited involvement of many adolescents with the Bible and suggest that they do not know how to enter into a larger involvement with it.

Young persons, ranging in ages from 12 to 16 years, were asked, "How important is it to read the Bible?" The invariant response was "Very important." To the question, "Why do you think it is important to read the Bible?" the vast majority responded, "It tells you how to behave" or "It helps you live a good life." At another point in the interview each was asked, "How often do you read the Bible?" The overwhelming majority responded, "Not very often. I can't understand much of it."

This brief scenario brings into sharp focus three issues which deserve our attention. First, what is regarded as "Very important" is most normally ignored. The young people engage "not very often" in an activity declared to be "very important." Second, in their responses the adolescents asserted that much of the Bible was "unavailable" to them. They were not saying that the book as such was not obtainable, but that much of the biblical language and imagery rendered the Bible inaccessible to them. Third, the majority of responses regarded the Bible primarily as a rule book for behaving and living a good (moral) life. In their responses these young persons suggested that they did not know what else to do with the Bible. If this is a dominant view among the youth, their understanding of the Bible is highly restricted. If adolescents are to engage the Bible in its richness and fullness, that view must be challenged.

To the question, "What do you think of or how would you describe 'Jesus?'" one catechetical student replied enthusiastically, excitedly and almost in one breath:

> Jesus is a man who was God's son, and uh, the Virgin Mary got him there, and then he started to teach about God and so the Jews didn't believe. So he went to the Gentiles and the Gentiles started to believe and he used to come back and forth to the Jewish city and the chief priest didn't like him and all so they started to want to plan on things so they could kill him. Well, God's plan for Jesus was for him to die for sins. So he died on the cross, the place to die for sins. See, in the Old Testament, they used to have an ark and there was a torn curtain and that means that only one person is supposed to go in there and take a perfect lamb, and Jesus was perfect. O.K. So when Jesus dies for our sins, for all our sins, they are forgiven. So that was just like the lamb but it's for, you don't have to burn a lamb for everything.

This response is not the occasion for laughter or ridicule. It illustrates a most critical and complex problem we encounter in assisting adolescents with the Bible. That young student possessed a large storehouse amply filled with an abundant supply of strange, peculiar, and disconnected bits of information about the Bible and the faith. He had arranged the information in a way that made some sense to him. He had done with it what he was able to do at the moment. Regardless of how we judge the sense he made, he told us how he "saw it." He had been involved in an act of interpretation; he had constructed for himself his own particular meaning for the information he had. And it is reasonable to conclude that he did not have an understanding, that he may have misunderstood the intent of the information.

That student did not, first, need more information. More disconnected information would but have added to the already confused and
chaotic picture. He needed, however, the assistance and opportunity
to sort out his information, to think about it, to ask questions of it, to
distinguish what is critical, to have questions asked of him, and to
attempt new orderings and interpretations. His need poses two questions. First, how can we assist youth to think anew, to interpret anew
and to give new order to the information about the Bible and the faith
they already have? Second, how do we bring new information and experiences to bear in such a way so that new insights and understandings are achieved?

The young people in our research project were also asked, "Do you
believe that everything written in the Bible happened just the way it
is written?" With few exceptions the adolescents, including the one
quoted earlier, replied in the negative. To the probe concerning how
distinctions of "true" and "untrue" are made concerning biblical materials, a variety of responses were given. "You just have to use your
mind." "If something seems really silly." "If something is just unbeliev-
able." These young people were not biblical literalists. For the moment, at least, they had discarded the criterion of literalism as a useful
approach to the Bible. But something more important is apparent. These
young people possessed few adequate working skills or criteria which
would encourage and assist them in a serious conversation with the
Bible.

One conclusion and one prediction are offered. The conclusion: youth
need to be and can be introduced to and initiated in new skills, tools,
and criteria which will bring them into a larger task of interpreting
the Bible than was possible earlier. The prediction: if they are not introduced to and initiated into that task they will either settle back into
a literalistic style encumbered with all the problems inherent in it or
will remove themselves from any serious and significant engagement
with the Bible.

Some Underlying Presuppositions

Christian youth should be introduced to and initiated into a larger
ongoing task of interpreting the Bible than was possible for them as
children. The Christian community, its pastors, educators, teachers,
and parents, must move intentionally to engage adolescents in a larger,
ongoing work of interpreting the Bible. The adolescent can *begin* to
participate in an ever-expanding interpretive task. We do not suggest
that the task will be learned easily and quickly, certainly not once-

and-for-all-times. Our emphasis here is on a *beginning*.

Some youth, of course, will make only a beginning. Some will find the task difficult, even painful. Some will want to back off, wanting nothing to do with the task. Indeed, some will not participate at all. Some will be reluctant and timid while others will falter and stumble. Still others, even though struggling with the task, will catch new, exciting, ever-widening visions of what it is to be the people of God in the church and the world. However, if Christian adolescents are not introduced to and initiated into that larger task, approaching and doing the task at a later age will be more difficult and problematic.

The Bible is our sacred text. There we encounter the witness to God's activity and to the faith of the church. There, the stories that belong to the church are our stories, identifying and describing us as the people of God. When we engage the sacred text in conversation, to interpret and to understand it, in strange, unexpected, and marvelous ways the Bible interprets us. How our youth engage in the task of interpreting the Bible will influence their lives profoundly. It can give direction to them as Christian people in both the church and the world, spurring their efforts to live under the Gospel and shaping their decisions and actions in daily life.

The Bible is always interpreted from within the context of human life. Therefore the conditions of human life at any given moment will highly influence both doing the interpretive task and its outcomes. For the Christian, interpreting the Bible is a critical activity set within the realm of that broad and encompassing task, that of attempting to make sense of human life and the world—its events, people, values, and behaviors. When we engage the Bible in critical conversation, we bring our experiences and how we think and feel about them. We bring our sorrows and joys, our hopes and fears, our commitments, and even our unbelief. In part, we bring the sacred text to bear upon all these, not for final answers, but for illumination as we attempt to make sense of the world. These are brought to impinge on our conversation even as the Bible comes to bear upon us.

Interpreting the Bible is informed and shaped by the processes of human development. In adolescent youth, these processes are in a state of transition. New abilities and possibilities belong to youth. They encounter particular sets of tasks and problems requiring some solutions. Solutions achieved will shape futures. Those abilities and possibilities, tasks and problems consume an extraordinary amount of the adolescent's time, energy, and interest. Again, these elements of human life will influence how the young person is able to engage the

Bible and what the outcomes of that engagement will be. Taking seriously the lives of adolescents with their accompanying strains and demands, we believe that the sacred text can be brought to impinge upon those lives. It can illumine their lives, giving clues and directions for tasks and problems. It can identify and describe young persons as the people of God. These adolescents can learn and know what it is for them to be Christians; they may dare to be, to do, and to become who they already are. To that end, this book is offered.

And What Follows?

In this book we describe an approach, including illustrative materials, which can encourage adolescent youth to engage the Bible and to learn a larger, more advanced task of interpretation. This book is not a curriculum for a study of the Bible. Rather, it is an appeal that we enter into a conversation together with young persons and with the Bible as an active participant.

The book is divided into two sections. Part One discusses the theoretical bases which inform the approach offered here. In chapter 1 we see that clarity of theoretical underpinnings guides us in setting objectives, and shapes and gives direction to our practice. Edward Everding has noted, "The interpretive act is comprised of three ingredients—the interpreter, what is interpreted and the relationship between the two."[1]

Chapter 2 then focuses on "what is interpreted"—the Bible. Our understanding and convictions concerning the nature of the Bible will have a determinative effect on how we engage youth with it and for what purposes. Here we state our understandings and convictions, recognizing that we have already engaged in an interpretive process and affirming that our interpretations influence the contents of this book.

In chapter 3 we consider "the interpreter"—the young person. What we understand the human creature to be and to be able to do will influence our human interactions. And so it is with youth and our interactions with them. Viewing adolescence as a period of transition, from childhood to adulthood that involves various process changes, we identify some developmental tasks confronting adolescents. We show that process changes and developmental tasks are primary concerns for them. That in actuality two contents, the Bible and the life-content of the young person, interact in the process of interpretation. Thus we ask: can the Bible illumine, inform, shape, and guide the teenager's responses and solutions to the process changes and developmental tasks?

Chapter 4 turns attention to a theoretical perspective of the interpretive process itself—developmental constructivism. We discuss major facets of the perspective which asserts that human life is a process of interpretation and is, at the same time, shaped by that process. It is our view that interpreting and learning to interpret the Bible is embedded in the broad, ongoing interpretive and constructive process of human life. Some implications of the perspective for our teaching activity are noted.

The period of adolescence offers the church a unique opportunity for doing Christian education. We can make a deliberate, concerted effort to introduce and then to initiate teenagers into a larger task of interpreting and learning to interpret the Bible. Our understandings of the Bible, of adolescents, and of the interpretive process demand the effort which we describe as a "conversation together in the faith." In chapter 5 we discuss the contributions and roles of pastors, teachers, and parents as shapers of the environment for this conversation.

Part Two, reflecting the third component of Everding's description, offers a framework which can facilitate our conversation together. In the several chapters of Part Two, biblical content and the life-content of youth, along with that of adults, are brought into a dynamic interaction and conversation with each other. Coinciding with adolescent concerns and tasks, six questions are explored:

- *Who am I?* (Attaining an identity).
- *Who tells me who I am?* (Achieving an identity).
- *Whose body is it, anyway?* (Accepting one's body).
- *What is it to be male or female?* (Developing sexuality).
- *What is required of me?* (Achieving a value system).
- *Am I my neighbor's keeper?* (Achieving social consciousness).

The several chapters are divided into four sections. First, each chapter—focusing on one question—begins with a brief introduction which places the particular concern in a broad human context. Second, a restatement of the specific process change or task describes the involvement of youth with it. Third, we suggest a group of activities or exercises which invite young persons to examine and explore the specific task or change and to become aware of and to describe their responses to it. Fourth, we suggest biblical passages which we believe can inform, direct, and shape adolescent responses.

Several comments concerning our selection and use of biblical material are in order. Our selection has been deliberate, suggesting those passages which do relate to the several questions posed. They can illumine the questions, and broaden and deepen teenagers' understanding of the issues and concerns involved. We are not suggesting that the passages contain finished and fixed answers. Significantly, the passages call adolescents to move beyond individualistic concerns, assisting them to view their lives within both the human family and the community of faith. We have not considered every thrust and dimension of a passage. We recognize that more can and should be said about a portion of Scripture than is said here. We therefore do not presume to have exhausted the force and richness of any set of verses. But we do direct attention to very specific elements of a passage, those related to the questions posed. We believe that our selection and use of suggested biblical material can encourage and assist youth in a larger task of interpreting and learning to interpret the Bible.

·2
The Bible we interpret

In any interpretive process, there are three significant components: the content or source to be interpreted; the person doing the interpreting, including the content of his or her life; and the relationship and interactions between the Bible and the interpreter. How we understand these three components will give clarity and guidance to our work with adolescents as they engage the Bible. In this chapter, we examine the content to be interpreted—the Bible.

Concerning teaching the Bible, we can easily assume that we all are talking about the "same thing." But are we? We can easily assume that we all desire to teach the "same thing." But do we? We think not. Responses to the question, "What is the Bible?" are diverse. The diversity represents understandings and commitments which are cherished and elicit deep devotion. These particular commitments direct individuals as they engage the Bible, and even give shape to the message of the Bible. And so, here we, the authors, share our response to the question, "What is the Bible?" indicating its implications for the task at hand.

Some Immediate Concerns

Several immediate concerns highlight the necessity of developing clear responses to the question, "What is the Bible?" They are:

First, what is it that we want youth to do with the Bible? The question may be put in another way: Why do we want adolescents to engage in the task of biblical interpretation? Two other questions, moving in opposite directions, may help to amplify our concern here. Are we interested primarily in somehow *getting the Bible into them*— however defined—with the hope that they will possess a wide range of answers to questions of God and human life? Or, do we want them to learn to *interpret* the Bible so that it will be a means (a means of grace?) to help them make sense of the world with its things, events, and people and of their lives as Christians? The point here is singular. It is necessary that we have clarity concerning what we hope may happen, else all our efforts may turn into useless exercises.

Second, it is imperative that we describe and share our own adventures in and with the Bible. We invite young persons into an engagement with the Bible; but is the invitation worth accepting? By describing our adventures with the Bible, by sharing its impact and demonstrating its shaping influence upon our own lives, we may cause the invitation to be most attractive. If we do not, adolescents may well regard our invitation as unimportant or only tangential to their concerns and needs. Many things compete for the time and attention of young people. They determine which items will receive their attention. Getting their attention by sharing our own adventures with the Scriptures may be the key which unlocks doors to new horizons for youth as they engage the Bible.

Third, we need to have a particular clarity concerning our understanding and conviction about the nature of the Bible. In this regard many questions about the Bible "stumble over" each other for attention. Is the Bible a source book of eternal truth and absolute answers? Is it the Word of God? In what sense is it the Word of God? What is the source of the Bible? What is the nature of the Bible's authority? What authority does it have over us as individuals and over the Christian community? These are difficult questions.

We need to recognize that whatever we say about the Bible is our interpretation, construction of, or conviction about, what the Bible says to us. Equally, whatever any other person says about the nature of the Bible is that individual's interpretation or construction or conviction. We are not suggesting that one interpretation is just as good as any other interpretation or that it makes no difference which interpretation one chooses. Not at all! Differences in interpretations in this matter are crucial. Differences lead to different conclusions. We simply wish to point to a reality. To our own particular interpretation we will be profoundly committed. Indeed, we will regard our particular interpretation as appropriate, right and true. Nevertheless, we assert that any statement, any theology of the Bible is a human interpretation or construction, not a divine-given. Thus, we ought not to claim more for our interpretations than is appropriate. Without question, we must be faithful to "where" we are at the moment, and yet always open to the unexpected new. Remembering that we are engaged in an interpretive process, we can live in the expectation that the Bible may break forth upon us in new and unimagined ways.

Fourth, biblical interpretation is both a private and a communal affair. An individual's interpretations or constructions of knowledge, reality and meaning are creations of the individual, and so it is with one's biblical interpretations. In a critical sense, interpretation of the Bible is a private matter. Yet, such an assertion is not a license for the individual, in solitude or isolation, to make of the Bible any thing he or she chooses. We are members of the Christian community, belonging to particular Christian traditions. A particular tradition has its own ways of understanding and interpreting the Bible, ways informed by both long engagement with the Bible and biblical scholarship. Our life in and our faithfulness to a specific tradition will shape our perspectives and interpretations. Our individual perceptions and interpretations should always be examined and judged by the tradition's perspectives and interpretations.

What Is the Bible?

Whatever we say about the nature of the Bible is our interpretation, emerging from our life in a particular tradition. We do not possess the Bible in and of itself. We do not bring it into our beings to digest it and to make it a part of ourselves. The Bible stands always as an event external to us. It cannot be reduced to something we own. It is an event to which we must respond, about which we must make some decisions and about which we must make interpretations. Whenever we engage adolescents with the Bible, we are asking them to act upon that event, to interact with it, to interpret it, to make sense of it, and to give sense to it—as they are able. We ask them to join with us in the adventure of interpretation.

An Interpretation and Witness

The Bible itself is an interpretation of and a witness to a past story of the church. In its many parts, the Bible is an interpretation and construction, giving meaning to particular events, things, and persons. It is a witness to the faith of a people over time. It expresses their understandings of the mighty acts of God. As the witness of the faith of a peculiar community, the Bible describes that community's attempt to make "sense" of God's actions and to understand and order their lives under those actions.

Within the Bible there is no one, uniform witness, but instead many witnesses. Their witness is not static. New events, new occasions, and new seasons call forth and require new interpretations and new witnesses. Over the centuries as the Bible took shape, generation after generation needed to make its own interpretations or constructions. New futures were opened. And each new witness became a part of the larger and expanding story of the people of God.

The Bible is, thus, many witnesses to God's redemptive activity in the world, to God's gracious dealings with the people. The stories we encounter in the Bible are not, in and of themselves, the actions of God. We meet something quite different. For example, the several Exodus stories in the Old Testament are not, in and of themselves, God's action of delivering the Hebrews out of Egypt. Even if someone on the scene had written a detailed, step-by-step account of what occurred, we still would not possess the action itself. Yet, something had happened to the Hebrews—something great, unexpected, and dramatic. What we have in the several Exodus stories are interpretations of that something, a people's struggle to make sense of what had happened to them. There we have a witness to the firm conviction that God had delivered them. As they retold the stories of the Exodus in their celebrations, the people not only remembered God's saving activity from Egypt; but also, through and beyond those stories, they encountered the redemptive Word of God in new situations. And so, succeeding generations told new stories of the old story.

The mighty acts of God are neither contained nor bound by a particular historical moment, though they occur in such a fragment of time. The acts of God transcend all moments. The Bible does not presume to give step-by-step detail of those actions or events. History as some mechanical, literal description was not the primary concern of biblical writers. Their task was far more profound—and far more exciting.

Only a few of the biblical writers participated in the events of which they wrote. Most did not. In any event, the actions of God stood outside them. The writers of the Bible never possessed those actions. God's activity possessed them.

God's activity impinged upon them, challenging them, making claims, and asking questions: "I am the Lord your God." "I will be your God, and you will be my people." "What does the Lord require of you?"

The biblical writers, standing in their historical moments, had the task of interpreting, of making sense of God's action for their day. They wrote stories, codified laws, developed genealogies, composed poems, and penned letters. All were efforts to understand, to give witness to, and to tell anew what God had done, what God was doing, and what God would yet do. Among and within all the efforts there were differing and varying emphases, concerns and understandings, a diversity giving witness to the God "above all gods."

The biblical writings produced through a thousand years, each in its time, were efforts to reflect anew, interpret anew, and tell new stories of God and God's people. The stories told were God's stories, and yet they were the stories of a people, stories describing and identifying a peculiar people. From generation to generation the stories differed. There was a continuity with the past, but each generation altered, rearranged, and even transformed something of the old. Each new generation in new seasons and circumstances, recalling its past stories and remembering from whence it had come, had to write its own stories of the God who acts to redeem. Each generation added to the collection of stories (witnesses), and tradition was added to tradition.

If we must speak of a consistency in the Bible, we must speak of the consistency of women and men who endeavored to be faithful witnesses to God's gracious dealings with a people. The early Christians embraced the Hebrew Scriptures as their own. Sharing in those stories, they knew from where they had come and to whom they belonged. They knew themselves to be in a long line of faithful witnesses. Yet, those Scriptures were not sufficient for them. They needed to write new stories. Those new stories, though in continuity with the past, were unlike any that had ever been told.

For those Christians, a mighty event had occurred. They had to write the stories of Jesus. They did not possess the event of Jesus; it possessed them. They were compelled to make sense of it and to interpret it even as it interpreted them.

Christians stood in a new age. They wrote new stories while rewriting some of the old stories with a new vision, bearing witness to Jesus. Their particular witness is the New Testament, a work composed of many witnesses and interpretations. That which had occurred could not be captured by one, single witness. Each writer, moved by particular concerns, insights, emphases, and problems, gave witness. Each wrote a somewhat different story. As the early church gathered, preserved, and cherished those witnesses, it gave shape to its faith and proclaimed its Lord.

When we encounter the Bible, we meet many witnesses and interpretations. We meet stories of a faithful people coming to terms with God's action. We encounter a faithful people endeavoring to arrange, order, and live out their lives as God's people. Their stories are our stories. They belong to us, describing us and identifying us. Remembering from where we have come and to whom we belong and remembering the past witnesses of the faithful, we must write and tell new stories in these days. And with our new stories, we take our places in the long line of witnesses.

The Word of God

Within the Christian tradition, it is imperative that we speak of the Bible as the Word of God. In so doing, however, we must exercise extreme care. The Bible itself, at no point, presumes "to capture" or "to encapsulate" God, a fact we do well to remember.

Some segments of the Christian community have declared that the Bible is the "inspired Word of God." In so doing, some wish to say that somehow and in some fashion the Bible has come from God or that it is the *direct* work of God. Inspiration, in this sense, gives a particular emphasis to the origin and nature of the Bible. At the same time, inspiration is frequently linked to a concern for "infallibility and inerrancy," insisting that there can be no "error" of any sort in the Bible. This view, which is itself an interpretation or construction, focuses greatly on the verbal form and detail of the Bible. It leads in certain directions. It suggests that if we know the words of the Bible we then know the Word of God. In fact, the words of the Bible are equated with the Word of God. The view therefore tends to seek consistency and uniformity, often overlooking the diversity of witnesses.

Others, claiming inspiration of the Bible, focus on the persons who produced the Bible. The writers of biblical material are viewed as having been inspired in some special way by the Holy Spirit to give "an accurate account." In such a view, the message of God has been given directly to individuals who faithfully recorded it. Thus, the reader of the Bible encounters the very words as "dictated" to the writer by God. And so again, to know the words of the Bible is to know the Word of God.

We want to move in a different direction as we speak of the Bible as the Word of God. We do not equate the words of the Bible with the Word of God. If we are not to read the Bible in some literalistic or mechanistic fashion, we must ask of the Word beyond the words. The Bible does not draw attention to itself. It always points us beyond itself to the God who, though hidden, chooses to show self, to reveal self through actions in human life. The biblical tradition(s) is not so much interested in God as "the divine being" as in the God who speaks and acts in human history. It devotes little effort to describing what God "is like" but tells marvelous stories of what God has done, is doing, and is yet to do. And thus, the Bible points beyond itself to the Word.

Preeminently for the Christian, the deed and the Word of God is Jesus the Christ.

Preaching and teaching are crucial and necessary events for the church. Whenever and wherever the stories of God and God's marvelous deeds are told, there God encounters us. There God is in our midst. As Luther suggests, the church is not a "pen-house" but a "mouth-house." God has entrusted self to the words, the lips, the voices of men and women, boys and girls.

And so, we speak of the Bible as the Word of God in a derivative sense. It is the Word of God derived from the historical sense of the Word—from the actions of God in human life. The Bible is the Word of God derived from the Word as proclamation. As a proclamation of God's deeds, which are the Word of God, the Scriptures participate in the nature of that which they proclaim. The Scriptures, therefore, can be called the Word of God, and they function in relation to preaching and teaching by sustaining the oral proclamation of the Word and by preserving that proclamation from error.

Therefore, we do not possess the Word of God by memorizing and reciting the Bible. In reality we never possess the Word of God at all. It possesses us. We may recite to others passage after passage from the Bible and yet never speak to them the Word of God. To speak of the Bible as the Word of God is to say that the Bible is always pointing us beyond itself to the living God to whom the biblical tradition bears witness. It points us beyond itself to the living God who continues to act and to speak not only in and through the Bible but also whenever and wherever the stories are proclaimed. We take our clues from the Bible as it points us beyond itself to the God who continues to break upon us in new and unexpected ways. Hearing the stories of God anew through faithful witnesses of the past, in our seasons we interpret and give witness to the God beyond the Bible.

The Book of the Church

The Bible is the book of the church and is the norm for the church's faith and practice. All statements of faith and all theology are to be measured against the Bible. Christian life and practice are to be measured against the Bible. Christian teaching and preaching are to be measured against the Bible. Such assertions clearly imply that the Bible has some authority over us as Christian peoples and in our Christian traditions. Yet, they do not imply that in the Bible we have a "road map" which leads us directly and unambiguously into the mind and will of God.

The church created the Scriptures. The Bible belongs to the church as community, and only then to us as individuals. It is in the church that the Holy Spirit is calling, gathering, enlightening, sanctifying, and preserving the people of God. As the church has determined the Scriptures, it has placed itself under the authority of the Bible. In our life in the church we then place ourselves under the authority of the church's book. The appropriate arena for our acting upon, interacting with, and interpreting the Bible must ultimately be within the context of the Christian community. All our individual interpretations must be brought under the scrutiny and challenge of the community.

Any discussion concerning the authority of the Bible is an attempt to define relations. It seeks to define the relationship between the Bible, the church, and ourselves. Authority resides in the living God, the Word beyond all words, who continues to act and speak in and through the Bible but not in the Bible alone. The authority of the Bible rests upon the activity of God to which, the church believes, the Bible is a faithful witness. As the Bible bears witness to that God, it has an authority for the faith and practice of the church.

The discussion of biblical authority introduces an element of trust. In the human operation of things, we have the tendency to give authority to those persons or institutions that we trust. The person or institution wishing to have authority over others must elicit trust and must produce a situation in which an individual can grant authority. The biblical tradition(s) witnesses to the faithfulness of God and demonstrates that God can be trusted to keep promises made. The Bible, proclaiming the Word and deeds of God, elicits trust in us and enables us to give authority to the Bible as the witness of God's redemptive, loving concern. The church has responded in trust to the God of whom the Bible gives witness and has placed itself under the authority of the Scriptures.

Interpretation of the Bible

What is involved in the process of interpreting the Bible? To interpret a biblical text involves seeking responses to three questions. First, what does the text claim that God is saying or doing? Second, what was the situation in which God spoke or acted? And third, so what? So what that God spoke or acted in that situation? What has it to do with me (us) or to say to me (us) this day?[1]

The Bible is preeminently a witness to the redemptive activity and Word of God. Thus, a primary task of interpretation is to inquire of what the particular text is saying about the divine activity. What are the claims of the text? What is its witness? What is it saying about God's activity? The Bible does bear witness to God's actions. Thus a primary concern for our interpretation is to focus upon what the biblical text is saying about God's activity. The interpreter needs to wrestle long and hard with the text itself, ascertaining as far as possible what that text is saying and claiming.

The whole biblical tradition bears witness to the reality that God acts and speaks in the context of human history. The interpreter of a biblical text must necessarily recover something of the historical context in which God was acting and speaking and from which the text itself emerged. A historical context impinged upon the biblical writers, influencing, informing, and giving shape to their interpretations and witnesses. From within the context of their human situation they sought to make sense of and understand what God was doing and saying. Recovering something of the past historical contexts, the interpreter can more readily understand the claims and witnesses of the various texts.

The question, "So what?" moves the interpreter in a new direction. To ascertain what a biblical text says about God's activity is not the end of interpretation. Having made some conclusion concerning what a biblical text in its historical situation is saying about God's action and speaking, the interpreter must grapple with the task of making sense of that Word of God which comes to her or him in the present context. If that is what God was doing and saying then, what is the Word of God doing and saying in the present? A new dimension of interpretation emerges. If such-and-such was the case, what are its claims today? What is it saying today about God? And what is it saying about us as we live out our lives in our days and circumstances? What is the Word beyond the words?

Biblical interpretation, taking seriously the "So what?" question, does not produce final, fixed, or static answers. Recognizing that the human situation is always changing with new events, new circumstances and new seasons, it calls for new interpretations, new stories, and new witnesses to what God is doing and saying. It is a process giving structure to our struggles, our efforts to write and tell new stories of our God and of us, the people of God. Biblical interpretation therefore is not a once-for-all-time activity but rather a dynamic process involving us in the continual task of creating meanings, interpretations, and stories for the Word of God as the Bible bears witness to God's activity. The results of our efforts will be at least somewhat different from those of past witnesses. We live in a new time. Moreover, the new stories that we create this day may be somewhat different from those given at a later day. Witness will be added to witness, tradition to tradition. Thus, we do what the biblical writers themselves did.

The church is always in the process of interpreting its Scriptures in the presence of new events and seasons. The interpretations given today, right and proper though they may be for today, may not be what is required for tomorrow. The church strives for new and faithful responses to the Word of God as it encounters the world and human life. And so, as the church calls us to engage in the ongoing process of interpretation, we are invited together into an exploration and conversation with the church's book that we may hear anew the Word of God— and, ourselves, tell new stories.

Some Implications for Our Task

We have not discussed all that can or should be said about the Bible. To produce a comprehensive discussion of the nature of the Bible has not been our intent. We have, however, shared something of our interpretation and understanding of it. We turn now to some implications of our discussion as we engage adolescent youth with the Bible.

To Engage the Old Stories

If youth are to interpret and learn to interpret the Bible, they must encounter the biblical material itself. We cannot interpret an event with which we are unacquainted or of which we have no knowledge. Without some acquaintance or knowledge, the event does not even "exist" for us. Equally, we cannot interpret the Bible if its contents are not available to us or if we have no acquaintance with them.

We may remind ourselves that adolescents, when children, were exposed to biblical material via the various agencies of Christian education. Thus, it is tempting to conclude that they do know the Bible or should know the Bible. Such a conclusion can mislead us. Yes, they were "taught" the Bible as children. But what they "carry" with them as adolescents is not the biblical material itself, but their interpretations of that material, interpretations created by themselves as children. Those interpretations are characteristic of children's abilities and limitations. Those already-achieved "interpretations" must be challenged. If interpretations created in childhood are not challenged and if adolescents are not encouraged to create new ones, they will carry throughout adolescence and into adulthood an understanding of the Bible created by children. In a new engagement with the Bible, the biblical material itself will offer the challenge.

To interpret or to learn to interpret the Bible requires that young people read, engage, and ask questions of it. At what point and in what manner we bring particular biblical material to bear is not an issue here. Rather, it is not sufficient that youth rely solely on past encounters with the Bible or on past interpretations of it. Neither is it enough that they rely solely on what others say about the Bible. The bottom line is: they must engage the Bible itself.

We are asking our youth to participate in a rather difficult task. Some have totally relied upon others to tell them what the Bible says or "means." They have had very little practice in asking questions of the Bible. In fact, some young persons consider it "wrong" to ask questions of the Bible or to question another's thinking about it. It is not uncommon to meet adolescents who assert that they already know "all about the Bible and God" for they were taught "that stuff when we were kids." Some of them have been "put off" by the strange and peculiar language of the Bible and by its descriptions of alien contexts. Thus, they do not know what questions to ask of the Bible. Some know neither what questions to ask of the Bible nor how to frame questions of and about the Bible.

In the engagement process, we encourage them to ask questions of the Bible. What is the particular passage saying? What claims does it make? What story is it telling? What witness does it make? What does it say about what God has done? What does it say about the human creature? We focus attention on the biblical material itself. We may need to give them information about the passage, its structure, its language, and the historical context from which it emerged. Although such information may assist youth in their explorations of the Bible, it does not serve as a substitute for those explorations.

To Tell New Stories

Following the example of the biblical writers themselves, we encourage our young people to tell and write new stories of the old stories. The biblical writers asked of the old stories the same questions which we must ask. If the old story describes the way things are, if its claims are true, and if what it claims about God and human life is appropriate, then what does it say to us today? What stories must we write, having encountered the witnesses of the Bible?

These questions and similar ones move us into another dimension of the interpretive process, a dimension that will receive greater elaboration at a later point. But at this point, however, it is sufficient to note that we cannot be satisfied if the old stories are merely remembered and recited. The old stories cannot be merely imposed on the present. One may recall and recite the old stories, and yet fail to encounter and bear witness to the Word of God. A step beyond reciting the old stories is necessary.

In asking them to take another step, we are asking youth to engage in an exciting and new, yet a risky and difficult, adventure, to interpret their lives under the Bible, and to write new stories of themselves as God's people. We can anticipate a great diversity of new stories. Even as we share and celebrate the diversity of old stories so we can share and celebrate the diversity of new stories.

By What Authority?

We seek to bring biblical material to bear on the lives of youth because we believe that the Bible does exercise authority over us. We want them to engage the Bible because we believe that it is the norm of Christian faith and practice. We want them to encounter the Bible because we believe that there they may encounter the Word of God.

The Bible holds no significant authority at all over many adolescents. Yes, there may be much reverence for the Bible as a book that tells what God did in ages past. Yes, they recognize something of the place that it holds in the church and regard it with some respect. They have heard many appeals made to the Bible. They may assert that it is important to know the things in the Bible even if they are unable to describe that importance. Reverence, respect, and asserted importance, however, do not constitute authority. For a large number of adolescents the Bible is a book of interesting stories from the past that have little connection with ordinary life. In making such assertions, we do not intend "to put down" adolescent youth. We are attempting to describe a reality that we must work with in awareness and patience.

Many of our youth ask serious and far-reaching questions. Why should the Bible have any authority over me? Why should I pay more attention to the Bible than to the many other voices claiming my attention, allegiance, and obedience? How do I know that the Bible is the Word of God? What difference does the Bible make in one's life? Far from being unfaithful or wrong, these are the right questions to be asked.

A rather critical matter needs to be noted at this point. Even though they have a long acquaintance with the Bible, youth are asking their *own* questions about the Bible. Their questions represent their strivings and struggles with the Bible. We are called upon to assist adolescents to achieve and to make appropriate, adequate responses to their questions. We cannot impose answers on them. We may declare that the Bible is the Word of God, or that the Bible is a faithful witness, or that the Bible has authority over us, or that the Bible is the norm for faith and practice. But our declarations do not "make it true" for the adolescent young person.

Yet, our declarations we must make. We must describe how the faith community understands the Bible. We must bear witness to the church's convictions about the Bible. Then we must continually describe our understanding of the Bible's authority over us. Moreover, we must demonstrate how and in what ways the Bible exercises that authority, and how and in what ways the Bible serves as a norm of faith and practice for us and the church. Knowing that we cannot impose biblical authority upon youth, we give witness to the authority by which we live. Both to articulate and to demonstrate that authority are magnificent gifts we offer to our adolescent youth as they determine what shall be their relationship to the Bible.

In Community

The Bible is the church's book. The church has put itself under the authority of the Bible. And the task of ongoing interpretation belongs primarily to the church. In a variety of ways we all encounter the Bible as individuals. We make individual interpretations of it. Yet, all individual interpretations are subject to the challenge, questioning, and even "correction" of the faith community. Indeed, we must recognize the diversity of faith communities and the implications of that diversity. Nevertheless, interpreting and learning to interpret the Bible is an activity belonging ultimately and most properly within a faith community.

It is appropriate that we urge adolescents to read the Bible privately. Yet, many attest to their utter inability to understand or to make meaningful sense of the Bible when left alone with it. It is necessary that we deliberately and intentionally so arrange an environment that adolescents engage the task of interpretation within community. Interpreting within community offers engagements and challenges that private reading cannot afford. Not only are common problems shared in community, but it is in community that we assist each other in interpretation. It is in a community of God's people that we hear the old stories of God's gracious dealings with people, and we write new stories of God's dealings with us in a new season, a new day, or a new circumstance.

·3
The adolescents who interpret

Adolescent youth live at a particular moment in their human development. As we engage them in a larger task of interpreting the Bible, they bring into play the content of their lives—their experiences, already-achieved understandings, values, hopes and fears, and certainties and doubts. They participate from within the context of adolescence with its demands, tasks, and possibilities. That content and context influences both the willingness of youth to engage in the interpretive task and how they participate in it.

When engaging youth in the broad arena of Christian education, we must strive for appropriate and adequate responses to the question, "Who are the youth?" Popular, simplistic, and overarching views of adolescents and adolescence may mislead us entirely. There are no simple, "foolproof" descriptions of adolescents. Yet, we need not be utterly bewildered by the multiplicity of legitimate descriptions. The rich diversity and complexity of adolescence does, however, place heavy demands upon adults but, at the same time, offers abundant opportunities for exciting and significant Christian education.

Adolescence: A Period of Transition

Adolescence is the period of transition between childhood and adulthood. Many transitions occur during the life span. The movements from infant to child, spouse to spouse-parent, student to employee, and employee to retiree are but several transitions that individuals may experience. During periods of transitions across the life span, such processes as the physical, intellectual, emotional, sexual, motivational, social, and moral are in the midst of change. Both internal and external demands call forth changes in processes. During transitions individuals must learn to respond to and cope with changes.

How they respond to changes in processes will greatly influence their overt behaviors as well as their values, self-understandings, and ideologies.

Adolescence is a most significant transition within the life span. During adolescence most of the processes appear to be in a state of change almost simultaneously. Rapid physical changes, development of reproductive capacity, entrance into the world of work, redefinition of values, development of independence from parents, construction of a realistic identity—these and many other changes occur. Thus, adolescence is seen as the time "period within the life span when most of a person's processes . . . are in transition from what typically is considered childhood to what typically is considered adulthood."[1]

It is important to remember that among individuals process changes begin at varying times and develop at varying rates. Some transitions occur faster or slower than others both within an individual and among individuals. For example, physical transitions may occur rather early for one individual without accompanying transitions in intellectual or emotional processes. For another individual, there may be transitions in intellectual processes without accompanying transition in physical or emotional or social processes. And still for another individual, transitions may be occurring in several processes simultaneously. The implication is clear. Adolescence is not to be defined merely by age categories. It is misleading, for example, to suggest that all thirteen-year-olds will act emotionally in particular ways or that all sixteen-year-olds are interested in the same things. Thus, in any group of adolescents there will be great diversity of both the transitions that are occurring and the rates at which they are happening.

Genetic and Environmental Interactions

Genetic and environmental forces interact to influence the process changes. During adolescence one's genetic potential becomes particularly evident. For example, all adolescents at some point experience a growth spurt similar in acceleration to the growth period that occurs from conception to birth. Since birth physical growth has been comparatively gradual and steady. Suddenly the body begins to grow rapidly. The timing of the growth spurt varies from individual to individual and appears to be under hormonal control. The end result brings short, average, tall, and very tall individuals along with slender, stocky, and average builds.

The adolescent must respond to and cope with those rapid changes in his or her body. More important than the actual height or weight of the individual is the adolescent's attitude toward her or his body. How one regards, thinks about, and feels about his or her body and its form influences greatly the individual's thinking and feeling about self.

Some intellectual abilities and talents also may be tempered by a genetic influence. Simply put, some individuals may not be able to do some of the things they might wish to do. Increasingly, adolescents must become aware of their weaknesses and strengths. Past dreams and hopes may need to be reassessed and rechanneled. New directions may need to be planned and taken. Again, the genetic influence may not be as important as the response the adolescent makes to new understandings of abilities and talents.

Environmental forces do interact with each other as well as with genetic components. They influence the process changes. Parental demands, societal expectations, peers, and the mass media with their high-powered advertisements are all possible influences. They all clamor with conflicting and contradictory voices to tell the adolescent what it is to be adult. The adolescent must select from that overabundant mass of environmental forces those that he or she will attend to, explore, test out, and incorporate into his or her own self. And the incorporation, whatever it may be, will shape behavior, values, morals, commitments, and ideologies as well as religious beliefs.

The period of adolescence may be short or long. Various segments of a society frequently impose time expectations on its young. Some segments afford a relatively short period for the transition from childhood to adulthood. Physical maturity, full-time entry into the work world, and marriage may be the criteria for adulthood. Other segments afford a relatively long period for the transition. For example, in a segment which places high value on increased years of formal education, individuals are given a longer time for the transition. In many instances, individuals who lengthen their formal education may remain dependent, at least economically, on parents, and may devote a number of years in preparation for full-time entry into the work world. The expectations of various segments of a society interact with adolescents in such a fashion as to speed up or slow down the transitions.

And so again, adolescence is not to be defined by age alone but as a "transition from what typically is considered childhood to what typically is considered adulthood." Clearly, genetic influences will determine, in part, what is "typically" adulthood. But it is equally clear that environmental influences, expectations, and demands determine what is "typically" adulthood. Thus, it is not possible to describe all adolescents in a monolithic fashion except to say that they are in transition from childhood to adulthood. And so, we expect both diversity and complexity during the transition period of adolescence.

Moratorium: Time for Exploration

Moratorium, in the present context, refers to a period of time that a society affords its adolescents for actively experimenting with various roles, ideologies, and behaviors. It is time given to the adolescent before she or he needs to make commitments in adult living.

The importance of this time, short or long, must not be underestimated. It allows time for the adolescent to explore alternatives, to give shape to self-identity, and to determine where his or her commitments will be anchored. The length of time, however, does not assure active use of the moratorium period by adolescents. They need to be aware of available options open to them. Interjected into this period must be information, experiences, and models which not only demonstrate options available but which give clues and directions to adolescents as they make commitments. Awareness of available options may create stress for adolescents as they confront contradictions. We should not attempt to protect them from contradictions. Contradictions cause disequilibrium, an unsettling experience, and yet motivate eventual commitments. The absence of a moratorium period propels the individual toward a predetermined set of behaviors and towards predetermined commitments. It encourages one to accept uncritically an ideology, a religious stance, and a role in society. Wise use of moratorium time moves the adolescent toward the status and responsibilities of adulthood.

Debate has reigned concerning the storm and stress character of the period of adolescence. Some insist that only through a period of storm and stress can optimal development occur. Thus, they would expect adolescence to be a period of upheaval. Others question the assumption. In the debate both sides concur that the adolescent must face many crises and challenges.

Mounting evidence suggests that the answer to the debate is not "either-or" but "both-and." The "both-and" response is dependent upon the amount of conflict present in an individual's life. Adolescents who experience storm and stress are most normally those who experience several process changes simultaneously in different areas. Too much is happening; too much is changing all at once; too many demands are being made. Storm and stress can be expected. If process changes occur in some orderly fashion, upheaval will be minimal. A typical sequential pattern of conflict areas might be anxiety over heterosexual relationships, followed by fear of rejection from peer group, and followed by conflict with parents. If, however, these conflict areas become superimposed upon each other rather than sequential, storm and stress is more likely to occur. And so, the adolescent is normally capable of coping with crisis situations with minimal storm and stress unless the number of crises is overwhelming and unmanageable. Successful resolution of each crisis or challenge provides confidence, courage, and stamina to engage in new and unique experiences and to resolve future challenges.

Intellectual Development

Adolescents can begin to engage in a larger task of interpreting the world and life because of a particular qualitative change that can occur from childhood to adolescence. The qualitative change is the development of a higher level of thinking. Our discussion here will focus on two aspects of change: first, the nature and emergence of a higher level of thinking; and second, "adolescent egocentrism."

What is qualitatively different about thinking at a higher level than thinking child-like? An illustration will demonstrate. Children ages four to twelve were placed in a room with a toy car. Each child was asked a simple question. How many possible routes or paths is this car able to travel in this room? The youngest children demonstrated straight paths. Older children began to use curves and "zigzagged" around objects. The still older children said that there's no limit to the number of routes or paths. You can go a short distance, a long distance, make as many turns as you like.[2] Those children stated a general rule. Their solution to the question was more complex, more flexible, and qualitatively different than the responses of the other children. Their response represents a qualitative change in thinking.

Another example will illustrate additional changes. Adolescents, ages 11 to 15, were asked to read the following paragraph and to respond to several questions.

All large cities have art galleries, and Italy is exceptionally rich in art treasures. Many people travel to Italy, especially to enjoy these old paintings, books and sculptures. Floods in the Florence area recently damaged many of these great works. Old paintings are rare, valuable and beautiful and should be kept safely stored.

Q. Are the Italians to blame for the loss of paintings and art treasures?

Q. Why do you say that?[3]

The responses demonstrate three levels of thinking. At the first level, a few adolescents gave restricted answers, "No, because they have lots of treasures." This answer, and others, focused on irrelevant information. At the second level which may be labeled "circumstantial," some adolescents concentrated on the "here-and-now," considering only the content of the paragraph. "I don't think they are to blame. I think it was just the weather and the rain had to come." At the third level, *imaginative* answers were given. Some adolescents moved beyond the content of the paragraph and developed possible hypotheses based, in part, on their experience.

> Well not entirely, but they were partly because they could have put them somewhere where they weren't damaged by the floods, but if there were no place to put them, they were not to blame.[4]

This last response, moving beyond the content of the paragraph, is more complex yet more flexible and more imaginative than the first two. It reflects a level of thinking qualitatively different than that expressed by the first two answers.

It is important to note that not all eleven-year-olds gave restricted responses nor did all fifteen-year-olds give imaginative answers. The quality of the level of thinking, therefore, is not solely a function of age. And so, in any group of adolescents from the ages of eleven to fifteen reacting to materials similar to those noted above, we would anticipate that some fifteen-year-olds as well as some eleven-year-olds would give restricted answers. Some eleven-year-olds as well as some fifteen-year-olds would give imaginative responses moving beyond the content and constructing many possibilities. And so, there is no one level of thinking characteristic of *all* eleven-year-olds or thirteen-year-olds or fifteen-year-olds.

The higher level of thinking being discussed here is called formal thought. The ability for formal thought opens for adolescents the possibility of a new, expanding, and more inclusive task of interpretation. A new quality in thinking may emerge. A key feature of formal thought is the construction of the possible. The formal thinker goes beyond the information given, the "here-and-now content," and thinks about many variations of the information. The formal thinker thinks of the many different arrangements which can be given to the content. He or she resists literalisms. The formal thinker is more fluent in thinking ideas about ideas, in using metaphors, in using propositional thinking, and in creating new possibilities and responses to life situations than is the non-formal thinker. Formal thinking provides for diversity, complexity and flexibility in one's thinking and problem-solving. It is most critical to remember that the quality of thinking will influence the outcomes of emotional, social, moral, and ideological change processes.

Formal thinking, however, does not develop automatically. If it does not begin to emerge at some point in the period of adolescence, its development at a later period is somewhat problematic and can be traumatic. If formal thinking is to develop, some environmental intervention must occur in the individual's life. Formal thinking is more likely to develop if the society or a community expects and demands it.

Teachers of youth have the responsibility to encourage and foster openness and flexibility in thinking. Adolescents must be challenged to explore questions and problems, to search out contradictory views, and to make appropriate distinctions between what is critical and what is not. Contradictions can be catalysts for new understandings of and commitment to a position, a value, a moral system, or a faith stance. Although a contradictory state may indeed be unsettling to some, the search process by which one comes to some sort of resolution demands flexibility in thinking and calls forth formal thought. The development and use of thinking skills is important so that adolescents can take stock of who and what they already are and to create appropriate visions of who and what they might yet become.

The development of formal thinking skills is not unidimensional. Nor is it universal and pervasive across all areas of life. There are many areas of life about which we think and to which we react, and we do not necessarily apply the same level of thinking to all areas. The development of formal thinking skills in one domain such as mathematics or physics does not assure that those skills will automatically transfer to other domains such as politics, history, or religion. One may be most able and proficient in formal thought in thinking as a nuclear physicist but be unable to exercise that thought in the realm of religion. Perhaps the society never placed particular demands on the individual. In addition to the demands of society or a community, a second major factor influences the development of formal thinking. That is the interest of the individual. We cannot *make* an individual interested in a subject or an area of life. We cannot *give* an individual an interest in a subject, program, or cause. We can demonstrate and share our interest, and thus may spark an interest in another. An individual's interest in an area, subject, or program will influence his or her motivation to develop formal thinking vis-à-vis the particular area. Strong interest will be a strong motivation. With little or no interest in an area, the individual will have but little engagement with the area. Again, and most important, we cannot *make* another interested. We can set the environment which *may* spark an interest. Whenever and wherever, we can challenge adolescents in all areas of thinking, encouraging and fostering them in the development of a higher level of thinking.

We turn now to a second aspect of intellectual development, that of adolescent egocentrism. The term, "adolescent egocentrism," is used to describe a typical behavior in early adolescence related to the thinking process. A major task confronting adolescents is developing the capacity to take account of other people's thoughts in appropriate and adequate ways. It is the capacity to assess appropriately other people's thoughts and to acknowledge those thoughts as belonging to the others. The assessment and acknowledgment is not easy for the adolescent.

During early adolescence in particular, when the person is undergoing physiological metamorphosis, entering several process changes, and being primarily concerned with himself or herself, the adolescent fails to differentiate between what he or she is thinking and what others are thinking. The adolescent acts as if he or she is on center stage and that all others around are an "imaginary" audience. The young person easily assumes that others are obsessed with his or her appearance and behavior as much as she or he. The adolescent tends to regard his or her thoughts as those of the "imaginary" audience. The results can be painful.

A personal anecdote of one of us will illustrate. My eighty-seven-year-old grandfather was visiting my family. My father, thinking that some whiskey might stimulate and raise his energy level, called my uncle, asking him to meet me after school and to send a bottle of whiskey home with me. My teacher delivered a message to me, telling me to meet my uncle after school. My uncle took me to the liquor store, purchased the whiskey, and gave the bag of purchased goods to me to take home on the school bus. I was furious. Upon arriving home, I cried, "Don't ever ask me to do that again! What do you think all those kids on the bus think of me?" With some distance of years from the event, I came to a realization. Not one person on the school bus asked what I had. Seemingly, none of them even noticed that bag I was carrying. But on that day I was sure they all knew what was in the bag, and I was convinced they were making judgments about me.

Or, hear the conversation between a mother and her daughter who returned from school with flowing tears.

"What in the world is wrong? What's happened?"

"All the kids were talking about me today and saying nasty things."

"All of the kids? Everybody? Who was talking about you?"

"Oh, a gang in the cafeteria."

"Did you overhear them talking about you?"

"No, they were sitting at a table across the room."

"Well, if you did not overhear them, did someone tell you what they were saying?"

"No."

"How do you know that they were talking about you?"

"I don't know what they were saying, but I just know that they were talking about me!"

What agony! And tragically, some persons never totally overcome "adolescent egocentrism."

Teachers with adolescents must help them to recognize and move beyond this "egocentrism." It must be challenged and called into question. It is necessary to help adolescents differentiate between "imaginary" and real audiences, to discriminate between the real and the imaginary, and to distinguish between their own thoughts and those of others. As the adolescent becomes more proficient at higher levels of thinking, he or she begins to take into appropriate consideration other people's thoughts and is able to engage in new, fresh, more satisfying forms of social intercourse.

We have defined adolescence as a period of transition, not rigidly confined to a particular age bracket but marked by process changes. It is recognized that not all adolescents will be at the same point at the same time in the transition. Also, we have considered the development of formal thought, that qualitative change in thinking that can occur if society demands it. We turn now to some developmental tasks which are characteristic to adolescence.

Some Developmental Tasks

We focus now on some specific developmental tasks to which adolescents should address themselves to make the transition to adulthood. Specifically, we have selected (1) the attainment of an identity, (2) accepting one's body, (3) developing sexuality, (4) achieving a value system and (5) achieving social consciousness. We recognize the difficulty of separating these tasks in practice but we chose these categories for ease of presentation.

Attaining an Identity *(Who am I? Who tells me who I am?)*

The "goal" of adolescence is to emerge from the transition with some continuity among the change processes and with a commitment to an ideology as well as to a role in society. When such occurs, the

adolescent has developed a sense of identity, a sense of "who I am."
There is no one continuity; there is no one commitment; there is no
one ideology; there is no one role in society. And thus, there is no one
description of "who I am" that is applicable for all adolescents—or adults.
But in a most profound sense, each adolescent is engaged in creating
a response to the question, "Who am I?" The response given is dependent upon many factors. A necessary ingredient is the adolescent's response to the question, "To whom do I belong?" To this question we
shall return later.

The child may begin adolescence with a good sense of "Who I am,"
with some sense of identity. The identity may be described in terms of
parents, school, a sports team, the name of a church, Boy Scouts or
Girl Scouts, and other associations; or as "a son," "a daughter," "a good
student," and other similar identifications. The child's sense of identity
may be most adequate for him or her. However, with the many process
changes during adolescence, the stability of that identity may dissipate. The adolescent then wonders anew, "Who am I?" Resolution of
this question leads to a new construction of identity, which in turn
influences commitment to an ideology or faith stance and shapes one's
role in society.

Adolescents need to experience crises and tensions which demand
that they consider and resolve the frustrating and often pain-producing
question, "Who am I?" Crises are important elements in the development of commitments, values, and faith stances. We may perform a
disservice to adolescents when we attempt to protect them from all
crises. In fact there may be times when we must produce crises for
them. Yet, in doing so we must take care that the produced crises will
serve the adolescents and that they are not the results of our frustra-
tions and needs.

In the process of attaining an identity, adolescents have been described in terms of one of four identity statuses.[5] Each identity status
is described by the adolescent's involvement in coping with crises and
making commitments. In the first status, some adolescents seemingly
do not experience any significant crises in confronting the question,
"Who am I?" Often, they remain utterly dependent on others for their
values, ideology, and ways of regarding the world and human life.

Rather than examining and questioning, they readily adopt family attitudes, values, and behaviors. Although they may be highly committed to a position, they have made that commitment without
exploration and question. They may comply with all the expected behaviors of the family. Sometimes a peer group or some other group is

substituted for the family. Such individuals are described as in a *foreclosure* status. Comfortable with themselves, these individuals experience little anxiety. They work with a relatively narrow range of solutions to life's concerns. Yet, often such people are authoritarian and sectarian. They do not see alternative solutions to a problem. Moreover, they are often impatient with and resistant to efforts to discover alternative solutions.

The foreclosure status is attractive to adolescents. It eliminates ambiguity, crises, struggle, and stress. It offers clear direction and final answers. The religious conversion experience of some adolescents must be described as efforts to achieve a *foreclosure* status. And it is necessary to point out that individuals in the foreclosure status often lose their strength and stability as adults in the presence of life crises which produce ambiguity.

In the second status, other adolescents may or may not experience crises or make any commitments related to the question, "Who am I?" The presence or the lack of crises does not concern them greatly. Because they simply do not know what to do with the changes taking place, or for any number of reasons, they do not attempt to make sense of what is happening to them and around them. Frequently, they appear rather carefree and can "take or leave" both people and ideas. With reference to the religious domain, they may announce an affiliation with some religious group, yet demonstrate little commitment to it. They are often impulsive and unsystematic in their thinking. Sometimes they are social isolates in the sense that they cannot or will not invest themselves in others and, thus do not establish enduring relationships. A critical characteristic of these individuals is the lack of commitment to individuals or values or ideologies. There is an unwillingness or inability to engage or to come to terms with the transition that is occurring. These individuals may be described as in a status of *identity diffusion*.

Third, the identity of another group of adolescents may be described as in the status of *moratorium*. Such adolescents are caught up in "soul-searching" and are on their way to constructing a stable identity. In fact, they will pass through many states of crises. As yet uncommitted to anything or anyone, they consciously move toward commitment. They have self-awareness that they are actively seeking answers, testing out various alternatives and attempting to decide "who I am" even though at the moment they are unable to make determinations. In the religious realm, they do struggle with fundamental religious questions. Is there a God? What difference does it make if there is a God? Somewhat utopian in their outlook, these adolescents are able to give verbal expressions to their conflicts. They may express rebellion toward authority figures, including the church and its doctrines. To outsiders they may appear to be "yo-yo's" in their behavior and emotions—up and down, up and down. Yet, their behaviors are not merely erratic. They are testing out alternatives, attempting to determine those things, values, groups, positions, and persons which can claim their commitments. Though somewhat anxious, they nevertheless have a good feeling about themselves, recognizing that they are struggling to determine who they are and where they are going.

And fourth, there is yet another group of adolescents who may be described as in the status of *achieved identity*. These adolescents have left the "status of moratorium" and have passed through crises. They have encountered and struggled with the changes. Having engaged in a "soul-searching" crisis, they have made some commitments. In the religious realm, they may have passed through a period of doubt and question. They have reevaluated previously held religious concepts and understandings. They have made deliberate choices relative to religious faith and participation. Identity achievers are somewhat autonomous and self-regulating individuals. In faithfulness to their commitments they are open and flexible, willing to examine and explore their commitments, and to alter or rearrange them if careful consideration dictates. As flexible individuals, they are able to respond without despair to changes and new responsibilities. They are learning to take control of their lives and to be responsible for their decisions. Identity achievers, as such, may not emerge fully in adolescent years, but they may give evidence of being "on the way."

The task of achieving an identity is critical and necessary. Not all adolescents may be at the same point "on the way." Exercising care, we can use the statuses of *foreclosure, identity diffusion, moratorium*, and *achieved identity* to describe adolescents. No one status may completely describe any one adolescent. Yet, the four statuses remind us that in any group of adolescents there will be diversity among them as they encounter the question "Who am I?" It may be that adolescents in the various identity statuses differ in their levels of thinking, in the way they view the world, in the way they make sense of the world and in the ways they put their worlds together. In any group of youth which is representative of the four statuses, one might anticipate conflict among the adolescents. They may be unable to understand, accept, and appreciate each other. However, it is important that they confront and challenge each other, that they provide contradictions for one another.

Accepting One's Body *(Whose body is it, anyway?)*

Adolescents confront the task of accepting that qualitative change that occurs when through the growth spurt and puberty the previously child-like body takes on a more adult form. As noted earlier, throughout childhood gradual increments in height and weight take place, but as hormones push the body to physical maturity a sudden growth spurt occurs. Clothes that did fit but a few months earlier are no longer wearable. Concurrently, the internal reproductive system matures, and the individual becomes capable of reproduction. Externally the shape of the body changes, and the physical characteristics of maleness and femaleness become visible. The body changes its form to a more adult-like appearance. The reactions of the individual as well as those of other individuals to the new body form are important influences in adolescence.

New sexual awareness and feelings emerge. How is the adolescent to respond to and cope with the new awareness and feelings? In the presence of conflicting suggestions, how is the adolescent to respond to a new awareness of maleness and femaleness? How is the adolescent to respond to and interact with others whose bodies are distinctively different from his or hers? In a society marked by conflicting expectations and a broad, yet contradictory, set of permissions, how is the adolescent to use his or her body to express maleness or femaleness? And what is it for one to be male or female? Answers to these questions do not come easily.

Not only must the adolescents deal with relationships between the sexes, but they must respond to and come to terms with their own bodies. Parents can tell stories of both males and females who, from the parent's point of view, devote extraordinary attention to their bodies: multiple baths in one day, fussing with hair, distress over skin blemishes, using the right cosmetic, and wearing the right clothes. The nature of the attention given may change from one segment of the society to another. In so many instances, the adolescent is motivated, even driven, by the desire to make his or her body attractive to others. Annoying as the behaviors of adolescents may be, they represent efforts by the adolescents to come to terms with their bodies.

Driven by popular images of the ideal body type, tall skinny boys and girls and short or fat adolescents are often unhappy with themselves. Female obese adolescents are often miserable, for the "ideal" demands a chic, well-proportioned feminine figure. These individuals may suffer from social rejection, for persons often make judgments of others based on their first perceptions of attractiveness. The female cultural "ideal" affecting one's self-esteem may sometimes motivate certain females to starve themselves to the degree that they become anorexic.

The male ideal demands big muscles, broad shoulders and chests, and well-proportioned arms and legs. Those who do not fit that ideal or who mature late are often distressed with their appearance. These individuals can be found frequently isolating themselves and spending endless passive hours in front of the television. Males and females whose body types depart from the "ideal" may be dissatisfied and wish they were different. These adolescents need acceptance and encouragement from others to help them recognize and accept the physical appearances that cannot be changed. On the other hand, when physical appearances can be changed, encouragement and support should be given.

Developing Sexuality *(What is it to be male or female?)*

The development of sexuality consumes enormous amounts of adolescents' energy and attention. At the same time, adolescent sexuality is of great concern to the family, church, and community. And yet, sexuality is an area of human life which many find difficult to discuss even though our culture is permeated by and replete with sexual expressions. Here we discuss sexuality in perspective with other basic human needs and concerns, note a sequence of development which can enhance the development of sexuality, and identify some factors which tend to influence sexual behavior.

We define sexuality "as the total personality identity of the individual person, the actual sense of his [her] learning experiences as being a male or a female."[6] This rather formal definition carries a number of implications. Sex gender, culturally defined sex roles, and sexual activity, either individually or collectively, are not to be equated with each other. Sex or sexual behavior is not sexuality. Self-identity in terms of sex gender is biologically based, but that base is not sufficient to encompass the totality of sexuality. An individual's sexuality is not some quality or quantity given at birth to be unfolded in time. Sexuality is the individual's created and achieved interpretation and understanding of himself or herself as male or female. As an interpretation, sexuality may always be in the process of being achieved. Sexuality is that which the individual is. The value that one gives to sexuality is directly related to value that one possesses for self. Sexual behavior in the first instance does not create sexuality. Sexual behavior is an expression of already-achieved sexuality.

We are suggesting that sexuality, not given or conferred, is learned, and learning implies the active participation of the individual. Sexuality begins not with puberty but at birth. Sexuality is constructed and learned along with the individual self. It continues to develop throughout the life span. An individual's sexuality is his or her response to the question, "What is it for me to be male or female?" The response at any point along the life span is highly dependent upon the individual's regard and feelings about self, about his or her body and of others. Adolescents are at a particular point in a change process concerning their development of sexuality. Significantly, the development of sexuality is not an isolated phenomenon, unrelated to other development or change processes.

In industrial societies young people are defined as sexually mature at puberty while they are defined as socially and psychologically immature. Such a perspective focuses primarily on the biological capacity for reproduction. However, unlike such needs as food and water, sexual activity is not necessary to sustain one's life. Sexual function among humans is *most* influenced by factors other than biological ones. Again, one's regard for one's self, one's sense of self-worth, one's regard for others, one's regard for his or her body, one's values, and one's cognitive abilities are more influential factors than the biological.

Adolescents need assistance in developing their sexuality. Certain capacities that develop within individuals appear to enhance the development of sexuality. *Autonomy from parents is a critical capacity.* Being able to function independently of parental presence or authority can influence the development of sexuality. The individual becomes ready to transfer the trust from a parental relationship to an intimate and trusting relationship among peers and eventually to one individual. Ideally, the desirable development is the movement into heterosociality (largely dating or coed groupings) with gradual movement into heterosexual commitment. Indeed, preoccupation with a heterosexual commitment without sufficient heterosociality may well interfere with the development of sexuality. Involvement in heterosociality prior to commitment allows time for the development of both autonomy and sexuality.

Other than the sexual act itself, there is very little that is universal about sexuality. The sociocultural environment highly influences sexual development. Each culture prescribes appropriate behaviors for males and females. Yet across cultures those behaviors vary. However, social-cultural sexual expectations can change. While the changes are in transition, disagreements about sexuality are evident. This is evidenced by the pro-choice vs. pro-life encounters.

Adolescent sexual patterns are more highly influenced by the expectations of the culture than by the needs of the adolescent. For example, the capacity to experience female orgasm may be a biological constant. However, in very few cultures has female orgasmic capacity been valued. The male's culturally defined sexual role has negated the female response. The culture prescribes legitimate sexual behavior for males and females. Similarly, motivation for sexual behavior among adolescents is largely a response to external pressures.

Throughout the life cycle sexuality develops on two levels, the intrapsychic and the interpersonal. The internal representations that determine what "sex symbols" "turn one on" and which anticipate the "results" of sexual activity are of the intrapsychic level. These erotic symbols and themes tend to be uniform within a culture. Children learn them by observing and listening to adult interpersonal interactions. They discern gestures, responses, and strategies expected in a social sexual encounter which shapes erotic response.

The interpersonal level contains the agenda of how one presents oneself overtly to another and how one responds to another's behavior in a way that aids a heterosexual encounter. The interpersonal is highly influenced by the sociocultural moment. That moment may prescribe acceptable or unacceptable sexual behaviors. The herpes epidemic may well serve to alter some sexual encounters. At the present, there are three major, specific cultural and social influences affecting adolescents as they develop interpersonal levels of sexuality. They are: (1) the debate concerning gender differences, including male-female social roles; (2) the expectation that adolescents be interested in sex; and (3) the adult social world observed by the adolescent, that is, an adult world more preoccupied with sex and more overtly sexually active than it used to be. The adolescent is compelled to make some response to, and some sense of, these influences.

Not all adolescents experience the same stress as they develop their sexuality. The least strain is experienced by those adolescents for whom there is a reciprocal facilitation or congruency between the development of the intrapsychic and interpersonal levels. Adolescents need to learn to articulate or describe their own intrapsychic and interpersonal interpretations. Thus they will be able to discern congruencies and incongruencies between their intrapsychic and interpersonal interpretations and be more able to direct their own sexual behaviors.[7]

We have already asserted that overt sexual behavior is not, in and of itself, sexuality. Nevertheless much overt sexual activity, while serving some immediate purposes, may serve a larger and more complex goal. Participation in sexual behavior may be an attempt to construct, achieve, and verify sexuality. The behavior may be destructive or constructive, but it is precisely at this point that parents must contend with the erratic and, at times, infuriating sexual behaviors of their adolescents.

But sexuality must not be discussed only in terms of sexual activity. Isolated sexual behaviors are meaningless and inane without some reference to the total persons. Adolescents must be assisted to ask larger questions. "What is it for me to be male?" "What is it for me to be female?" Various segments of the society answer these questions by producing a list of stereotypic male-female roles. Increasingly, the list is being challenged, and adolescents must respond to the challenge. Attempts to move from sexuality based on female-male stereotypes to a more inclusive human sexuality reject such stereotypes. They urge that males and females accept and share in both traditionally assigned masculine and feminine sex-roles. Recognizing that biologically males and females are different, the attempts urge the acceptance of a human sex-role orientation without reference to female and male stereotypes. As we work with adolescents, we must hear the question of another, "Is it possible to find a creative and Christian way to foster a liberated conscience which is a union of masculine and feminine characteristics?"[8]

The development of sexuality is not an isolated phenomenon, unrelated to other aspects of development. In actuality, the development of sexuality is influenced by a number of factors: a regard and appreciation for oneself; a regard and appreciation for one's body; a regard and appreciation for others; the development of autonomy; the development of moral judgments; the participation in heterosocial activities; the ability to make congruent intrapsychic and interpersonal interpretations; the ability to ask and engage in the larger questions of sexuality; and to be in control of and responsible for one's own behavior. Sexuality is complex and powerful. With the complexity, adults must engage adolescents.

Achieving a Value System *(What is required of me?)*

An individual's answer to the question "What is required of me?" is shaped by his or her value system. One's value system consists of general beliefs by which each person judges that some means or end action is personally or socially desirable in relation to its opposite or converse. For example, one prefers equality to inequality, honesty to dishonesty. One is not born with a value system. Individuals develop their own values that guide them in resolving conflicts as well as making decisions. Values function as standards or criteria that guide the thought and action of the adolescent.

Several factors appear to facilitate the process of change in the value system of adolescents.

First, adolescents are involved in a search for fidelity. Abhorring falsity and hypocrisy, they look for people and ideas to have faith in.

Second, adolescents can develop the ability to form more generalized concepts. They are beginning to understand the role of history and the impact of the present on the future; to get some feeling for social change, recognizing the possibility that people and social institutions may alter and be altered; and to weigh the wider costs, benefits, and actions of decisions. Adolescents are beginning to realize the importance of using principles and frameworks for judging particular events.

Third, in the process of developing an identity, the development of a philosophy of life is critical. Ideals and values are an important component to integrate into a philosophy of life. Thus, the value system contributes to answering the question "Who am I?"

In childhood the value system consists primarily of concrete items. Judgments of behavior are often made on cleanliness and obedience. The change processes that occur in adolescence foster a move to more abstract concepts such as equalitarian, responsible, imaginative, and courageous. Secular trends and historical events affect an adolescent's value system. Participation of our country in the Vietnam War had a large effect on the value system of adolescents during that historical period. An abstract value system is more likely to emerge within adolescents who are faced with contradictions. Alternative viewpoints will help them reflect on their present interpretations, and respond with feelings and reactions in light of other possible interpretations and to various situations and conditions.[9]

Achieving Social Consciousness (*Am I my neighbor's keeper?*)

The development of a concern for others begins in infancy. However, the potential for developing a larger concern for others emerges in adolescence. Development of a concern for others is learned and demands the integration of affective, cognitive, and motivational processes.

Infants are born with the capacity to make an affective, empathic response. Newborns in the hospital nursery, upon hearing the cry of another infant, will respond with crying. The cry of the infant is a selective stimulus as newborns will not cry to other imitative crying stimuli. Young babies transfer to themselves the emotions of their caretakers. These empathic responses appear to be innate.

An early-developed empathic response can be seen in an emotional reaction to someone experiencing pain or discomfort. A child cuts her/his knee. It hurts. Later, seeing other children fall and cut their knees, the observing child feels an emotional reaction. Another empathic response is motor mimicry. One listens to a stutterer trying to talk. The listener's lips begin to move slightly, trying to help the stutterer speak. Furthermore, eventually an individual imagining how another individual feels in crises situations responds empathically. These responses are primarily internal and not necessarily related to a concern for the other. These particular empathic responses must undergo transformations for one to have a genuine and enduring concern for others.

Cognitive processes interacting with these empathic responses enable the transformations. The first cognitive influence is the infants' recognition that they are distinct persons, separated from other individuals. Having learned this separateness, preschool children note that others have emotional states different from their own, and they role play these different emotions. In late childhood, children become aware that emotional states in others may last for a long time. They experience or see that individuals going through crises situations may be emotionally troubled over a long period of time. With further cognitive development one comprehends both the plight of the individual as well as that of an entire group or class of people. With this last cognitive response, egocentrism subsides, a sociocentric viewpoint emerges, and a larger concern for others becomes possible.

Integration of the cognitive with the empathic transforms the responses to compassion or sympathetic distress; and when individuals acknowledge that they caused or were responsible for the other person's plight, guilt emerges. The earliest "guilt over action experience" probably occurs when young children are faced with the fact that their behavior caused the distress of another. Later "guilt over inactions" emerges when the individual is able to recognize that an act which one should have done but did not do caused distress in another person.

Other guilt responses can occur. Guilt over survival may occur, for example, when all passengers are killed in an automobile accident except the driver. Guilt over affluence may emerge when one becomes aware of the affluent life one has while many others are living in destitute situations. For such guilt to occur the individual must be able to imagine vividly the circumstances of the other's life while admitting that there is no justification for his or her own well-being. Thus empathic distress may be transformed into sympathetic distress or guilt, depending on the causal attributions of the observer.

Where is the motivational component? Does empathic distress contain an altruistic motive, a desire to help another? Am I my brother's and sister's keeper? When empathic distress is aroused by another person's misfortune, a major goal of the empathic distress is to help the other, for gratification can be obtained only by reducing the other's stress. Adolescents must become aware of the plight of others. They can know and feel the needs of others within their own communities. They can develop the capacity to imagine and become aware of the plight of more distant others. These awarenesses enhance the development of the larger concern for others.

In summary, the young adolescent has had the capacity for empathic arousal since birth. While cognitive capacities have developed during childhood, a new, larger cognitive ability can develop in adolescence. This is that awareness of others as having distinct identities, life circumstances, and inner states. This allows one to compare others' well-being with one's own. The integration of this cognitive capacity with the affective altruistic motive can provide a motivating force for moral action, a concern for and intervention in the welfare of others.[10]

Some Implications for Our Task

We have identified and discussed several process changes and five developmental tasks of adolescents by which we can gain understanding of the transition period from childhood to adulthood. Our selection is not intended to be all-inclusive. Though we have discussed, by necessity, the changes and tasks in a sequential way, there is considerable overlap among them. Moreover, they act upon and interact with each other. Thus, adolescents are involved in a dynamic and complex work of responding to, and of achieving adequate and useful solutions for, the changes and tasks. The presence and demands of process changes and developmental tasks, and the efforts to respond to and achieve solutions, constitute a major portion of adolescents' life-content. It is about that life-content that adolescents are most normally concerned. Pastors, teachers, and parents can facilitate the adolescents' work of responding and of achieving solutions, thus assisting young persons to make the transition from childhood to adulthood. Here we want to consider implications of this present chapter for our task.

First, whenever we engage adolescents with the Bible, they bring their life-content to bear on the engagement. Their life-content influences their interest in the Bible, their willingness to engage it, and their ability to interpret it. Their life-content affects that which youth hear from the Bible. Adolescents, as well as all of us, engage and interpret the Bible from within their life-content. It is imperative that we deal knowledgeably and sensitively with the life-content of the adolescents with whom we work. Knowing that we can better respond to the question, "In what way might the Bible impinge upon, inform, and shape the adolescents' responses and solutions to the process changes and developmental tasks belonging to the period of transition?" A failure in this matter is a failure to take seriously the adolescent and is to isolate the Bible and the adolescent from each other.

Second, we have defined adolescence as a period of transition involving process changes and developmental tasks. Thus, adolescence is not to be defined solely by a specific age-span. Not all adolescents experience process changes and meet developmental tasks at the same age, in the same sequence, and with the same intensity. Not all enter and move through the various identity statuses at the same time and in the same sequence. Thus, within any group of adolescents we can expect a wide range of diversity, even if all are of the same age. As we engage adolescents with the Bible, we can expect a diversity of willingness, interest, and ability to interpret as well as differences in the nature of interpretations. Therefore we need to be sensitive to and patient with the diversity. We must arrange the learning environment to respond to that diversity and to encourage its expression. Moreover, we should assist the members of the group to accept, rejoice in, and learn from the diversity among them.

Third, adolescents can learn a larger task of interpreting the Bible because they have the possibility of developing a higher level of thinking—that of formal thinking. With the emergence of formal thinking, they can deal more adequately with the metaphorical language of the Bible; they can imagine a variety of possibilities concerning a passage; they can deal with stories as stories. They can resist literalism for the sake of literalism. They can ask new, complex, and penetrating questions of the Bible. They can consider many "sides" of a passage. They can imagine and consider relationships between themselves and the biblical material. And they are able to move beyond the words of the Bible, so as to hear the Word. The development of formal thinking with reference to biblical material does not occur automatically. It is our task to expect, to demand, and to encourage such thinking on the part of adolescents as they engage the Bible.

Fourth, there are times when we are to produce conflict and to create contradictions for adolescents. They must cope with changes. They must develop solutions to tasks. Evenly or in upheaval they are moving through crises. We are called upon to help and encourage adolescents to work through these crises, rather than ignoring them or running away from them. We are called to help them risk responses and solutions. Our help may demand that we produce conflict, create and identify contradictions, and even contribute to painful and unsettling experiences. The biblical witness will frequently do the same.

·4
The interpretive process

Interpreting the Bible and learning to interpret the Bible by Christian people are done within the broad, ongoing interpretive and constructive process of human life. All of human life is shaped by that process. Boys and girls, women and men, acting upon and interacting with their own experiences and the world with its events and things and people, make interpretations of all them. Giving some order to those interpretations, they construct knowledge, reality, and meaning—of self, the world, and human existence. The ongoing process is an essential and critical activity of the human creature. Christian life itself is an ongoing process of interpreting and constructing one's life under the event of Jesus. The work of interpreting the Bible and learning to interpret the Bible, an essential activity for the Christian, must be viewed within the framework of that critical and essential activity of the human creature.

Here we will discuss the perspective of developmental constructivism which describes the ongoing interpretive processes and activity. It can illuminate and inform our work as we engage adolescents in learning a larger task of interpreting the Bible. It addresses directly the third component of the interpretive process—the relationship and interaction between the content to be interpreted and the interpreter. It describes the human activity of interpreting, ordering, and constructing knowledge, reality, and meaning. It gives us clues concerning our role in the teaching event, suggesting what we as teachers can or cannot accomplish and suggesting what we can do to aid the process.

Developmental Constructivism[1]

Briefly, the perspective holds that the individual, acting upon and interacting with his or her own experiences and the external world, is an active and determining participant in the process of constructing and learning to construct her or his own knowledge, reality, and meaning of the world and human life in it. The constructive process continues across the life span, not limited to one age group or to one point in a person's life. What is constructed and how it is constructed will differ from person to person and will differ for an individual over the life span. Differences will result from varying ages, abilities, experiences, values, and commitments.

Creators of Knowledge, Reality, and Meaning

Throughout the life span the individual is offered—and confronted by—an enormous amount of experiences, bits of information, and stimuli from the world and life in it. So massive is the supply that the individual cannot possibly give attention to all of it. An effort to do so would spell disaster for the individual. To protect the self from the destructive flood of information, stimuli, and experiences, the individual must select out, consciously or unconsciously, only a portion of what is available. He or she must determine what items will be selected for attention and consideration because selection is necessary for survival.

The selected items are then given some interpretation, invested with some meaning, set into some order, and constructed into some kind of a whole. In so doing, the individual endeavors "to make some sense" of the world. She or he has created a resultant picture of human life, of self, and of the world. And it can be said that the picture *is* the individual's knowledge, reality, and meaning.

The picture created has been achieved with but only a portion of that vast supply of available experiences, data, and stimuli. The individual has not used all that is available. Recognizing that no two people will make exactly the same selections from available supply, we can anticipate a vast and rich diversity of constructions or pictures. No two persons will view the world and human life in exactly the same way. It is not possible for any one of us to view the world and human life without some personal prejudice or bias. Each one of us works and lives from within the framework of his or her own picture or interpretation of external reality. Regardless of how well the constructed reality or picture approximates external reality, it functions as the "real thing" for the individual. We never see the world and human life as "it really is" but always through our interpretations or constructions.

An individual regards his or her achieved construction or created picture as the "real thing" as long as it is satisfactory and adequate for life in the world. When it proves to be inadequate, new constructions may be required. At the same time, it can be expected that an individual will protect and defend his or her constructed reality, at times even under most severe attacks and challenges.

The achieved construction, which is an internal picture, exerts tremendous influence in two directions. First, it is a powerful determinant in how the individual will act upon and toward the world. The construction with its values, norms, and meanings influences a style of action. It gives clues to the individual for meeting and coping with the world and human life. Second, it influences how the individual will permit the world and its events and people to impinge upon him or her. It influences the determination of what is regarded valuable and worthwhile. It influences the determination of what information and experiences merit attention. The achieved construction, functioning in these two directions, serves to inform future constructions, and thus the individual's future.

The perspective maintains that a constructed reality, and thus knowledge and meaning, cannot be given to an individual from the outside, cannot be "poured into" an individual by another. It cannot be delivered to or imposed upon one person by another. Meaning, truth, and values are not "substances" or "quantities" or "qualities" which can be deposited in one individual by another. Moreover, they cannot be transmitted from one person to another in a one-to-one correspondence. Meaning is not some "substance" or "quality" located in things, events, words, persons, or experiences. Rather, the individual actively engages in interpreting and in giving meaning to and investing meaning in events, experiences, and things. The individual makes sense of these things, giving them value, worthwhileness, and a place in his or her life.

A Continuing and Recycling Process

Even the very young child, provided with experiences and stimuli from the external world, selects out particular items for his or her attention, interpreting, ordering, and giving meaning to them. Thus, the child is engaged in the constructive process. The results are rather gross, simplistic, highly undifferentiated, and, in some respects, rather rigid. Early attempts at the constructive activity are circumscribed by limitations in cognitive, affective, and social abilities as well as an exceedingly narrow range of experience. However described, the child's construction is still his or her achieved reality. For the moment at least, it is adequate for the child's life in the world. The child has no need of a more complex and differentiated reality.

Through time the individual is active in elaborating knowledge and in altering, rearranging, and even transforming already achieved constructions. New information, experiences, and situations demand greater complexity in constructions. In the presence of the new, the already achieved may prove to be insufficient. The new may challenge it, unveil its inadequacies, and press for reconstructions. The individual may choose to engage the challenge or opt to ignore, deny, or flee from it. In either case the individual makes the choices. In new situations and with increased cognitive, affective, and social abilities and an expanding range of experiences, the individual will most normally create some alterations, rearrangements, and even transformations of already achieved constructions. Thus, new or somewhat different constructions of knowledge, reality, and meaning result. They are characterized by greater complexity, differentiation, and flexibility.

In the continuing process there is a recycling effect. An individual "mulls over" and reflects about past events, behaviors, experiences, information once received, and constructions already achieved. He or she thinks about them repeatedly, acting upon and interacting with them cognitively and affectively. The past is retrieved, re-encoded, reworked, and reordered. The past is reinterpreted and comprehended in new and different ways. There are new pictures of the world. There is new knowledge, reality, and meaning.

The continuing, recycling process is marked by two characteristics. First, there is a stability and continuity of knowledge, reality, and meaning with the past. The past cannot be ignored; it influences the shape of the present as well as the future. Second, there is the possibility of change and flexibility. The recycling process enables the individual to reinterpret, reorder, and reconstruct the past even as the past contributes to the interpretations and constructions in the present. The past is reshaped even as it shapes the present.

This discussion of the continuing, recycling process leads us to two significant conclusions. First, already achieved constructions of knowledge, reality, and meaning are not to be regarded as complete, fixed, static, or final. They are tentative and subject to ongoing alterations, rearrangements, or even transformation. At any given moment, an individual may highly value and be profoundly committed to his or her construction of knowledge, reality, and meaning—and that properly so. But in the process there is increased elaboration of knowledge, reality, and meaning with greater differentiation, complexity, and flexibility. In turn, commitments and values become more complex and differentiated. There is greater flexibility in the sense that there is increased understanding and appreciation for differing views.

Second, there is no need and it is inappropriate, at least initially, to make value judgments of "right" or "wrong" concerning another's achieved constructions. Within the range of his or her experiences and within cognitive, affective, or social abilities, the individual interprets, orders, and constructs as she or he is able and not as someone else may wish. Whatever the construction, it is the individual's attempt to make sense of the world and human life. It belongs to her or him. It may be the "very best" that can be achieved at the moment. Resulting constructions may be most inappropriate and inadequate for life in the world or in a particular community. Thus, they would prove destructive to the individual and may require alterations or transformations. But for each individual there is a particular range of abilities and experiences within which the constructive process can occur.

Constructing in Community

The perspective under discussion here gives a primary emphasis to the individual as an active participant in the constructive process. Nevertheless, the interpretive and constructive process is not the work of the individual "doing an individual thing" in splendid isolation. The activity always possesses social or communal dimensions, though the extent will vary from time to time and from person to person. Regardless of variations, the individual is always dependent upon the external world or community to make available information, stimuli, and experiences.

Cultures, societies, and particular communities are themselves constructions of knowledge, reality, and meaning. They are modes of interpreting, thinking, and feeling about the world. They are ways of behaving toward and in the world. They are ways of acting on and interacting with the world and life in it. One's culture as well as particular communities set limits. They define and describe ways of thinking, feeling, valuing, and relating which are acceptable and which are expected of members. They determine behaviors that are both acceptable and expected. Social predilections or expectations, community values, and norms become a part of the individual's knowledge base. They serve to mediate, to give meaning to, and to influence the individual's own constructions of knowledge, reality, and meaning. Language, especially the particular language of a particular community, influences how the individual discriminates and describes the world, its things, events, and people.

A culture, society, or community can be expected to initiate and encourage its members into a particular way of thinking, feeling, behaving, and valuing. It will cause particular information and experiences to impinge upon members, while deliberately excluding other data. A particular community will consciously and deliberately do those things which will assist and encourage members to internalize and take for themselves its way of interpreting and constructing. Consciously, intentionally, and deliberately it will provide socialization experiences.

Socialization experiences in a particular community are not one-way actions summarily imposed upon individuals, producing carbon copies. The individual, within the context of abilities, range of experience and already achieved constructions, acts upon and interacts with the data from the community. In conversation with that data and with others in the community who also bring their abilities, ranges of experiences, and already achieved constructions, individuals develop and create commonly held and shared interpretations and constructions. Shared and commonly held constructions result not from external imposition but through interaction with others. Resulting from the dialectical conversations, the very shape and life of the community may be gradually altered, rearranged, or even transformed.

There may be a high degree of commonality among a community's people. In the last analysis, even shared and communal knowledge, reality, and meaning belong to the individual. They are the interpretations and constructions achieved by the individual within the context of community. And so, diversity of understanding, meaning, and valuing will be present in every particular community. Each community must determine the amount of diversity which can be tolerated or enjoyed without losing its life. At the same time a community may lose its life and vitality if no diversity is permitted. That lack would leave no room for others who do not fit perfectly. Such a community will be tyrannical.

Role of the Cognitive Domain

The perspective maintains that what is constructed and how it is constructed is a function of the individual's developmental level with its peculiar abilities and limitations. The developmental levels of the cognitive, social, and affective domains and the interactions between the three are critical determinants in the constructive process. In the perspective, the cognitive domain receives special attention.

Preschool children do not have the cognitive (thinking) abilities possessed by elementary children. In turn, elementary children do not have the cognitive abilities exercised by many adolescents and adults.

Among adolescents and adults there is a wide range of cognitive abilities. Those differing cognitive abilities are dominant determinants of how data, stimuli, and experiences are selected out for attention and consideration, and of how they are interpreted, ordered, and constructed into some whole or picture. Interpretations and constructions do reflect cognitive abilities. Simple and undifferentiated constructions of knowledge, reality, and meaning are indicative of an individual's cognitive abilities. More complex and flexible cognitive abilities make possible more complex and flexible constructions. An individual may not exercise the full extent of his or her cognitive abilities in the constructive task. Nevertheless, an individual's ability to construct is circumscribed by the limits of cognitive development. Whatever an educational event may be able to achieve is limited and defined by the cognitive abilities of the students.

The emphasis given to the cognitive domain neither ignores nor detracts from the affective and social domain. They, too, influence and give direction to the individual's determination of what is valuable and worthwhile. They play a profound role in a person's commitments. They are powerful forces in the constructive process; they can energize or abort the process. At times, affective and social dimensions can be so overwhelming and so powerful that they short-circuit cognitive abilities. They may render the cognitive abilities ineffective. On other occasions they may provide the necessary challenges and conflicts which prompt the individual toward alterations, rearrangements, and even transformations. The cognitive domain and abilities can be abused. Total reliance on cognitive abilities can ignore or blot out the influences of the social and affective domains. To be "too" cognitive is to over-intellectualize, ignoring and denying dimensions of what it is to be human.

There remains much to be learned about the interplay and influence of the cognitive, social, and affective domains upon each other. A major thrust of the constructivist perspective is clear, however. How one deals with, gives meaning to, and structures social relationships as well as affective dimensions is highly contingent and dependent upon the individual's level of cognitive development. A person can ultimately deal with strong emotions of love and hate only in ways congruent with cognitive abilities. A person can take on the roles of others only in ways congruent and consistent with cognitive abilities. A person cannot be expected or compelled to use cognitive abilities which she or he does not possess. But whatever those abilities, the cognitive domain exercises a powerful role in the constructive process.

Implications for Our Task

It is within the context of developmental constructivism that we wish to explore the work of helping adolescents learn a larger ongoing task of interpreting the Bible than was possible for them as children. In the remainder of this chapter, we will examine and elaborate on the perspective's implications and contributions for our task.

First, the Christian tradition, viewed from within the perspective discussed, is itself an interpretation, an ordering, and a construction of all life under the event of Jesus. The Christian tradition possesses and is identified by a rich treasury of particular contents: its sacred texts, liturgies, symbols, actions, hymns, and past stories. It is a way of regarding, feeling, and thinking about all life in the presence of the gospel. Informed and guided by a particular Event, Christian tradition is a construction of all life with its hopes and despairs, successes and failures, experiences and behaviors. Its varying theologies are constructions or attempts "to make sense" of God's activity in the world.

Christian tradition, per se, is not divinely given or imposed; it has not been delivered finally and once-for-all-times. Christian tradition is achieved by Christian people endeavoring to be faithful to the gospel. It is a continuing process. Clearly, the present construction of Christian tradition is not a replica of the tradition in past eras. Generation after generation of Christian people in new circumstances, in the presence of new demands and challenges in living, and in the company of problems, horrors, and failures have remembered the story of Jesus and the stories of Christians past. In recycling—remembering and interacting with the past in the present—they have constructed and told new stories of themselves as the people of Jesus. New interpretations, constructions, and stories have opened new opportunities for them as Christian people. Succeeding generations of Christians have altered, rearranged, and, on occasion, even transformed something of the past tradition. In continuity with the past, each generation of Christians leaves behind a somewhat different tradition than it received, thus adding tradition to tradition.

As individual Christians ask, "What is it for me this day to be a baptized person?" and as Christians in a community ask, "What is it for us this day to be Christians together in the church and the world?"[2] they will continually come to new understandings and will create new constructions. They will discover that answers given yesterday, while right and proper for that time, may not be adequate and appropriate today. They will discover that answers given yesterday must not be regarded as finished, complete, and final but as tentative—even as the answers given today are tentative, freeing Christians for new responses tomorrow.

Viewing Christian tradition as an ongoing construction of knowledge, reality, and meaning in continuity with the past, we recognize that we can never present it to anyone in a complete, final, and finished form. We have no neatly wrapped package to offer. Christian tradition is always in process. The tradition in which we live, which identifies and informs us, and which we cherish must be regarded as somewhat tentative. Today, Christian people endeavoring to live out faithfully their baptism are giving shape to the continuing and future tradition. As we engage adolescents in learning a larger task of interpreting the Bible, we invite them to take their rightful place in the community of the faithful. They can participate in that ongoing tradition in ways not possible for them earlier, asking and responding to "What is it for me this day to be a baptized person?" and "What is it for us this day to be Christians together in the church and the world?"

Second, another implication for our task of helping adolescents learn to interpret their lives and the world under the gospel is that we can expect adventure in a community. To learn to interpret the Bible is always an adventure in a community, for the Bible does not belong to individuals but to the church, the community of God's people.

Every particular Christian tradition or community is itself a particular interpretation and construction of the larger Christian tradition. From the tradition's rich treasury of sacred texts, liturgies, symbols, actions, and past history each particular tradition has selected particular content to which it gives primary emphasis and attention. The selected content has shaped the past character of the community and continues to give shape to its present and future characters. Each lives in the world as a particular knowledge, reality, and meaning of life under the gospel. In a very special way, each is a construction of the larger tradition. To every response given, the gospel stands over and against it, calling it into judgment and challenging its faithfulness, and thus asking for new interpretations and constructions.

Each particular Christian tradition has both the right and the responsibility to introduce and initiate its people into its way of thinking, feeling, and doing. Those ways must be declared, demonstrated, and articulated; they cannot be summarily imposed. Into an ongoing conversation with content selected for primary attention, a Christian community brings to bear its past and present stories, its thinking and understandings, its ways of doing and its commitments. From the ongoing conversation marked by challenge, judgment, and critical think-

ing, as well as support and encouragement, the community creates
new interpretations, new orderings, new ways of doing things, and new
constructions which, in some measure, are held and shared in common. As Christian people share in life together and dialectically engage their personal and common lives with the contents of the faith,
there is the Spirit of God, calling, gathering, enlightening, sanctifying,
and preserving God's people.

Our life in Christian community is to be marked by our participation in the ongoing conversation not *of*, or *about*, but *in* the faith.
Adolescents are to be encouraged and enabled to join with us in the
conversation in the faith as they are able. They do belong to the household of faith. They stand at a critical moment with their particular
concerns and needs. In new and exciting, yet frightening and frustrating ways, they are called anew to interpret and construct their lives.
We believe that their participation in the ongoing conversation in the
faith can assist them profoundly in their task. The Christian community must offer a wide array of data and experiences. It must probe and
challenge as well as support and encourage. It must leave space for
testing, building, tearing down, and rebuilding. In our work with adolescents, we cannot compel. We cannot determine how the task will be
done or what will be its results. We cannot determine what content or
experiences will be selected for attention and consideration. We can
create, however, an environment which may maximize participation
in the Christian adventure, assisting us all together to achieve shared
and commonly held knowledge, reality, and meaning of life under the
gospel.

Into the conversation must be brought the contents of the faith.
And so, the Bible must play a major role. Christian adolescents, when
children, were already thinking about the Bible, interpreting it, and
constructing knowledge and meaning of it. Children are limited in their
engagement with the Bible. With their particular cognitive abilities,
they are unable to understand much of the Bible as it intends itself to
be understood. Children are unable to deal adequately and appropriately with the biblical language. Nor can they fully come to terms
with the realities to which the Bible points. Yet the already achieved
constructions of children could dominate the adolescents' continuing
interpretation of the Bible.

Therefore it must be declared forcefully that those constructions
achieved in childhood, while appropriate for that time, are limited and
narrow. To encourage adolescents deliberately or by default to continue in them is a disservice both to the youth and to the church. With
the onset of adolescence there is the possibility for a larger and more

inclusive thinking. Let us highlight and underscore a particular concern. We are concerned about the quality of thinking. We want adolescents to bring the best thinking possible to bear on their engagement with the Bible. We must challenge them to engage in a larger and more inclusive thinking than was possible for them as children. It is a thinking that makes possible more complex, flexible, and differentiated interpretations and constructions of human life and the world as well as the Bible. With a larger and more inclusive thinking, adolescents can be initiated into a larger task of interpreting the Bible. They can be challenged and assisted to *begin* to learn the larger task.

Third among the implications of our task is the role of the young person. The adolescent is an active participant in the interpretive process, constructing his or her own understanding, knowledge, and interpretations of the Bible. As much as we may desire, we can neither give to nor impose on adolescents a beautiful map to follow through life. We cannot give them a ready-made value system, a finished Christian view of the world, or an understanding and knowledge of God. Yet we can offer useful and appropriate information and experiences. We can shape the environments of home, church, and community in ways that help to bring about the actualization of certain possibilities. We can model and share our faith, our understanding of God, our values, and our ways of doing things. But maps to be followed, values calling forth commitment, purpose giving direction, and an understanding of God giving hope and confidence—all of them, in a most critical and profound sense, must be constructed by the adolescent for herself or himself. Of the results, we may rejoice or despair, give thanks or weep in disappointment, but always we must encourage or challenge. In any event, the adolescent has done for himself or herself what only he or she can do.

Adolescents are not newcomers to the broad interpretive and constructive task of human existence. They have been active participants in the constructive process since birth. They have built many "realities," periodically discarding some and rearranging others or tearing others down and building new ones. They have constructed many views of the world. They have also constructed many "knowledges" of right and wrong. Our youth have already made and remade interpretations of the contents of the faith. They have constructed many understandings of God.

What may have been adequate for them as children, however, should be inadequate for them as adolescents. The demands of adolescence may challenge, attack, or even destroy already achieved constructions. Adolescence requires something other than did childhood. We do not

meet adolescents as "empty slates" waiting to be filled by our "scrib-
blings." In our relationships with them we dare not dismiss or ignore
those already held creations of knowledge, reality, and meaning. We
must not set them aside in our eagerness to get on with our agenda.
The already achieved constructions and understandings give clues, influence, and help to determine altered and new constructions. We must
make every effort to achieve a knowledge and understanding of the
adolescents' present understandings. The information for such an
achievement must come from the adolescents themselves. We must ask
them; we must listen to them. Such an achievement will enable us to
discover what new information and experiences are necessary. It will
inform us in giving both encouragement and challenge and producing
conflict which may enable the creation of more adequate constructions.

Adolescents are beginning to appraise their lives and the life of
the world with its things, events, and people in new ways and with
new abilities. They are required to make a "new sense" of the world
and human life, and of themselves. They are challenged to create new
interpretations, new constructions of knowledge, reality, and meaning.
Beginning with constructions already achieved and receiving new information, events, and experiences, they begin to engage in the constructive process in new and ever expanding ways. The beginnings
may be difficult, confusing, and painful, full of false beginnings and
new beginnings. But all of that is part of the adventure. And part of
that adventure can be a new and vigorous engagement with the Bible.

Fourth in our task of aiding the interpretive process in maturing
young people is how we perceive their—and our—functions. Examination of the perspective of developmental constructivism confronts us
with both the cruciality and complexity of our understanding. The perspective, translated into our concern, offers no short-cuts, no easy ways.
It offers no certainty that our efforts will achieve our hopes.

The examination, however, provides us with utter clarity concerning one aspect of our task. Translated to the work of initiating adolescents into a larger task of interpreting the Bible, the perspective makes
clear what parts of the work belong to us as pastors, teachers, and
parents and what parts belong to adolescents.

In any educational event we may supply students with data, stimuli, and experiences judged to be necessary, useful, and appropriate for
the task at hand. We may exercise careful and deliberate control over
what is presented. Through verbal articulations we may demonstrate
a particular construction of data and experiences, the construction of
how we see things. We may exercise deliberate and intentional control
of the educational environment in an effort to maximize the possibili-

ties of our desired outcomes. But with all our careful, deliberate, intentional efforts, we have no sure way of controlling, determining, or predicting with complete accuracy what information or experiences will be considered worthwhile or will be selected out by the student for attention and consideration. Even when we know what data has been selected, we have no way of ultimately controlling how the student will interpret and order them and construct them into a whole. Ultimately, the student controls what will be learned and how it will be learned.

The student actively participates in constructing his or her own knowledge, reality, and meaning. The teacher is not merely a dispenser of information and experiences, and certainly not of pristine truth. Carefully and intentionally the teacher must provide pertinent and useful content. But more is required. The teacher must demonstrate his or her own interpretations and constructions, setting forth values and commitments—all which become important data for the students. At the same time students should have opportunity to question and challenge that data. Students are to be encouraged to articulate verbally their own constructions, to test them out, and to rebuild if necessary. Their constructions, too, are to be challenged, probed, and critically examined by the teacher and other students. Our task as teachers is to assist, enable, and encourage students to participate in the ongoing process as deep and wide as they are able. With the best of good intentions and hopes, we cannot do that job for them. We can provide a rich and encouraging environment, but each student must do the task for himself or herself as he or she is able.

Regardless of all our wishes and hopes, we cannot "make" adolescents interested in the Bible. We cannot make them engage the Bible in conversation. The adolescent is in ultimate control in this matter. We cannot compel, we cannot force a particular knowledge or understanding of the Bible. The adolescent is ultimately responsible for his or her own constructions of knowledge, reality, and meaning. Our task is to provide an environment which is inviting and encouraging. It is our task to challenge, to ask questions, and to probe. It is our task to provide the opportunity for building, tearing down and rebuilding, for testing, and for devising and revising. It is our task to share, articulate, and demonstrate our faith and our understandings. We must encourage adolescents to take up the tasks which belong to them. We must do the tasks which belong to us.

·5
Shaping the environment

It is precisely with adolescents that we should participate in a deliberate, conscious, ongoing event of initiating them into a larger work of learning to interpret the Bible. With us we invite them to participate in a conversation together in the faith. Pastors, teachers, and parents share the primary responsibility for shaping the environment in which the conversation can occur.

Let us identify briefly some dimensions of our task as shapers, returning to them in a larger discussion.

First, in the conversation we greet and acknowledge adolescents as pilgrims with us on the way. We are all pilgrims in the faith. We belong to the household of God, responsible for and to each other. And so, we share together in the conversation.

Second, we must abandon all attempts to impose on adolescents fixed and static answers assumed to remain unchanged forever. We do not pass on finished and complete interpretations of the biblical witness. We do share the church's past and present understandings. We share our understandings and our convictions. In our conversation together, collectively and individually, we may come to new and fresh interpretations, understandings, and knowledge.

Third, we will bring appropriate biblical material to bear on the thinking, feeling, and experiences of adolescents. Our selection gives focus and guidance to our conversation. To the Bible we listen. We probe it, challenge it, ask questions of it. We make interpretations of it even as it interprets us.

Fourth, we recognize that interpreting the Bible occurs within the context of the present. When we encounter a biblical story or passage, we do so with our past and present stories, our present understandings, and our present beliefs and values. Knowing and describing our present stories adds a richness to our conversations with the Bible. Thus, we will assist adolescents to construct and tell their present stories.

Fifth, we will not be satisfied if adolescents learn merely the information in the Bible along with the ability to recite it. We will challenge them to go farther. What might it say now? What claims does it make about and on you? What will you do with those claims?

Sixth, we will give space and encouragement for attempting and testing out new interpretations and understandings of self and the Bible. There will be room for building, tearing down and rebuilding, for devising and revising, for constructing and reconstructing. And thus, the conversation continues.

The Present: The Beginning Point of Interpretation

The present context and situation is the beginning point of all interpretation. We have a present because we have a past. Yet, we live in the present. We always interpret through the lenses of the present. And so it is as we meet the Bible.[1] We bring with us our hopes and despairs, successes and failures, certainties and confusions, joys and sorrows, and excitement and weariness. All impinge upon our conversation. Our understandings of ourselves and others, the nature and quality of our human relationships, our values and beliefs, and our commitments play influential roles in our conversation with the Bible. Our present, in particular and profound ways, gives shape to what the Bible says to us, to its message for us.

Adolescents, as well as all of us, need the opportunity to probe, to explore, and to tell their present stories. They need to share those stories with others. Some devote little effort to understanding and describing their present. Some, so victimized by circumstances, flee from the reflective process. Others, so bombarded by things present, are unable to tell a clear and cogent story. Others are unable to tell any story for they do not know its parts. And yet others, possessing a powerful sense of self, cherishing values and commitments, and knowing from where they have come and to whom they belong, tell beautiful and thrilling stories which are careful blends of joy and sorrow, of clarity and confusion, and of giving and receiving. As adolescents engage the Bible, they bring to bear their stories, however they are described. Those stories serve as beginning points for interpreting the Bible's stories.

Adolescents are compelled to construct new stories of themselves, others, their world, their values and commitments, and their relationships. Many stories constructed in childhood are no longer adequate or useful. Though the task may be difficult, unsettling, or frightening they can, with new abilities and an increasing range of experiences, begin the construction of new stories. There is a gift we offer, the gift of the opportunity to share with us and each other both their present stories and their adventures in creating new stories.

We discover that adolescents attempt several but conflicting stories as they struggle with questions of right and wrong, or strive for some understanding of sexuality, or seek to develop a faith posture, or work to understand themselves as individuals yet bound to each other. With amazing and breathtaking rapidity they can change their stories without any notice to us whatsoever. We may be baffled and frustrated by adolescent unpredictability. They are building, tearing down, and rebuilding. They need a community to hear, accept, and support them, not to control or ridicule them.

Adolescents bring their stories, their life-contents to bear in conversations with the Bible, interpreting it from within the present. Their conversations can be expanded, enriched, and increased if they are assisted to construct and tell their present stories. They become more aware of what it is they bring to the encounter. They become more aware of and sensitive to the issues of their own lives. They gain practice in questioning, distinguishing, and imagining. Thus, adolescents are more able to converse with the Bible, to ask questions of it, to explore several facets of the same passage, to imagine and probe various interpretations, and to listen. In the conversation the Bible challenges, asks questions, and makes claims, describing and identifying them. It prompts youth to consider anew their stories and assists them in constructing and telling new ones. And so, the Bible informs their present stories and becomes a part of their present.

As adolescents strive to examine and explore their life-content and to tell their present stories, we must do all possible to establish an environment marked by freedom, acceptance, support, as well as challenge. They need the freedom to give voice to understandings of their lives and of the world with its things, events, and people. They need the freedom to speak of their thinking, feelings, values, commitments, and behaviors without fear of reprimand or ridicule. Reprimand and ridicule must be regarded as unacceptable in the conversation. We may not always like what we hear. We may even be appalled by what we hear. We may readily discern the possibilities of destructive and devastating consequences. But if we do not hear adolescents, how can we engage them in a conversation that is significant to them? They are telling us "where they are" and what they are about. And too, as they hear themselves telling their own stories they may come to new understandings and insights and may discover a demand for change and alterations.

Closely related to their need for freedom, adolescents seek the acceptance of others. Acceptance does not imply agreement. We should accept adolescent expressions for what they are at the moment, attempts to come to terms with life. They belong to the individual and are part and parcel of his or her present self. And they are the adolescent's gifts of sharing with us and others. An environment marked by unacceptance contributes to fear and retreat, and to untruthfulness and duplicity. An environment marked by acceptance contributes to daring and sharing, to imagining, and to forthrightness.

Adolescents need our support. It is not that we will necessarily support their conclusions or behaviors. We encourage them in their efforts to tell their stories and to make sense of their lives and the world. In so doing we foster mutual support among adolescents for each other. In their joys and sorrows, hopes and despair, certainties and confusion, successes and failure they should know that they can count on our concern, care, and love.

An environment marked by freedom, acceptance, and support makes possible an environment marked also by rigorous challenge and penetrating probes. Gently yet persistently we are to ask the hard questions. Why do you choose "this" over "that?" What ideas and persons have influenced your thinking, feeling, and behavior? Why do you listen to them? What are the consequences of what you are saying and of your behavior? We can identify contradictions in their stories and call for greater clarity. With questions we challenge them to probe and explore more deeply their present, assisting them to become more aware of its parts and complexity and to distinguish what is crucial and what is not. Moreover, adolescents can learn to challenge and probe each other with sensitivity and kindness. In the activities of challenging and probing, we enable adolescents to participate more fully and consciously in the interpretive process.

All interpretation occurs within the present. The context of the present is brought to play in the process, which gives shape to the process itself and influences its results. And so it is as adolescents converse with the Bible. Understanding their present stories and willing to probe and explore their own stories, adolescents can engage the Bible with new sensitivity, vigor, and excitement, and can hear its old stories which become new.

Selecting Biblical Materials

In the chapters of Part Two we have suggested the use of a number of biblical passages. We have the task of selecting appropriate biblical material and bringing it to bear on the thinking and feelings of adolescents. As we have listened to them tell their stories, and as we have joined with them in questioning and probing, we have found that we are better informed to make selections.

Other passages could have been selected. Whenever we propose to bring particular biblical material to bear on the lives of adolescents, we need to respond to several questions. For what purpose do we wish to bring a particular passage to bear? Why would we want them to know anything at all about a specific portion of the Bible? Why should they be interested in the material? What do we hope that they might do with it? These are not irrelevant or irreverent questions. They demand a critical appraisal of what we are doing and why we are doing it.

Let us express our concern in another way. For what purpose would we want adolescents to consider the story of Sodom and Gomorrah? Why would we want them to know about the kings of Israel and Judah? What is the point of having them trace the journeys of the Apostle Paul? For what purpose do we wish to engage them with the Revelation of John? We are not suggesting that these biblical materials are unimportant or insignificant. Rather, what purpose do we have for selecting them? What do we hope will be done with them?

There is another side to our concern here. Let us give an example. It is determined that we will use the several Exodus stories with adolescents. It is a rather simple matter for them to learn many of the details of the stories and to recognize differences. But let's ask some "first" questions. In what ways are those stories significant for us? What value do we give to them? Do they tell us anything worth listening to? Do these stories in any way inform, shape, and interpret our lives? If those stories do not play some significant role in our lives, why should we bring them to impinge on adolescents?

Earlier we discussed some of the changes and tasks confronting adolescents, including new abilities which assist them in a broad, yet complex, interpretive process. Adolescents have the work of constructing new understanding, knowledge, and meaning of themselves, human life, and the world. It is that work which dominates their lives. They are seeking clues, information, and experiences which can illumine and offer direction. A major conviction expressed in this book is that the Bible can illumine, inform, shape, and interpret adolescents on their way to adulthood.

Yet we are not suggesting the ploy that some may wish to use: Let's find a need that adolescents have and then supply them with an answer from the Bible. First of all, things are not that simple. Second, we must not attempt to reduce the Bible to a book of final, static answers covering the range of human problems. And third, adolescents will always be active participants in creating their own responses.

Therefore we do not ask the Bible for simple and static answers. Instead we ask questions of the Bible, wanting to hear the Word beyond the words. What claims does the Bible make of me and all human life? How does the Bible view and regard me and all humankind? How might those claims, view, and regard inform and shape who I am, my regard and use of my body, my struggles with moral decisions, and my dealings with others? Working with such questions, hearing the claims of the Bible, and considering its responses, we receive new clues and directions as we frame our responses. In amazing ways the Bible interprets us.

Adolescents live in a period of transitions. They have tasks to accomplish. They have changes with which to cope. They seek assistance. Adolescents' conversations with the Bible can be profoundly informing and forming events. As we select biblical material two concerns must guide us. First, what is the significance of the material for us, and how does it inform and form our lives in both the world and the church? Second, it should have the possibility of informing and forming the lives of adolescents moving to adulthood, yet living in the present as members of human society and the household of faith.

An Unhindered Opportunity

Adolescents are to be given the unhindered opportunity to act upon, interact with, reflect upon, to interpret, and to make sense of biblical material as they are able. We will give direction, assistance, and challenge, remembering the active role that they play in the interpretive process. We may wish to tell them what a particular passage "means" or "should mean" for them. But, even with all good intent, we cannot impose on another what something "should mean" for him or her. Instead we may describe how the church has understood the passage in the past and how it understands it now. We may share our own understanding of the passage. Such efforts are necessary and desirable. They remain, however, our contributions in the conversation together, upon which adolescents will react, reflect, and interpret.

An unhindered opportunity does not imply the lack of direction and goals. We should take care not to produce a "directionless" conversation. To present a biblical passage followed by the unspecified question, "What do you think about it?" simply leaves the adolescent in a vast sea without any point of reference. We can give direction without assuming or attempting to impose an answer which must be discovered. We give a task on which to focus. For example, we judge that a biblical passage might assist adolescents struggling to be individuals yet fearing exclusion from their peer group. We give directions to focus attention: "As you read and work with this passage, what do you understand it to be saying about who an individual is? How does it define an individual? What does it suggest as a course of action when group demands stand in opposition to the individual's values and commitments?" Or, some adolescents declare they want to be individuals without interference from anyone. We select biblical material and give directions: "How does this passage define an individual? What does it say about life and community? From the viewpoint of the passage, can we be individuals apart from other persons? Why? Why not?"

Directions for assigned tasks need not confine and constrain. They serve as guidelines and focus. They ask adolescents to meet and engage the biblical material. They ask that another voice be heard and appraised. They invite adolescents to act upon, interact with, to reflect upon, and to interpret the biblical materials. The participants are free to bring their thinking, feelings, and experiences into play as they work with the material, making sense of it as they are able.

Many interpretations will be inadequate, will miss what we understand to be the thrust of the passage, will be inappropriate vis-à-vis the passage, and will be simplistic and at times even preposterous. We must resist the temptation to make statements of "right" or "wrong," or to give the "correct answer." Adolescents need the opportunity to work and struggle with the biblical materials as they are able, if they are to learn a significant task of interpreting the Bible. We must not deprive them of that opportunity by our desire to preserve them from "error."

We walk a narrow and difficult line. The "unhindered opportunity" does not assume that adolescents possess in and of themselves all the skills and tools appropriate for biblical interpretation. It does not suggest that adolescents, by their own struggles, can "pull out" of a passage "its correct meaning." It does not ask that we be satisfied with initial interpretations or that we accept them as end results. It does not assume the posture of "anything goes." A careful listening on our part enables us to chart new approaches responsive to the needs, concerns, questions, and interpretations of adolescents.

Participants may need more information than can be gleaned from the passage itself. We have the responsibility to make available and to present critical information. We may need to discuss the context of the passage within the Bible. Information related to the historical and cultural contexts from which the passage emerged may be desirable. With new information, we then pose new questions: "Does this information help you to understand the passage in new ways? Does it prompt you to alter or change what you have already said about the passage? Are there new questions you would ask of the passage?" New information given and questions posed offer a more informed "unhindered opportunity" to explore the passage anew.

We can assist adolescents to probe the material more thoroughly, to look at it "from all sides" and to continue the making of fresh and larger interpretations. We may call attention to an overlooked element of the passage and ask if it might inform their thinking and feelings in new ways. We ask them to focus on a specific item that may give a new "twist" to already achieved interpretations. We may bring two distinct items of a passage into sharp conflict. And we help them to distinguish and identify the most critical elements of a passage.

Two matters stand out in sharp relief. First, one brief encounter or a "once-over-lightly" with a biblical passage is not sufficient for the task before us. We need to devise ways by which adolescents may return time and time again to the same biblical material, using on each occasion new information, improved skills and tools, and new experiences and understandings as they construct new interpretations. They need the opportunity to explore a biblical passage as thoroughly as they are able at the moment, even if our desire for wide biblical coverage must be set aside. To move from one biblical passage to another in rapid succession prevents thorough exploration. Second, the approach described here requires significant commitment of time and energy on our part. But then, we are involved in a work which is critical for adolescents as they live in the world and the church.

Interpreting in Community

The work of interpreting the Bible is to be done within a Christian community. The Bible belongs to the church. Interpretation of the Bible is not solely a private matter. The Christian community, in whatever form it takes, has the right and responsibility to examine, to critique, and to challenge any and every private interpretation of the Bible. And so, our interpreting the Bible with adolescents must be done within the context of some Christian community. About all our interpretations of the Bible, we must ask if they are faithful witnesses to the activity of God. That question can be asked most appropriately within the context of community. It is precisely in the Christian community that the Holy Spirit calls, gathers, enlightens, sanctifies, and preserves the people of God.

It remains the case that each individual is ultimately responsible for his or her interpretations of the Bible. Nevertheless, we need other Christians to assist us in our interpreting. Adolescents need the assistance of members of the household of faith, including their peers. Sharing the interpretive task within a Christian community, our youth can assume the responsibilities of assisting, caring, challenging, and supporting each other. They can listen to and react to the interpretations of their peers. Interpretations made and shared can be examined by all together. Adolescents are able to challenge the adequacies of each other's interpretation and push for clarification. They can suggest changes and alterations. In all this they will give encouragement to each other.

Some young persons will encounter difficulty in performing the tasks just outlined. Nevertheless, they are tasks that need to be learned, and they can be. The environment that we shape for them can facilitate their learning. As adolescents participate in these tasks, consider what is happening. First, they are learning to do what all Christians are to do for each other—to assist, care, support, and challenge. Second, they are interpreting and learning to interpret the Bible as a people of God, together. Adolescents learn to interpret as they risk interpreting. In so doing, with others, they are learning to do what every Christian community is to do continually—achieve new understandings of what it is for us to be Christians together.

In community, we can encourage our youth to bring their understandings of the biblical witness to impinge upon their present by asking how the biblical witness may influence, inform, and shape their lives: what is the relationship between your understanding of that witness and your present story or life-content? What does it claim to say about you? We cannot make the relationships or connections for the adolescents. They must do that task for themselves, but we can set the context in which they can make the effort.

How might we set that context? "Together we have been examining and studying this biblical passage. We have suggested some of the things it says and that it claims. We have made our interpretations of it. Now if what this passage claims is true, if what it is describing is the way things are or ought to be, then what does it say about you? What does it say about who you are? What does it say about the way you regard or treat your body? What does it say about how you regard and treat others? If what it says is true, what claims does it make on you and your life? And if what it claims is true, what are you going to do with it?"

The "if what" question can be a powerful ally in our work. It gives adolescents a larger space in which to practice and learn the interpretive task. It frees them to examine the biblical material and its implications from all sides without the demand to determine the question, "Is it true or not true?" It gives freedom and encouragement for continual exploration and interpretation of the Bible. And when it is asked, they are asked to reflect anew on their life-content and to view it through the lenses of the biblical witness. In so doing, they are encouraged to interpret and shape their lives by the sacred text of the church. In community, listening to each other, sharing with each other and challenging each other, they help each other to frame their responses to the "if what" question.

Adults as Participants

Adults can provide a rich, exciting environment. As educators we can provide an abundance of helpful exercises and activities such as those suggested in the following chapters. Yet, when we engage teenagers in the task of interpreting and learning to interpret the Bible, we should be full participants. We, too, are pilgrims on the way. Our participation can be of profound value to adolescents without dominating or stifling them. Indeed our participation may be a gift of immeasurable worth.

First, by our full participation we serve as models for adolescents. We are models of pilgrims on the way, not models to be "aped." Nor are we models of perfection or "answer-possessors." By telling our present stories, sharing our understandings, values, beliefs, and commitments, we describe our journey in the faith, articulating what we judge to be critical and necessary. We identify those influences that have informed our lives. We demonstrate how and why we put our lives together as we do at the moment. In this witness to the faith we offer to adolescents new information, a new experience, and a new event. Young people will think and feel about our sharing. They can interact with, interpret, and act upon it. From our sharing adolescents may gain clues and directions to enhance their own journeys.

Second, we should participate in the activities and exercises suggested in the following chapters. We can produce a collage, design a bumper sticker, fill out charts. We share and discuss these with the group, inviting them to do the same with us and with each other. By our participation we provide models for the adolescents' participation. Moreover, as we become active participants, the activities and exercises become the occasions for sharing our own stories. They afford opportunities to tell of our encounters with the Bible, of our understandings of a particular passage, and of its influence and significance for us. As we tell about our encounters with the Bible, once again we offer clues and directions to enhance adolescents' engagements with it.

Third, what we share, our descriptions, must be open to the same questioning, probing, and challenging that we do with adolescents. They should have the opportunity to ask questions of us, to challenge our statements, to ask for clarification, and to weigh our values and beliefs. As we respond we demonstrate how we participate in the interpretive process. We give clues for adolescents' participation in the process. Our willingness to be open to probes and challenges can assist and encourage adolescents to move in the same direction.

Not at all incidental, our participation can have exciting possibilities for us. We, too, engage in the ongoing process of interpreting. We have the opportunity for continuing reflection, interpretation, and articulation. We hear new stories and witnesses to the faith. We engage the Bible anew. In unexpected, sometimes amazing, ways, we gain new insights. Seeing our lives in new ways, we reinterpret our past stories and give new shape to our present ones. We see new visions. Our opportunity to participate with adolescents in a conversation together in the faith becomes their gift to us.

In this chapter we have considered the contributions and the role of pastors, teachers, and parents as shapers of the environment for the conversation. We want to make a strong and necessary statement concerning the influence of that environment. As we developed our understanding of adolescents earlier we emphasized their life-content, those process changes, tasks, and concerns which dominate and characterize the period of transition. When adolescents engage the Bible, they bring with them a life-content that exerts powerful influence on the engagement. The life-content, interacting with other elements in the interpretive process, influences both the adolescent's willingness and ability to engage the Bible. And it plays a determining role in the interpretations and understandings achieved. We described one perspective of the interpretive process, highlighting the role of the adolescent as an active constructor of his or her interpretations and understandings. The ultimate task of constructing belongs to the individual. Although life-content and active constructing will play powerful roles as adolescents learn to interpret the Bible, the environment we provide for the process will also be powerful and determining.

Depending upon the arrangement, shape, and content of the environment, it provides specific and particular information and experiences that claim attention and consideration. It sets forth what is critical and necessary and thus gives focus to the task. It provides models for thinking and feeling, and ways for dealing with things, events, and persons. The environment itself is a demonstration of what is desired. It can challenge already achieved interpretations and understandings. It can call forth from its inhabitants a vigorous participation in an interpretive task larger than they had experienced before. We know our goal: to introduce, initiate, and aid adolescents in a larger task of interpreting the Bible than was possible for them as children. We should consciously and deliberately so arrange the environment for our conversation together so that the possibility of our goal will be maximized.

PART TWO

doing the task

·6

Who am I?

This chapter focuses on the question, "Who am I?" Detailed in its descriptions, the chapter serves as both framework and point of reference for the chapters to follow. Therefore the directions will be more detailed than those in the following chapters. We will set forth explicitly our underlying assumptions concerning the materials and methods that we have selected. And we will also state explicitly our purposes for the procedures we follow.

In this chapter we introduce the marking system that is used throughout the remainder of the book to identify certain materials. The word "Bridge" represents a verbal statement that can be used in assisting participants to shift from working with the exercises, activities, and explanations to engaging the biblical material. The material which appears in italics and/or is enclosed in brackets sets off directions for the leader and/or gives ideas for the conversation with the study participants. The material set off with bullets is in list form and often may be used in the same manner as the italicized and bracketed material. The material enclosed within quotation marks contains quotations and statements which may be directly addressed to the youth. Material which should be copied to hand out to the young people is boxed; when making copies, do not copy the bracketed material. The closed squares indicate the beginning of a new activity while the open squares indicate the different steps within an activity.

The chapter that follows this one, where our question is "Who am I?" poses a companion question: "Who tells me who I am?" Both questions relate to the task of "achieving identity." We have separated the two questions so as to provide, first, the opportunity for adolescents to reflect upon and to describe present understandings of themselves. The second question is designed to alert youth to the many voices which claim to tell them who they are. And it raises another question, "To whom will I listen?"

Responding to "Who am I?" is a continual life task. We are never done with that question. At any given moment we may possess a clear and personally satisfying answer. Then, in new circumstances and situations we are required to achieve new answers. Who am I as a spouse? Who am I as a parent? Who am I as a widow or widower? Who am I as one who has lost his/her job? Who am I as one with most of my life behind me? We are always in the process of achieving identity, of creating answers to "Who am I?"

From our range of experiences and the pool of information available, each of us selects out those items, persons, and events to which we give our attention. We ask what these have to do with us. We examine, make sense of, interpret, and give meaning to them. In so doing, we construct an understanding—a picture—of ourselves, of who we are. With that understanding, we manage our lives among the world of persons, things, events, and ideas.

Achieving identity may be accomplished evenly and smoothly over the life span. In concert with their past, persons may achieve rearrangements, reconstructions, and even transformations of identity with little stress and anxiousness. Ever mindful of who they are and from where they have come, young people engage the task with flexibility and confidence, and in the expectation and anticipation of change. Yet, specific moments and dramatic events can be severe challenges to our self-understanding, calling into question who we are, our values and worth, our commitments, and our past decisions. The resulting confusion and pain can be profound. In such circumstances the demand is clear. We engage the task anew, striving for satisfying and appropriate understandings of who we are.

Toward Attaining Identity

A major task of adolescents is to strive toward attaining an identity which they claim as their own and for which they are responsible. The child entering adolescence will have an identity, an understanding of self adequate for childhood. However, identity achieved in childhood can dissipate rapidly during adolescence in the presence of new demands and experiences. New understandings must be constructed.

Adolescents have new cognitive, affective, and social abilities. They can think and feel about themselves and their world in ways not possible during childhood. With a widening range of interpersonal relationships, they must ask new questions of themselves as social beings. They must ask new questions of themselves as male or female. They encounter varied and conflicting value systems and must ask questions of themselves as moral beings. They encounter powerful and differing ideologies and must ask new questions of their commitments. As they respond to new questions and demands they give shape and substance to who they are.

Identity is not some isolated dimension in human life. It is the composite of responses to critical questions and demands. Commitment to an ideology, understandings as male or female, selection of social roles to be attended, commitment to a value system and creation of social relationships—all impinge upon and interact with each other as we construct who we are. Thus, when we ask "Who am I?" we are not searching for a "secret self" or "real self" residing somewhere deep within us. Rather, we inquire of our decisions, responses, thinking, feeling, and commitments as we live in the world of persons.

One does not emerge from adolescence with a fixed identity for all time or with finished and well-polished responses to the question "Who am I?" Nevertheless, during adolescence major dimensions of the response may be drawn. Significant commitments may be made. Some directions may be determined.

The identity statuses discussed earlier represent major routes adolescents may travel in efforts to solve issues of "Who am I?" Along their way, they need both encouragement and assistance. First, they need the space and freedom to describe as clearly as possible their present understandings of self. The task for them is difficult and requires patience. Descriptions may be occasions for surprises, joy, excitement, pain, or sorrow. Without realistic appraisals adolescents may be trapped in their own bewilderment and confusion. In their efforts to describe, adolescents may recognize new questions to be asked and new possibilities for themselves.

Second, they need encouragement and assistance to reflect critically upon their understandings. Probes and challenging questions are in order. Are there things in your description which make you happy or sad? Are there things you wish were different? What would you need to do to make things different? What persons or ideas or events have influenced your understanding of yourself? Do you think that your friends would describe you in the same way?

Third, adolescents need the encouragement and assistance of adult models who reflect critically about themselves. How do we as adults describe ourselves? What things do we hold as valuable and worthwhile and why? What persons, ideas, or values influence our understanding of ourselves?

Fourth, adolescents need to examine and explore alternative responses and understandings. They need assistance and practice in anticipating consequences of alternative responses. If you were to make certain changes, how would your life be different? If you do not make certain changes, what might you expect in the future? How do your behaviors tell others who you are? If you were to change your behaviors, would that change who you are?

Adolescents meet and respond to a host of questions and issues as they construct an understanding of self. In so doing they frequently lack a clear understanding of their present selves. A lack of clarity prompts them to wander aimlessly in the realm of trial and error, hoping that in some unknown way they may hit upon the right answers. Whatever young people's understanding of present selves, it will greatly influence and shape their continuing response to the question, "Who am I?" Achieving appropriate descriptions of their present selves, adolescents are greatly enabled to make conscious choices and to create new and responsible responses as they determine who they are.

Describing Present Understandings of Self

A new adventure with the question, "Who am I?" must begin with the adolescent's present understanding of self. It may be clear, beautifully constructed, powerful, vivid, exciting. It may be a big box of jigsaw puzzle pieces belonging to several puzzles, which need to be sorted and put together. Whatever the understanding, it influences behaviors, values, and commitments. It influences how new experiences and information will be interpreted. It is a critical element of the conversation of the adolescent with the Bible. With some clarity of understanding, the adolescent's engagement with the Bible can be dynamic and exciting.

Not all adolescents are able to articulate for themselves a clear response to the question, "Who am I?" Some experience extreme difficulty in describing themselves. Some are hesitant in talking about themselves. In many instances they have had little experience or practice in the art of self-reflection and in the task of self-description.

Without some self-reflective abilities and some understanding of present self, adolescents may experience dramatic shifts in emotions and feelings, knowing not what is happening to them but experiencing the pain of it all. Some will engage in a variety of unusual behaviors, neither understanding what they are doing nor why they are doing it. They announce newly embraced positions, having little sense of implications. There is, then, the need to assist adolescents to tell their stories of who they are at the moment and to learn to do so with increasing precision and self-reflection. The goal in this section is to provide opportunities for adolescents to describe themselves more adequately and accurately. Exercises and activities (experiences) are suggested. They can lead the adolescent to a more realistic understanding of "who I am" at the moment. The exercises and activities (experiences) offered here are arranged into two categories: (1) environmental aids; and (2) oral and written expressions.

Environmental Aids

Environmental aids are concrete, "hands on" material, which can assist adolescents in developing their descriptions of self. A concrete item that initiates conversation about itself provides a non-threatening beginning to conversations and eventual descriptions of self.

1. Comic Strips. The characters in comic strips can be delightful aids for adolescents as they reflect upon and describe their present selves.

■ *We supply the group with a wide assortment of comic strips. Our directions give guidance, freedom, and space for the exercise.*

"Make several selections of comic strip characters. Think carefully as you choose. Later we will share our selections with each other, including some reasons for our choices. First, select the one you like most. Second, select the one who is most like you. Third, select the one you wish to be like. Fourth, select the one you like least."

As the various choices are shared, what might we hear? "Gee, I feel like a Charlie Brown, but I would like to be a Lucy." "I like Andy Capp. Nobody messes with him." "That cat, Garfield, is great. He just does what he wants, no work and stuff." "Boy, I don't like the one about Momma. She's always trying to make the kids do what she wants." "Beetle Bailey is fun. He fakes out everybody." "I'd like to be like Snoopy. He's cute and lovable."

□ *We probe, challenge, and push for clarification.*

"In what ways are you similar to that character?"

"Why would you want to be like that character?"

"Can you think of any changes that are necessary so that you may be more like that character?"

Such probes and questions are not concerned primarily with the specific comic strip character as such. Rather, they call upon the ado-

lescents to reflect upon their choices and to examine their own thinking, feelings, understandings, and values.

Adolescents can actively participate in developing an accepting
environment marked by probes and challenges. We will need to exercise care as we guide adolescents in doing so.

> "Mike, would you have identified Jane with the character she se-
> lected? Why or why not?"
>
> "Jane, do you wish to respond to anything that Mike has said?"
>
> "Ann, do you have any idea why Sue chose the character she did?
> Do you have any questions for her?"
>
> "Sue, do you think that Ann understands your thinking and feel-
> ing about the character?"

There are some risks in such probes and challenges. Some rude-
ness may creep in. Some unintentional hurt may occur. Yet, we dare to
take the risk. We are asking adolescents to listen carefully and sensitively to each other, to reflect upon what each other says, and to take
the perspective of another. We are asking them to learn from each other.
These are not easy tasks to learn. Practice is necessary.

There are two other uses of comic strips that we might make. First,
if two or more adolescents choose the same character, for example, as
the one they like the most, they could discuss their selection with each
other. They would have the opportunity to share their thinking, feelings, and understandings with each other and to discover if they share
a common interpretation of the character. Are they attracted to the
same character for the same reasons or for different reasons? In their
conversation they will assist each other in further self-reflection and
articulation.

Second, their choices of comic strip characters could generate interest and conversation in their church congregation by a collage or
series of collages created by a group of adolescents from comic strips.
Collage titles could be "Comic Strip Characters Most Like Us" and
"Comic Strip Characters We Would Like to Be."

2. From the Outdoors. The group members take a short walk in the
outdoors. The assignment is simple.

> "Each of you is to bring back one item which expresses something
> about you—a hope, a feeling, a thought, or a value. We will share
> our stories about the items when we gather again."

What is brought back will depend, in part, upon the season of the year. In any event, the collection will be varied and surprising: a bright flower, a twig with but one leaf, a smashed soda pop can, a rock, a piece of rotting wood, a weed, dried leaves, and even an earthworm.

The use of such objects can provide a "safe situation" for some adolescents. By directing attention to a thing, they can exercise some control over the situation. Holding the object in hand, pointing to it, and talking about the object itself, the individual can describe himself or herself. In describing, discussing, and talking about the object the adolescent, at the same time, reflects upon and discusses who she or he is. The object is both a "prop" and aid as the individual learns the art of self-reflection and self-disclosure.

A variation of the activity can be useful. Each person brings his or her object in a paper bag so that no other person knows its "owner." One person, taking each item from its bag, asks the group to tell the stories that the item *might* tell of the owner. After all items have been discussed by the group, the owner of each tells his or her own story. The activity facilitates reflection, articulation, and understanding. First, the group members are encouraged to fantasize about the "unknown owner" and to practice the art of putting one's self "into the shoes of another." Second, in such efforts they are bringing into play their own understandings and feelings. "If you had selected that item, would those have been your reasons for doing so?" Third, all hear and experience different interpretations of the same item. "How would you account for the different interpretations that have been made?" Fourth, the owner is provided the opportunity to share his or her own interpretation. A significant question can be posed to the owner. "Has your story been influenced by what has been said earlier? If so, in what ways?"

3. Arts and Crafts. The use of arts and crafts materials offers a wide variety of opportunities for adolescents to reflect upon and to respond to the question, "Who am I?" We provide them with abundant supplies of paints, crayons, felt-tip markers, finger paints, old magazines, paste, tinker toys, and other materials. Adolescents will use these materials—even finger paints—imaginatively and creatively.

Each individual, choosing the material with which he or she wishes to work, is encouraged to make a collage or to shape a hunk of clay or to use finger paints, creating something which gives some expression to who he or she is. Not all in a group must do the same thing at the same time. Each is encouraged to do as he or she wishes. The resulting creations will vary greatly. Diversity will be the rule. Some results will be simple; others, complex and intricate. In any case, adolescents, using "hands on" materials, are striving to give some expression of themselves.

Each individual is given the opportunity to share and discuss his or her creation. In this activity a series of significant behaviors frequently occurs. Initially, an individual will hold his or her creation as far away from the body as possible, pointing to it, describing it and talking about it as if it were totally detached from self. In so doing, he or she is creating a "safe space" in which to talk. The individual is testing out what is permissible and acceptable. Discovering broad limits of a "safe space," he or she often draws the object closer to the body, pointing not only to the object but to himself or herself. Finally, the conversation becomes focused on self, not the object.

Questions for clarification, probes, and challenges will occur.

"Is this how you think and feel about yourself?"

"Is this how you would like to think and feel?"

"What influences or experiences contribute to your thinking and feeling?"

Group members can participate in the questioning and probing. They can make interpretations of each other's creations, thus offering challenges and new possibilities.

Let us suggest two uses of collages. First, the group has produced individual collages, responding to the question, "Who am I?" These are retained and stored. Several months later a second collage on the same theme is produced by each person. Each individual can then compare her or his two collages, noting similarities and differences in the expressions of self. Each can be encouraged to reflect upon and discuss the experiences, thinking, feelings, and events which have contributed to the differences. Such an activity can be used with other themes, "Who is God?" or "Who is Jesus?" or "What is the church?" Comparing several interpretations of self or God or Jesus, the adolescent may be enabled to recognize several dimensions of the ongoing process of interpretation.

Second, the development of a collage may be a group endeavor. Using the theme "Who we are," the group may give a communal expression of itself as a part of the community of the church. Such an expression can be shared with the entire congregation in the form of a banner or an altar hanging.

4. Popular Music. Popular music, especially the words of popular songs, can be used to assist adolescents to reflect upon and to articulate understandings of self. We invite each person to bring a recording of the popular song which reflects or gives expression to some feeling or thinking or understanding of self. The group listens to the various songs. Each person discusses his or her choice. Questioning, probing, and challenging continue to play significant roles.

"Is that the way you want others to regard you?"

"Do the words express a hope of yours?"

"Do you enjoy being with those who are similar to the descriptions in the words?"

"How would you react if someone treated you in ways suggested by the words?"

Two or more individuals may choose the same song. They can be given the opportunity to discuss among themselves their choices and the reasons for them. They may discover that they have differing interpretations of the songs. The differences become the occasion for new reflection upon their thinking and feeling. And too, they may discover commonalities among themselves which were not recognized before.

5. Bumper Stickers. The slogans on bumper stickers are often thought-provoking as well as humorous. They can be used as aids in helping young people sort out feelings about themselves.

■ *On paper provided, invite the participants to write (with felt-tip markers or crayon) a slogan for a bumper sticker. The slogan should express something about themselves. This activity should be done privately, without any conversation or sharing between the participants. After all the slogans have been completed, collect and post them on the wall.*

□ *Invite the participants to guess the owner of each slogan. They may "attach" several owners to each slogan.*

"What causes you to say that _____ is the writer of this slogan?"

□ *Have each participant to identify his or her slogan.*

"What do you think of _____'s description of your slogan? Does that description agree in any way with your description of it?"

"How would you describe or discuss your slogan?"

"Did your understanding of your slogan change in any way because of what others said about it?"

6. Which Animal? Animals are sometimes used to portray character-istics (and even appearances) of humans. This activity can help youth to look at themselves in a different and unusual manner.

■   *Invite each participant to select the animal which is most like him or her. On the chalkboard or on newsprint, list the selected animal alongside the name of the participant.*

"In what ways are you similar to this animal? What characteris-tics does this animal have which are similar to yours?"

"Are any of you surprised that _____ selected his/her particular animal? Why?"

□   *Invite each participant to select the animal which he/she desires most to be like. Again, list the selected animal alongside the name of the participant.*

"What about that animal is attractive to you?"

"Can you tell us why that characteristic is attractive to you?"

Oral and Written Expressions

Oral and written exercises and activities can assist adolescents to reflect upon who they are and to describe their present selves. Such exercises and activities, however, are marked by particular difficulties which we must take into consideration. Nevertheless, appropriate use of them can move toward our goal.

1. Oral Expression. While the goal is to assist youth to reflect upon and describe themselves as individuals with some degree of accuracy and clarity, to begin the conversation by talking "out loud" about themselves directly is usually not very fruitful. In fact the activity can be frightening. Adolescents may be afraid and reticent to reveal them-selves. They may not know what is permissible or what will be toler-ated. They fear ridicule and "labels."

Adolescents are making new discoveries in thinking, feeling, and understanding. To adults, those "discoveries" may be regarded as "usual" or "routine" or "old" or "expected." But such is not the case for young persons. Some regard their "discoveries" as having been discovered for the first time. And as exciting and thrilling as these discoveries may be, they can also be disturbing and perplexing. Furthermore, adoles-cents may not always know how to talk about the "new." They are not always certain that others will understand and appreciate their discoveries.

Frequently with a group of adolescents we move into a circle and ask each in turn to describe himself or herself. Responses are neutral, often concrete, and highly guarded. The end result of the activity is of little value to them or to us. Initial, direct encounters with the demand to describe themselves orally are both risky and difficult for adolescents. Yet, they need to learn to talk "out loud" about themselves. They can learn to take the risk of talking "out loud" about their thoughts, feelings, discoveries, and understandings. The learning occurs over time, often very slowly. It occurs in a safe, non-threatening, and accepting yet challenging environment. The exercises and activities described earlier can aid in that learning, encouraging adolescents in reflective and larger oral expressions.

2. Written Expressions. Experiences in written expressions provide a reflective and safe arena for adolescents who endeavor to articulate descriptions of themselves. Some can give beautiful expressions in writing of their feelings, thinking, and experiences. There is a major difficulty, however, which we must take into consideration. Apart from the fact that some may not be interested in writing, *the task of writing itself may be extremely difficult for others.* Thus, with written exercises we do well to provide several exercises, differing in difficulty and complexity.

- **Descriptive Statements.** *Those willing to attempt written expressions can be invited to write a poem, a paragraph, or an imaginary dialogue. The directions are simple.*

  "Write a piece which expresses something about you and which you are willing to share with the group. It may be a poem, expressing some thought or feeling you have. It may be a paragraph about an important event in your life. It may be an imaginary conversation between two of your friends discussing you. It may be new words for a popular tune you like. These are just a few suggestions. You may think of others."

  Such directions have several implications. First, the adolescent can determine what he or she wishes to share with the group. Second, it is not necessary that all write about the same thing at the same time. Third, the directions take into account a diversity of interest and ability, thus encouraging individuals to participate as they are able. Fourth, the adolescents are responsible for their choices. They determine what they will share.

- **Descriptive Words.** *On paper provided, invite each participant to write three short lists of words that others might use to describe him or her. Participants should imagine that one list is written by a friend, another by a teacher, and another by a parent. As the ado-*

lescents are willing, the lists of words can be shared with the group for discussion.

"With which list are you the most pleased? Which list do you think best describes who you are? Why?"

"With which list are you the least satisfied? Which list do you think is the least accurate in describing who you are? Why?"

"How well do you think your friend or teacher or parent understands who you are? If you think that there is some misunderstanding, how do you account for it?"

"Is there something you can do to correct the misunderstanding?"

☐ *Invite the participants to write another list of words. From the previously prepared three lists, they are to select six words which "best" describe who they are. Some may not wish to share their lists.*

"Do you like your list of words? Does it please you? Are you comfortable with it?"

☐ *Finally, invite each participant to produce another list, using words by which they would like to be described.*

"Are there any differences between this list and the last previous list?"

"If there are differences, what changes would you need to make so as to be the person you would like to be?"

■ **Imaginary Conversations.** *For an adolescent to write and/or relate an imaginary conversation between two of his or her friends may be an easier task and a safer venture than to write and tell explicitly about self. There is a "safe space." While sharing the conversation, in a difficult, painful, or challenging moment, the adolescent may need to say, "That's what my friends might think and feel. It is not necessarily what I think and feel." Nevertheless, he or she has taken the risks, however small and guarded, to give expression to self. Frequently, what we think and feel about ourselves may be just what we imagine others to think and feel about us. Other activities similar to the imaginary conversation may be used:*

"Write an imaginary conversation between two of your teachers. What might they say about you?"

"Write a paragraph of a friend's letter describing you to someone else."

The written expressions are shared with the entire group. Here, as in other moments of sharing, there should be agreement on the "ground rules." Any expression is permissible and respected as belonging to the individual. Ridicule is not acceptable. Whatever is offered is to be regarded as a gift to the group and is to be taken seriously. We do not argue, suggesting that the individual ought not to think and feel a certain way. But we do probe and challenge. An environment marked by sensitive probing and challenging can encourage and assist adolescents in appropriate self-reflection and in making distinctions in their thinking and feeling; and it suggests new possibilities. It is an arena in which broader and more complex interpretive skills can be developed.

Engaging and Interpreting the Bible

As we introduce biblical material into the conversation, we need to build a verbal bridge between that material and the adolescents' previous activities. The bridge will facilitate movement from one interpretive process to another. Our directions will also facilitate that movement. They should assign specific tasks relative to the biblical materials.

1. Genesis 2:4b–24. The creation stories in the book of Genesis, especially the second story (Genesis 2:4b–24), are profound responses to the question, "Who am I?" We choose these stories not because they are in the first book of the Bible and not with any assertions that they are historical accounts of creation. Rather, they are the response(s) of a people who struggled with the question, "Who are we?" These stories, simplistic and concrete in language, tell about the human creature and about what it is to be human. At the same time these accounts introduce major themes encountered throughout the Bible. From their own engagements with these stories, young people can gain clues and directions as they respond to the question, "Who am I?"

Bridge: In the activities and exercises we have told stories and painted pictures of ourselves. We have shared these with each other. Now, we want to examine a portion of the creation stories in Genesis (Genesis 2:4b–24) that makes some claims about who we are. We want to identify and describe those claims. We want to ask what those claims have to say to us. But first let's share what we already know, think, or feel about the creation stories as we remember them.

Most adolescents have some opinions, impressions, and questions concerning the creation stories. Frequently the already-held understandings are not informed by critical engagements with the text but are influenced by casual encounters with the stories or by others' comments about them. Some of the opinions and impressions do not reflect the stories at all. Left unexamined, they will influence additional interpretations of the stories and can interfere in the development of more adequate interpretations. So first, invite the young persons to give expression to already-held opinions, impressions, and understandings.

■   *Using the chalkboard or newsprint, invite the participants to develop a list of opinions and impressions. Simply list the items without comment. Do not discuss the list at this point but reserve it for later use.*

Some comments will relate to the seven days of creation or to Adam and Eve as the first man and woman. Such items as the human creature in the image of God, the sources of evil, the nature of sin, and the dominance of man over woman may be noted. Some adolescents will question the stories as history. Some will express their acceptance of the stories while others will declare their unbelief concerning them. In the exercise we are becoming familiar with the adolescents' thinking and views. We discover items which require greater clarification. We can be sensitive to their concerns and questions as we bring critical elements of the text to bear on the conversations. Ultimately, the understandings of the young people are to be considered against the text itself.

Bridge: We have made a list of our understandings, impressions, and questions of the creation stories. Now, let's turn directly to the text itself (Genesis 2:4b–24). We want to identify and describe the response of the text to the question, "Who am I?"

Our directions should give specific tasks to be achieved. They give focus to adolescents while working with the biblical material. Our directions can assist participants to learn to ask questions of the Bible. Thus, youth are encouraged and enabled to encounter a text itself.

■   *Divide the group into pairs or small groups. Each is to read, study and discuss the text, and prepare its responses to the questions below. [In any assigned task, remember that reading abilities may vary greatly. Some young people may have learning disabilities. In such cases it may be necessary that the teacher read aloud the biblical passage.] At an appropriate time, the responses will be shared in the total group.*

"How does the passage describe the human creature?"

"What does it claim to be true about the human creature?"

"According to the passage what is it to be human?"

Working in pairs or small groups, adolescents can assist and encourage each other in conversation with the Bible. They can pose for each other questions about the text. They can offer possible responses of the text to the assigned task. They can share with each other their own explorations, and they can question and challenge each other. In their interactions, they will return time and time again to the text.

□ *Invite the total group to develop a composite response, using the findings from the work in pairs or small groups. Using the chalkboard or newsprint, list the items offered.*

"We want to develop a group response to the several questions, a response which reflects the passage and with which we can all agree. If you think that a suggested item does not reflect the passage, voice your objections. Give your reasons. It may be that a particular item may be eliminated."

Our participation as adults is most crucial. We may need to give additional information, give a definition, point out the text's particular use of a word, or draw attention to an element overlooked. In so doing, we bring the group into a new encounter with the text. Moreover, we should participate in developing the various lists. Our contributions should be open to the same questioning and challenging as those of the adolescents. Thus, we join with the adolescents in a conversation together.

The passage gives a multifaceted definition or description of the human creature and of what it is to be human.

- All things, including human creatures, are created by God. What is created by God belongs to God.
- *Adam* (=man) is formed from the dust of the earth. *Adam* is made of the same "stuff" as all other things.
- *Adam* is created to share in the life of God. God breathes the breath of life into the lifeless form and *adam* becomes a living being.
- But the story is not completed. *Adam* is not complete in and of self. *Adam* is not human. The living being is alone.
- The animals are created in an effort to find a companion for the living being.
- There is the creation of woman, made of the same "stuff" of adam and all creation.
- The living beings join in community, and they are human. It takes a living being to make another living being human. Until there is community, there is no human being. [*There are sexual overtones and undertones in the passage, but the emphasis here is on community.*]

- The living being had to give something of self so as to create community.
- God created both male and female.
- Human beings are to live in the created world, to enjoy it, to keep it, and to tend it.
- Human beings are to live in community, in relationship with the whole of creation.

Adolescents will give their own expressions to the various elements of the text. Some responses will be larger and more complex than others. Whatever the expressions, part of our task is to ask constantly, "Is that what the story is saying? Does that reflect the story?" And again, we will draw attention to elements of the passage overlooked.

To add other dimensions to the biblical response to the question, "Who am I?" we can engage the group in an exploration of the first creation story, Genesis 1:1—2:4a, asking of it the same questions as of Genesis 2:4b–24.

- Man is created in the image of God.
- Man is the last of God's creation.
- "Man" is defined as male and female. God created male and female.
- God's creation, including male and female, is good.

These items can be incorporated into the composite response of the group pertaining to Genesis 2:4b–24.

□   *Having completed the composite responses, the participants can return to the first list developed, the list containing their already held opinions and impressions.*

"Let's compare the two lists that we have produced. Are there any contradictions or disagreements between the two lists?"

"Is there any item on the first list that should be challenged or questioned? Why?"

"In the light of your study of the passage, is there any item on the first list which is a misrepresentation of the story? Why?"

In this last exercise, we are asking participants to reflect upon and examine their already held understandings and impressions in the light of a new experience, that of studying and discussing the text itself. We are asking them to examine their understandings against the text and to consider necessary rearrangement and alterations in their impressions of the passage.

We move on to a most crucial and necessary step in the interpretive process, that of interpreting the story in relationship to self and of interpreting self in relationship to the passage.

Bridge: We have made a list, containing statements which the passage claims to be true about human beings. We have agreed that the various statements or items do reflect what the story is saying. If the claims of the story are true, if its descriptions are true, what does the story say about you and me? If the claims are true, what do they tell us about ourselves?

■ *By use of specific questions, lead the group in discussion. Encourage the participants to ask questions of each other, to ask for clarification, and even to challenge.*

"What is significant about the claim that we have been created by God and belong to God? Is that claim important to you? How?"

"If we are human only in community, what does this passage say about us when we act as if we do not need anyone else, or think that we ought not be responsible to anyone, or say that what we do is nobody's business but our own?"

"If the claims of community are true, can we live in relationship with others if we do not give 'something' of ourselves? When we will not share our lives or take the risk of sharing, can we live in community?"

"The story claims that we are made of the same 'stuff' as all other things are. What does the claim say about our relationship to all creation? What is it for us to keep and tend the creation?"

"What does the story say about us as male or female? Is one more important than the other? Does one have dominance over the other?"

We are asking adolescents to translate the ancient stories of the church into new stories of themselves. Not all will do so with the same ability. Not all will arrive at exactly the same place at the same time. Nevertheless, they share the adventure with each other, supporting, giving clues, challenging, and encouraging each other on the way.

Returning to adult participation, we tell our stories as we interpret our lives under the text. We describe and share how the passage informs and shapes our responses to the question, "Who am I?" Our sharing is our witness as we attempt to make sense of our lives as God's people. Our witnesses are new experiences for the adolescents, new experiences about which they can think, feel, and reflect. Receiving that which we share with them, adolescents may discover new clues and ways by which to interpret and understand themselves.

2. Genesis 3:1–24. In Genesis 2:4b–24, we meet one biblical description of what it is to be human, to be persons. We can regard it as a description of God's intention for the creation. The early Hebrews recognized that there was a sharp contradiction, a discontinuity between that intention and the reality of human existence. When we turn to Genesis 3:1–24, we encounter a different description of the human creature. This passage does not define the source of evil. It recognizes a world marked by evil and the destructiveness of evil. It describes the human creature in that world, picturing human creatures as *being* sinful and as *doing* sin.

Bridge: Genesis 3:1–24 is the second part of a larger story. In the first part (Genesis 2:4b–24) we have a biblical description of what it is to be human, to be persons. It is a biblical response to the question, "Who am I?" We can regard it as an expression of God's intention for the creation. In the present passage, we hear a different story; it makes different claims. We want to examine this passage, identifying the parts of its picture of the human creature.

■ *Divide the group into pairs or small groups. Each is to read, study and discuss the passage, having the task of describing the passage's understanding of the human creature. Each will produce a list of items. It will be shared with the total group which will produce a composite description. The composite description should be reproduced on chalkboard or newsprint and will serve as the beginning point for discussion.*

Adolescents may become fascinated with the serpent, the prohibition concerning the tree, the fruit of the tree, or the clothes of the man and woman. There may be need to refocus their attention on the task of describing the human creature. Such may be especially necessary during the development of the composite.

• The man and woman are hiding in the bushes. They are hiding from God. In the garden or world God gave them to enjoy, keep, and tend, they are hiding from the One who created them. There is the suggestion that they are afraid of God.

• At first, man and woman were not clothed. They were naked and not ashamed. Now they have made clothes for themselves. There is the suggestion that they are hiding from each other. Clothes may be a means of hiding.

• When God asks what has happened, the man blames the woman; the woman blames the serpent. Moreover, the man even blames God. The man and woman did not want to take responsibility for their own behaviors.

• Their life in the world would be harsh and difficult. Work would be a burden. Relationships between human creatures and all creation become strained or broken. The earth from which man and woman were made becomes an enemy rather than a friend.

• Man was to dominate woman. The dominance of man over woman is a result of sin.

• Adam and Eve are expelled from the Garden. Cherubim and a flaming sword guard the tree of life, preventing their return to it.

Other images or items may be offered as the young people develop composite descriptions. All should focus on description of the human creature.

□   *After the composite description is completed, lead the group in a discussion which will encourage them to interpret themselves by the text.*

"We have made a list of statements and items which reflect this passage. We have agreed that all are appropriate. If what the story is saying is the way things are, how does it describe us? What does it say about you and me?"

"What things in your life parallel the descriptions in the passage?"

"The creation stories claim that man and woman belong to God. In the passage they wanted to do their 'own thing.' They are hiding from God. Perhaps, if they hid long enough God would go away, leaving them alone. Are there ways that we attempt to hide from God? Why would we want to hide from God?"

"They were ashamed of their nakedness. They did not use clothes to hide from God but to hide from each other. In what ways do we practice the art of hiding from each other? Why do we want to hide from each other? What happens to truthfulness and honesty in relationships when we hide from each other? Might it be appropriate at times to hide from another? Why? Why not?"

"In the story the man and woman did not want to take the blame and responsibility for their own behaviors. They blame someone else or some other thing. Can you think of ways in which you have blamed others for your decisions or behaviors? Why do we want to blame others? What happens to our relationships with others when we blame them for our behaviors? Do we solve our problems when we blame others? Or, do we create more?"

"What's the ultimate condition of man and woman? Who or what have they become?"

With the last two questions above, we can assist our young people to explore a biblical understanding of sin. The simple response may be,

"They are not who they were created to be, not who God intended them to be. They are sinful beings. And as such they will act in sinful ways." The concept of man and woman as *being* sinful and *doing* sin begins to emerge. We can move farther. This passage describes a community which has been shattered, persons hiding from God and each other, persons blaming each other and God, persons refusing to take responsibility for themselves, and a world that has become an enemy. It is the vision of a people in "alien and hostile country." It is all one biblical understanding of sin. Then, what is it to be saved? What is salvation? To be saved is to be *brought back* to the intention of God, to be *brought* to humanness, and to be *brought* to the "Garden."

Following their engagement with the text, adolescents could participate in one of several activities.

- *Divide the larger group into two groups. One will construct a collage depicting Genesis 2:4b–24; the other, depicting Genesis 3:1–24.*

- *Provided with appropriate materials, they could prepare a slide show with accompanying script, illustrating both parts of the second creation story. Their production could be shared with other segments of the congregation.*

- *Invite each to write a paragraph retelling the Genesis 3 story. In the paragraph, they are to use the personal pronoun "I" rather than "man" and "woman."*

A Brief Overview

Let us state again the primary purpose of this chapter. Dealing with the question, "Who am I?" this chapter functions as a framework, model, and point of reference for our use of succeeding chapters with their specific questions. We have described in some detail the flow that our conversation together can take. We have given rationale and explanations for our choices of methods, materials, and exercises, and we have identified the purposes to be served by our selections. The following chapters will not contain the same degree of detail.

In concluding the chapter, we will highlight some of the salient features of the conversation proposed. First, adolescents are to be greeted as active participants. They bring major contributions to the conversation. Their contributions are themselves and their life-content.

Second, activities and exercises offer space, freedom, and encouragement for adolescents to think about, feel about, reflect upon, and respond to significant questions. These events assist adolescents to participate in the conversation with increased understanding of themselves and to create new understandings in the light of the biblical witness.

Third, the conversation should be characterized by acceptance, appreciation, and support of contributions made, yet characterized by challenges, questions, and probes. Knowing that they will be heard and taken seriously and knowing that they have the freedom to test out possibilities, adolescents will receive our challenges and respond to them.

Fourth, adult leaders will be active participants in the conversation. They will provide necessary information; they will assist adolescents to make distinctions and to distinguish between what is critical and not critical. They will participate in the activities and exercises; they will tell their stories; they will bear witness to their lives in the faith. And so, adult leaders are models for the adolescents.

Fifth, the conversation is a conversation in community. In community we support each other; we challenge each other. We build up each other; we assist each other to achieve new understandings. Moreover, the Bible is the community's book. Interpreting and being interpreted by the Bible is profoundly a communal task.

Sixth, the conversation will lead adolescents to a serious engagement with the biblical text itself. We cannot interpret the Bible if we do not know what it is saying and if we do not know its claims and witness. There can be no substitution for a serious working with the biblical text. Knowing the claims and the witness of the text, adolescents can ask, "If those claims and proclamations are true, what do they say about us, and what claims do they make of us?"

And seventh, the conversation does not begin with some "assumed" conclusion at which all must arrive at the same time. We expect a diversity of conclusions and understandings. Adolescents in the conversation participate as they are able, and they achieve understandings as they are able. As young persons continue their conversation with others in the faith, we hope they will always come to new interpretations and knowledge of themselves as the people of God.

·7

Who tells me who I am?

How we respond to the question, "Who am I?" is highly determined by our response to the question, "To whom do I belong?" Those to whom we belong, with whom we ally ourselves, to whom we listen, to whom we give respect, and to whom we make commitments inform and give shape to who we are. In that sense we are formed by others. They give us identity and present us with acceptable values, norms, and behaviors. We are dependent upon others to tell us who we are. Our family, church, clubs, friends, and political party define and describe us in some dimensions while at the same time announcing expected norms and behaviors. Our connections serve to shape our values and actions. Using clues furnished by others, we may define ourselves as successful, witty, or charming. We ally ourselves with a fad, a movement, or an ideology, and in turn our ally defines us. The other person who loves us makes us lovable. The spouse to whom we commit ourselves shapes who we are—our values and our behaviors.

Voices, a great multitude of them, cry out for our attention and allegiance. Conflicting and contradictory, they claim to tell us who we are, to tell us what is valuable and desirable, and to guide our actions. The issue is not, "Can we or should we ignore these voices? Should we reject them all?" We cannot. Yet, we cannot give heed to all of them. We cannot ally ourselves with all. We must make decisions. We must determine the voices to which we will listen. We determine with whom we will ally ourselves, to whom we will commit ourselves. We are responsible for the choices. In making them we determine *who* will tell us who *we* are, and thereby give shape to our futures.

To Which Drummer(s) Do You March?

Adolescents need to achieve an independent self, a self that is of their own making and for which they are responsible. With some frequency they assume that they can achieve that independent self alone—all by themselves, without reference to anyone or anything. They often demand no interferences. They declare themselves independent, being in charge of their situations. Loudly claiming their independence, they immediately relinquish it to others. Adolescents frequently fail to recognize just how subtly their understandings, values, and behaviors are shaped by external sources. They do not readily recognize that their preferences of clothes, music, and activities are greatly influenced by others. They do not readily understand that their notions of sex, drugs, alcohol, popularity, and adulthood are significantly shaped by those with whom they ally themselves. They are not always conscious of the utter conformity demanded by their peer groups. Unaware of, even mindless of, the shaping influence of others, they lose a significant control of their lives.

With an easy confidence adolescents, asserting that their friends do not tell them what to think and how to act, will argue that they can change friends or groups any time they wish. Well, perhaps such may be the case, but they fail to recognize the pain and the difficulty in doing so. They fail to recognize that a change will require new understandings of themselves and that, in some sense, they themselves as persons will experience change. New friends and groups make new demands. New friends or groups will call forth a change in ways of doing things, in opinions, in understandings, and values. And the new demands give new shape to the self.

Once again the issue is, "To whom will we listen? With whom will we ally ourselves? To whom will we make commitments?" To put the matter somewhat differently, many drummers call the adolescent to join their marches. Obviously, the young person cannot follow all. Because humans live in community, it is not possible to opt for no drummer at all. Quite simply, the adolescent must choose the drummer(s) with whom he or she will march. When the choice of drummers has been made, the march is determined. To be sure, new choices may be made, but each choice sets the direction of march.

Adolescents need to become increasingly aware of those external influences which inform and shape them as persons. That is, they need to recognize and identify who or what tells them who they are. They are to be encouraged to examine critically those persons, ways, and values with which they ally themselves, asking, "Why these and not others, and for what purposes?" Adolescents need others to challenge and to ask them hard questions about their choices. By leading and encouraging adolescents through such tasks, we may well create for them conflict, pain, and stress. Yet, as they critically examine the drummer(s) with whom they march, the nature and destination of the march, and their own choices, adolescents can gain appropriate control over their lives as they construct an independent self *in concert* with others.

The ability to anticipate, to imagine the consequences of our decisions and actions is a human task to be learned. Adolescents are not particularly adept in the activity. They have had little practice in learning it. In imagining possible outcomes of their choices they do confront difficulty. They can be ever so certain that what has happened to another cannot possibly happen to them. Says one, "Well, I just know that it can't happen to me." And "it" does happen. Even under the best of circumstances, an adolescent may opt for the wrong drummer with devastating results. We do not consign them to those results. Rather, we assist them to explore the decisions they have made, asking what influenced those decisions and what factors they overlooked or ignored. And thus, we engage them in the practice of learning the art of imagining and anticipating the destination of the marches they join.

Some adolescents never consciously experience both the thrill and the anguish of the question, "Who am I?" Uncritically, they adopt for themselves the values, norms, morals, opinions, and behaviors of parents or some other significant person or group. Because they mirror someone else or some group, they experience little anxiety or stress. Characteristically, such adolescents neither understand nor have patience with the struggles that others encounter. Clearly they have chosen a drummer to follow. They have made a decision. Who and what they are as well as acceptable behaviors and opinions are utterly defined and prescribed by another.

Other adolescents, unable to make choices and commitments, attempt to follow many drummers all at the same time, drummers marching in both opposite and colliding courses. Bewildered and confused, these young people have little sense of belonging to anyone or anything. Unable to articulate a description of themselves, they are anxious and fearful.

Still others, recognizing that decisions and commitments must be made ultimately, simply delay choice-making. They examine, try out, and appraise various drummers and marchers. They explore and test out alternatives with a degree of consciousness and deliberateness.

And still other adolescents make choices. They commit themselves to follow some drummer(s), possessing a measure of understanding of where the march will lead and of its consequences. Time and time again they reexamine their choices and commitments, willing to make necessary and desirable changes.

Many drummers clamor for the attention and allegiance of adolescents: parents, friends, peer groups, the media, the church. The adults may well be able to appraise accurately the purposes and motives of the various drummers. We may judge some to be good and helpful; others, evil and destructive. We may see with clarity several sets of consequences. Our appraisals and judgments must be announced and shared with vigor. But still, from the clamor adolescents must determine for themselves the drummer(s) they will follow. We cannot command them to follow a certain drummer. We cannot compel them to take up a particular march. But we can assist them to recognize that they do follow certain drummers. They will, however, make their own decisions and commitments. And in so doing, they determine who or what it is that tells them who they are.

Adolescents Responding to the Question

In this section are exercises and activities which encourage and assist adolescents to engage the question, "Who tells me who I am?" Adolescents as well as all persons look to others for approval and acceptance of their opinions, thinking, and behaviors. They rely upon others for clues of what is appropriate and expected. The activities and exercises here are to assist adolescents to identify and describe the drummers to which they march, to consider the implications and the consequences of their choices, to ask of the appropriateness and value of their choices, and to discuss the assertion that others do tell us who we are.

1. To Whom Do I Pay Attention? Most adolescents depend upon other people to define them, to tell them "how they are doing," to verify, support, and direct them. In all the issues confronting them, adolescents may turn to a variety of persons and things for guidance, confirmation, and support. Yet, there are some adolescents who have a "significant" person on whom they can rely.

■ *Prepare a mimeographed sheet to be used by the adolescents. The list on the following page can serve as a model. You may wish to add items or to delete certain items noted here. Inform the participants that some discussion of their response will take place in the group.*

The list below includes a number of issues about which you must make some judgments and choices. For each issue, put an "X" under the person or thing to which you give the most attention in forming your opinions. Also, for each issue, put "V" under the person or thing which you think tries most to influence your opinions and actions.

Issues	Friends	Religion	Parents	TV	Teachers	Magazines
Dating patterns and behaviors						
The right clothes to wear						
How to be popular						
Sex and sexual behavior						
Use of alcohol, drugs & tobacco						
Notions of right and wrong						
Tastes in music						

See exercise on preceding page.

❏   *Responses will create a "checker-board" effect in most instances. It is possible that a participant might identify one person or source for all issues. In any event, invite the participants to share some of their responses.*

"Why do you give most attention to the person or source on the issue of _____?"

"In what ways is the person or source important to you?"

"How does that person or source inform your opinions on the issue of _____?"

"In what ways does that person or source tell you who you are?"

"If you did not follow the opinion of the source or person to which you give the most attention, how would your opinions and behaviors change? What would happen to your relationship with that person?"

"On certain issues, you said that you give more attention to the person or source but also noted that another person or source tries to exert the most influence over you. Why do you pay attention to the one over the other? Do you experience any conflict or difficulty in the situation? If you were to follow the one who tries to exert the most influence, how would your opinions, understandings, and behaviors change?"

"You have indicated the person or source to which you want to give most attention on the issue of _____. Are you happy and comfortable when you do that? Would you rather give more attention to another person or source? If so, why don't you? Are you letting someone or something tell you who you are, tell you what your opinions ought to be, and tell you what your behaviors ought to be, even if you don't like what they are telling you?"

"How do you decide to whom you will listen and to whom you will give most attention?"

Using such questions as above, we can encourage the participants to converse with each other, asking questions and challenging each other. In a conversation together, the adolescents can assist each other in achieving clarity of their choices and even the consequences of those choices.

2. The World of Mass Media: Magazines. The world of mass media consumes significant amounts of time and attention of adolescents. Through a multifaceted world, it announces values and norms. It prescribes goals, modes of actions, and behaviors. In a variety of ways it seeks to describe who the human creature is. It does claim to tell us who we "ought" to be and describes how we might become those persons. Seeking a portion of adolescent spending, it describes pathways to popularity. Adolescents often give allegiance to some part of that world, following it without critical reflection and without significant questioning.

■ *Invite the adolescents to bring into the group discussion a copy of the magazine they most often read. Have each discuss his/her magazine, stating the usual content of the magazine, noting the type of content which receives the most attention and indicating their reasons for reading it.*

"In what ways does this magazine attempt to tell you who you are? Do you like what it claims to tell you about you? If so, why? If not, why not?"

"How much attention do you give to the advertisements in the magazine? What do the advertisements claim to tell you about you? Describe some of the claims."

"Would you want to be the person(s) that this magazine describes? Why? Why not?"

"What are the values reflected in the magazine? In what ways do you share the values expressed in the magazine?"

"How do your parents react to this magazine? What do they think of it? Why do they react in such a way?"

□ *Invite others who are familiar with the magazine to share their opinions of and reactions to it.*

"Why would you or why would you not read the magazine?"

"What questions would you have for people who read this magazine frequently? What impressions would you have of the person who reads this magazine frequently? Do the magazines that people read tell you something about the persons?"

In the discussion there may be a variety of reactions concerning a particular magazine. Also, the participants will indicate ways in which a particular magazine is helpful to them.

"Does the magazine that you read tell something of you to others?"

"Do you permit the magazine to tell you who you are? What clothes you ought to wear? How you should behave on dates? What will make you popular? What it is to be male or female? How to act in various social settings? What is valuable?"

"Why would you want to be the person(s) described in the magazine?"

"Why do you follow many of the suggestions or directions given in the magazine? Why do you follow the advice given in the magazine?"

"Does this magazine in any fashion tell you who you are or ought to be?"

3. The World of Mass Media: TV. Television programs can have subtle influences. They announce values, acceptable ways of behaving, and descriptions of the human creature. Adolescents need assistance in developing a critical stance vis-à-vis all mass media.

■ *Arrange for the group to view together a popular television program. Prepare a list of questions which will serve as a guide to their viewing. Also, the participants should be encouraged to use the same set of questions in viewing the advertisements surrounding the program.*

> How does this program describe the human being? What does it say about people?
>
> What values are expressed in the program?
>
> What does it say about men?
>
> What does it say about women?
>
> Does it make suggestions about how we are to act so as to be popular or successful?
>
> Does it suggest how we ought to treat people?

☐ *A discussion, based upon the program and its advertisements, follows.*

"How does the program describe the human being? Men? Women? Would you want to be described in those ways? Why? Why not?"

"What are the program's claims about popularity and successfulness? Would you want others to describe you on the basis of those claims? Why? Why not?"

"In what ways does the program suggest that we can deal with people? Would you want others to deal with you in that manner?"

"Do you think that there are persons who permit television programs to tell them who they are? How they ought to act? Can you give some illustrations?"

"In what ways, if any, do television programs influence you? your understanding of who you are? your visions of who you would like to be? your behaviors? Why do you turn to the television to help you in these ways?"

"What sort of a person would you be if you followed the suggestion of many television programs?"

4. An Additional Possibility with Mass Media: TV. Ask the adolescents to view at home their favorite television program, using the previous list of questions to guide their viewing. In the group, they can share their findings. By such a method a wide range of television programs can be discussed. The participants will probably be familiar with all the programs identified. Thus, they will be able to "add to" one individual's description, and they will be able to challenge each other. Also, they can ask questions of each other. Why do you watch that program? What do you "get out of it"? The discussion questions listed above can be used in the conversation.

Each participant is asked to identify the television character he or she would most want to be like. Each is invited to discuss why he or she would want to be like that character. Why would one want to be like that character? What values does that character express? What would it require of one to be like that character? What would be the consequences of being like that person?

5. Conformity and Mindlessness. Conformity and mindlessness function in ways to inform and define who we are and how we behave. Life in a group or community will require sharing and acting upon some commonly-held values and goals. Some commonality and conformity will be necessary. Those who make conscious decisions about their group or community affiliations are more able to recognize the control which the group or community exercises over their lives. They are more able to recognize how the group or community does define and describe them. Yet, others join groups, following the demands of the group with utter conformity, not realizing what is happening to them. With mindlessness, they simply follow. Persons mindful of and aware of the conformities which they choose can exercise appropriate control over their lives.

■   *Without any comment or explanation at the beginning of a group meeting, give a series of directions. "I want everyone to stand in a straight line across the room facing me." After the participants have complied, give another direction. "No, I would rather have your backs toward me, so turn around." After the participants have complied, give another direction. "No, I would rather have you stand in a line against the wall facing me." Continue the process until there are sustained objections from the group. How long will the group conform to your directions without overt complaints and resistance?*

"I have been giving you a lot of directions without any explanation whatsoever. Why do you think I have been doing this? What was my purpose in doing this?"

"In my directions or commands I was controlling your movements. I was exercising control over you. Why did you do what I told you? Why did you not object or resist from the outset? Did you have any idea why you were doing these things?"

"Was the fact that I told you to do those things a sufficient reason for you to do them? Why? Why not? What would happen to you if you did everything I told you, simply because I told you?"

"From time to time, we do follow what another person or group tells us to do. We follow blindly, without question or resistance. We may do that for many different reasons. We may be afraid to ask questions. We may fear that the person or group will not like us if we do not follow what is expected. We may think that by following we will be liked or popular. When we act in such a way, who is controlling our lives? Who is telling us who we are?"

"Can you think of instances in which you have followed blindly another's or a group's directions or expectations? What have been the results when you have done that? Would you be willing to share an example from your life or from that of others?"

"How often are you willing to question or resist the suggestions or expectations of your friends on such matters as the clothes you wear; whom you date, your dating and sexual behaviors; your use or non-use of alcohol, drugs and/or smoking; your values; etc.?"

"Who tells you who you are and how you should act? To whom do you pay attention? Why?"

6. How My Friends See Me. Adolescents are not always aware of influence that friends exert on them. They need to become aware of a friend's influence and its consequences.

- *Have the adolescents produce a collage or finger paint with the title, "How My Friends See Me." Directions could include the following How would your friends describe you? What kind of picture would they paint of you? The "products" are to be shared and discussed with the group.*

"You have described how you think your friends would describe you. In what ways do your friends tell you who you are? In what ways do your friends influence what you think, how you behave, and what you believe to be important?"

"Do you always like or feel comfortable with what your friends tell you about you, with what they expect of you, and with what they want you to do? If you disagree with them, what do you do?"

"How important is it that you be and do what your friends expect?"

7. The Lyrics of Popular Songs. The lyrics of popular songs to which adolescents listen and that they sing describe the human being in various dimensions. The lyrics suggest ways of dealing with one's self and with others. At the same time, the lyrics often give expression to the feelings and thoughts of adolescents. The words of popular songs can function as subtle shapers of persons, defining and telling them who they are and suggesting modes of behavior.

- *Previous to the session(s) which will consider song lyrics, have each adolescent provide you with words of his or her favorite popular song. Prepare mimeographed sheets containing the various lyrics so that all will be working with the same set of materials. Using the chalkboard or newsprint, invite the participants to make two lists concerning the lyrics. One list should be the images of the human*

*being as suggested by the several lyrics. The other should include
the suggestions from the lyrics concerning behaviors.*

"We have produced a list of images concerning who the human
being is. Do you like the images? Do you think that they are good
and right? Why? Why not?"

"Would you want to be described by the images present in the lyrics? Why? Why not?"

"Can you be described by those images? If so, in what ways? In
what ways do those lyrics serve to tell you who you are?"

"If you don't like those images or if you don't want to be described
by those images, why do you sing and listen to these songs? How
can you listen to these songs but not be influenced by them?"

"How do your parents react to the songs that you like? Why do
they react that way? Do you think that it is appropriate for them
to react in that manner? Why? Why not?"

"We have also produced from the song lyrics a list of suggestions
telling us how to deal with ourselves and how to deal with others.
Do you judge that those suggestions are good and proper, or bad
and hurtful? How would you evaluate each of the suggestions?
Why?"

"Do these suggestions express some of the ways that you behave
toward yourself and others? Do they suggest some of the ways you
would like to behave? Why would you want to behave in those
ways?"

"If you were to act or behave in the ways that the songs suggest,
what do you think would be the consequences of your actions? In
your relationships to your parents? In relationships to your friends?"

"Do the words of the songs express how you feel and think at times?
Do they encourage you to continue to feel and think in that
manner?"

"In what ways do you permit these songs to tell you who you are
and what you ought to do?"

■ *In conjunction with the use of song lyrics, invite the young people
to bring posters of their favorite musical groups. Hang the posters
around the room.*

"What is it that attracts you to or excites you about the group?"

"Does this group suggest ways that you should think or behave?"

"How do you react to the group on the poster that _____
brought? Why?"

"In what ways might a musical group influence a person's dress,
ways of thinking, values, or behavior?"

Engaging and Interpreting the Bible

The question, "Who tells me who I am?" is profoundly related to the question, "Who am I?" In reality, the first question is the primary one. We are dependent upon others. They do inform and give definition to ourselves. In this section, we present seven exercises by which we may bring biblical material to impinge upon adolescents as they work with the question, "Who tells me who I am?" The biblical material as presented in the exercises can assist adolescents to fashion useful and appropriate responses to the question. The exercises approach the question in two directions. First, they pose the question, "To whom do I listen?" asking about responsibility for decisions made and consequences that result. Second, they ask the question, "To whom do I belong?" asserting that belongingness determines the answer to the question, "Who am I?" The exercises here, to be used in some relationship with exercises in the first half of the chapter, differ in terms of complexity, difficulty, and demands. Thus, choice on our part will need to be exercised.

1. Proverbs 1:8–19; 4:10–19; 4:20–27. These passages make appeals to adolescents, identified here as "my son." There is the appeal that "my son" will hear and heed the instruction and teachings of the parents. There is the appeal that "my son" not permit "himself" to be enticed to walk in certain ways. There is the appeal that "my son" recognize the consequences of "his" decisions. These passages assert that those with whom we ally ourselves and whom we follow tell us who we are and "make" us as they are.

Bridge: We have been working with the question, "Who tells me who I am?" We know that many voices attempt to tell us who we are. We want to consider three passages in the book of Proverbs (1:8–19; 4:10–19; 4:20–27) which offer one response to the question. As we study these passages, we want to identify their major concern and to describe their response. I will read the passages as you follow the text. As I do so, ask if what you are hearing is similar to anything that you have heard elsewhere in your relationships with others.

■ *Read aloud the first two passages (1:8–19 and 4:10–19). Discussion can be in the total group.*

"Have you heard similar things from your parents, teachers, and other adults? Can you give some examples?" [*My parents try to pick my friends. Adults are always telling me with whom I ought to associate. They tell me that if I hang around with people who use drugs, I will start using them.*]

"How do you feel or react when adults tell you such things?" [*I get angry. I do not feel trusted. I know what I am doing so they ought to keep out of it. I do what they tell me.*]

"Why do you think that adults say such things to us?" [*It is for our own good. They are trying to help us. They are being bossy. They are afraid we will get into trouble.*]

□   *Invite the participants to read the two passages again, asking "What are the major concerns of the passages? What claims do these passages make?"*

"In Proverbs 1:8 and 9 there is the appeal that one should hear a father's instruction and not reject a mother's teachings. What is your reaction to these verses? Do they suggest that we should never disagree with our parents? If we do disagree with our parents do we have a right to ignore what they say? If we do not give heed to our parents, to whom do we listen? Why? Why do we not want to listen to our parents at times?"

"In these two passages there is a warning constantly given. What is that warning? How would you describe it?" [*Be careful about whom you follow or to whom you listen. Some people destroy themselves and those who associate with them. Walking with some persons is like stumbling in the dark, not knowing what one is stumbling over. You become like those with whom you associate and to whom you listen.*]

"Can 'my son' walk with sinners or evil doers without becoming as they are? Will those persons tell 'my son' who he is? Will they 'make' him as they are? Why? Why not?"

"What influences your understanding of what is attractive, popular, successful, being adult, valuable, right and wrong? Do those influences (persons, things, ideas, etc.) tell you who you are? Do they influence your behaviors? Can you give some examples?"

"In the passages, if 'my son' follows the evil persons and listens to them, can he avoid being as they are? Can you avoid being like the persons to whom you listen or with whom you associate? Do you, at times, attempt to be as some advertisement wants you to be? Why?"

"Both passages claim that consequences follow from our decisions to listen to or to follow certain persons, ideas, and various voices. Who is responsible for the choices? Who is responsible for the consequences?"

"How would you translate the concern and warning of these passages into our life today? Is that warning appropriate for us today? Why? Why not?" [*Advertisements claim to tell us what it is to be male or female, what makes us adults, how to use our bodies, how to use other people, and what is desirable. Our friends often encourage us to do various things. We often behave in certain ways to get people to like us and to prove that we are adults.*]

☐ *Invite the participants to read the third passage, 4:20–27, asking, "What is the appeal of the passage? What does it say about responsibility for decisions and consequences?"*

"What does the passage say about to whom we should listen?" [*We will listen to someone. Let us listen to the wisdom of others. Let us listen to those who are concerned about us, about our well-being. Let us listen to those who seek to assist us and support us.*]

"Who is responsible for the decisions for listening and following?"

"Can we ever avoid listening to someone? Can we ever avoid being who others tell us we are? Can we listen to all the voices calling for our attention?"

"How do we determine to which voices we will listen?"

☐ *Adolescents can be assisted in further reflection on the texts through a written exercise. Arrange for small groups. Invite each group to "rewrite" 1:8–19 and 4:20–27, using contemporary terminology, examples, and imagery. The various statements can be shared and discussed within the total group.*

2. Acts 4:1–22. This passage follows an accounting of several events in the ministry of Peter and John in Jerusalem. They had healed a man in the name of Jesus. In the temple they had proclaimed the story of Jesus. They had proclaimed the resurrected Jesus. Their proclamation, the gospel, set them in opposition to the religious leaders. In the present passage Peter and John suffer some consequences of their preaching and hear threats of possible future consequences. Before the religious leaders, they make a choice. They declare to whom they will listen.

Bridge: Considering the question, "Who tells me who I am?" we have discussed the assertion that the persons to whom we choose to listen tell us who we are. Also, when we choose to give heed to persons, ideas, or things there are consequences which result from our choice. In Acts 4:1–22, we have a story of Peter and John who had healed a lame man in the name of Jesus and who had proclaimed Jesus as the resurrected Lord. This passage begins with another incident in which the two men are teaching and preaching about Jesus in the temple at Jerusalem. Let's follow the story, asking how it responds to our question.

■   *Have the participants work together in pairs or small groups. Prepare the following questions in a written form. They will guide the adolescents' engagement with the text.*

"Why were the religious leaders annoyed or upset?" [*Proclaiming Jesus as the resurrected Lord, Peter and John were in opposition to accepted religious views. They challenged the religious* status quo.]

"What were the consequences of the two men's activity of teaching and preaching?" [*First, they were arrested and taken into custody. Second, many believed.*]

"On the following day, facing something of a trial, did Peter and John alter what they had been preaching?" [*They proclaimed the power of Jesus' name. They made certain accusations against the religious leaders.*]

"What did the religious leaders demand of Peter and John?"

"What was the response of the two men? What risks did they take by their response?"

□   *Invite the group to share and discuss their findings and conclusions. Encourage them to develop a description of the story with which all can generally agree. Assist them to relate the problem faced by Peter and John to their own life situations.*

"If you had been the two men, what decision would you have made? Why?"

"Can you describe some situation in which you have faced the same kind of problem? How did you go about making your decision?"

"If Peter and John had agreed to listen to the religious leaders, how would you describe them?" [*They did not listen to God. They went against what they believed was right or true. They let the leaders tell them who they were.*]

"Can you describe a situation in which you have not said or done something you believe to be true or right because you feared the consequences? Did you fear that another would be upset with you or shun you?"

"What happens to us as persons when we act in such a way?" [*We are letting the other person tell us who we are. The other person "makes" us like him or her.*]

"Can we ever be at a point when we do not have to listen to anyone at all? Why? Why not?" [*As human beings, we need others. We will always rely upon what some persons say to us. We have to decide to whom we are going to listen, to whom we are going to pay attention. Our choices will always have consequences.*]

"Peter and John declared that they would listen to God rather than to the leaders. They wanted to be faithful to God. We are Christians. Time and time again, we must decide if we will listen to God. What is it for us to listen to God?" [*We ask continually, "What is it for us to be God's people?" God tells us that we are God's people, that God loves us and cares for us.*]

"Who are we as we listen to God?" [*We are a people striving to be faithful to our Lord.*]

"Can you describe possible consequences when we choose to listen to God? What consequences have you experienced?"

As we engage adolescents with this passage as suggested here, most serious questions are asked. How do we hear God? Where do we hear God? When do we hear God? Our responses should always point adolescents to those situations in which the church understands God to be active. We should not point them to themselves, their feelings, and their private opinions. Rather we point them outside themselves. Where Christian people discuss and ask questions in their efforts to be faithful, there is God calling, gathering, enlightening, sanctifying, and preserving the people of God. In the Bible, we hear the witnesses, testifying to what God has done, is doing, and is yet to do. There we hear the promises of God. As others stand before us in pain, sorrow, need, and oppression, there is our Lord calling us to compassion, love, and actions of justice. In the sacraments we hear God's promises. We hear God declaring who we are, forgiven sinners and God's people. As the gospel, the story of Jesus, is told, there God speaks to us.

3. Joshua 24. The passage is one account of Joshua's farewell message to the Hebrews. He had succeeded Moses as their leader and had guided them as they secured the land of Israel for their own. He was near the end of his life. He recognized that the people needed to make a choice once again, a choice of whom they would serve and to whom they would listen. The choice would determine who they would be and the shape of their lives.

Bridge: We have been discussing the assertion that those to whom we pay attention, with whom we ally ourselves, and whom we follow tell us who we are. They define us. About those persons, things, and ideas which we follow, we must make some decisions. Our decisions always have consequences. In Joshua 24:1–28, there is an appeal to the Hebrews that they should make a choice. They had made similar choices before. In a new day and new circumstances, they needed to make a choice anew which would have its own consequences.

■ *The study and discussion of the passage can take place within a large group. The questions below, designed to give direction and focus to the engagement with the text, should be shared with the group before the initial reading.*

"In the first portion of the passage (vss. 1–13) Joshua recounted God's dealings with the people of God. Why did he do that?" [*He reminded the people of who they were, God's people. He reminded them of what God had done for them and that God had faithfully keep the promises made. He reminded them that God had a claim on them.*]

"In verse 15, what was the choice that Joshua wanted the people to make? Why might Joshua have thought that the choice needed to be made?" [*The choice was between serving the God of their fathers, the Lord Jehovah, and the "gods" of the people, the Amorites, who also live in the land. The Hebrews had not always been faithful to the Lord. They did, on occasion, seek after other "gods." There was the possibility that they would serve the "gods" of the Amorites.*]

"What was Joshua's decision? What was the people's decision?"

"In the passage, on three different occasions Joshua asked the people to make the decision (vs. 15, vss. 19 and 20, and vs. 23). Why would Joshua have asked them to do the same thing three different times?" [*He wanted them to consider the consequences. There are demands and expectations of God's people. To serve the Lord would require much. If they chose to serve the Lord, they were to live as God's people. To whom they listen determined who they were and the shape of their lives.*]

■ *We can assist adolescents to consider this ancient story as a part of their present stories. Questions and probes can encourage them to reflect upon the present and to describe that present.*

"Joshua was concerned that the people would go searching after 'other gods.' What are the 'gods' that we search out, that we serve?" [*Popularity, acceptance by a specific group. Independence. Possessions. Success. Attractiveness. Getting what we want.*]

"Where do we hear the voices of those 'gods' calling us?" [*Advertisements. Lyrics to popular songs. Expectations of peer groups. Voices telling us that our personal pleasure is of prime importance. Voices telling us that we should be free to do whatever we want to do.*]

"When we listen to those voices and serve those 'gods,' what are the consequences?" [*They tell us who we are. They make demands upon us. They shape our lives.*]

"Who is responsible for the decisions 'to listen' and for the consequences of having done so?"

"In what way is Joshua's call for a decision a call to us? Do we have to make the same kind of decision?"

"Where do we hear the voice of God?" [*In responding to this question, we do not point adolescents to their feelings, private opinions, or individualistic religious experiences. We point them to those events which the church understands to be the activity of God: the sacraments, the Bible bearing witness to what God has done, is doing, and is yet to do, the Bible bearing witness to the promises of God. We point them to the neighbor in need of love, compassion, encouragement, and justice. We direct young people to the preached Word, declaring the works of the Lord, and to a congregation of Christian people asking questions of what it is to be God's faithful people.*]

"If we make the decision for the Lord, what might be some of the consequences—in our personal behavior, our attitudes, our values, and our treatment of others? Can you think of ways in which we might encounter suffering as we make our decision for the Lord?"

4. Luke 15:11–32. This passage is the familiar story of two sons. It bears witness to God's gracious dealings with God's people. At the same time, it is a response to the questions, "Who am I?" and "Who tells me who I am?" It is on that response that we will focus.

Bridge: We want to study and discuss the biblical story of two sons (Luke 15:11–32), often labeled the "Parable of the Prodigal Son." While it describes how God deals with people, it gives several responses to the questions with which we have been working, "Who am I?" and "Who tells me who I am?" Before we begin our study of the story, let's share some of our reactions to and impressions of the story as we remember it.

■ *For a short period of time, invite the participants to share their responses to the several questions below. The responses can be written on a chalkboard or on newsprint and can serve as points of reference for later discussion.*

"Which character in the story do you most like? Why?"

"Which character do you least like? Why?"

"Which character is most like you? Why?"

"Which character would you want to be like? Why?"

■ *Prepare the following list of questions in some written form. The questions, designed to guide study and discussion are to be used by the participants in pairs or small groups. It should be noted that the younger son's request for his inheritance was proper. He was not "wrong" in making the request. Copy only the questions.*

What was the point of the younger son's going to a "far country"? Why did he want to go to a "far country"? [*He wanted to be independent. He wanted to do what he wanted to do, without any questions from anyone. He did not want to be a son.*]

What happened to him in the "far country"? [*He did what he wanted to do. He spent all his money in "riotous living." He had friends as long as he had money to spend. His friends told him he was "O.K." as long as he had money. When he had no money, they told him he was "not O.K." They told him who he was.*]

Ultimately, he had to hire himself out. He tended the swine and ate their food. Who or what had the young man become? [*He had become one of the pigs. Those with whom he associated and ate told him who he was.*]

What was the bargain that the young man decided to make with the father? [*He was attempting to determine who he would be. He tried to determine that he would be a servant.*]

What did the father do with the bargain? [*The father did not even hear the bargain. The father was not interested in any bargain. The father restored the young man to sonship. Only the father could do that.*]

The father declared that the son who was "dead" was now "alive." How did the "dead" man become "alive"? [*The father's love made him a son. The young man could not be a son unless the father declared it. The father made him "alive." The father told the young man who he was, "My son." To whom we listen can be the difference between "life" and "death."*]

What was the bargain that the older son attempted to use on the father?

What did the father do with that bargain? [*He made the same response as to the younger man, "You are my son." The older son needed to be reminded of who he already was. Both the younger son and older son "belonged" to the father.*]

If the claims of this story are true, in what ways does this passage suggest that God deals with us? [*God wants us to be God's children. We do not bargain with God. God is not interested in any bargain that we might wish to make. God tells us who we are. God makes us the children of God. We belong to God.*]

☐ *Invite the participants to share their study and discussion of the passage in the large group. Give particular attention to the last question above. We can assist the adolescents in further reflection on the story and their relationship to it by additional probing and activities.*

"In what ways do we play the role of the younger son? What happens to us, what do we become when we play that role? How are we like the younger son?"

"In what ways do we play the role of the older son? What happens to us, what do we become when we play that role? How are we like the older son?"

"Do those with whom we associate tell us who we are? Do they 'make' us who we are?"

"If it is true that others tell us who we are, what does that tell us about decisions?"

"Prepare a collage, depicting how you think God sees you and depicting who God says you are."

5. Luke 18:9–14. This passage is the familiar parable of the Pharisee and the tax collector. The Pharisees composed one of the three Jewish parties in Jesus' day. Their religious stance gave primary emphasis to conformity with the external Law, the rules and regulations assumed to be God's rules and regulations. For them, God's love and grace was promised only to those who conformed in their behavior with the Law. Tax collectors were a part of the lower echelon of civil workers and collected taxes for the Roman government. For the most part they were regarded as extortioners. Among the Jews, a tax collector was not admitted into their society. It was a disgrace for a "good" Jew to be a friend of a tax collector or to associate with one. One charge leveled against Jesus was that he visited and ate with tax collectors.

Bridge: The parable of the Pharisee and the tax collector (Luke 18:9–14) has several elements which could rightly claim our attention. In the previous activities and exercises, we have explored the question, "Who tells me who I am?" We have discussed persons, ideas, and things that tell us who we are and that shape our lives. At times, we think that we are the only ones who determine who we are. This parable also explores our question and gives a response to it.

■ *Divide the larger group into pairs or small groups. For study and discussion of the passage, we give three sets of questions which will serve as guides.*

> Who is telling whom who they are? (For example, to whom is
> the Pharisee speaking?)
>
> Do you think that the Pharisee was being truthful in what
> he said? Why? Was the Pharisee attempting to determine for
> himself and God who he (the Pharisee) was?
>
> Do you think that the tax collector was being truthful in what
> he said? Why? Was the tax collector attempting to determine for
> himself and God who he (the tax collector) was?

☐ *Invite all to share their findings and conclusions in the larger group.
List the adolescents' contributions on the chalkboard or newsprint.
Encourage discussion, probes, and challenges among the
participants.*

"Are there any disagreements among you concerning items that
have been contributed? Why? Why not?"

"Do these various items reflect the material in the parable?"

"Who is telling whom who they are?"

There are a number of significant elements at play in this story.
Our use of them will assist youth to engage the passage in a more
thorough way than suggested earlier.

- The truthfulness of both the Pharisee and the tax collector was not
  questioned.
- It is assumed that both were correct in describing their characteristics and behaviors.
- The Pharisee, while addressing God, "prayed with himself." In a sense
  he was talking to himself about himself. He was defining himself,
  as he compared himself with another. He was telling God and himself who he was, a good man, better than another. He was thus attempting to define the tax collector also.
- The tax collector, standing apart with downcast eyes, was doing the
  same as the Pharisee. He was telling God and himself who he was,
  a sinner.
- Jesus, the teller of the story, does not accept either man's definition
  of self. Jesus tells who they are. Jesus' response in both cases is the
  opposite of each man's description.
- Jesus (God) has the "last word" in telling us who we are.

  "Consider the people that you know and put yourself in the picture
  also. How would you describe present day Pharisees?" [*Better look-*

ing than . . . ; from a better family than . . . ; better dressed than . . . ; more smart than . . . ; more boyfriends/girlfriends than . . . ; a better job . . . ; a different color than . . . ; better behaved than. . . .]

"Can you state some examples of how our 'better than' or 'more than' become standards by which we compare ourselves in a favorable light to others, how they become occasions for disliking, looking down upon or ignoring those who do not match up to our standards?"

"How would you describe present day tax collectors? [*I am not accepted. I am ugly and unattractive. I can't do anything right. I get into a lot of trouble. I can't get along with others. At times, I am mean to others.*]

"What do you think Jesus would say to the present day Pharisees and publicans (tax collectors)?"

"If this parable appropriately describes how God deals with us, who will have the 'last word' in telling us who we are?"

"What do you think is the 'last word' that God says about you and me?"

We can encourage and assist adolescents in reflecting upon the passage and on their relationship to it:

■ *Invite them to write their individual parables of present day Pharisees and tax collectors, using the framework of Luke 18:9–14.*

❏ *Divide the larger group into two groups. Have each group prepare a short "playlet" depicting the parable. The two groups can compare and discuss the playlets.*

6. Genesis 12:1–3; Psalm 8; Romans 6:1–5. These three passages focus upon some activity of God. God acts and "something" comes into being. The three passages claim that God has acted upon a people in particular ways. In so doing, God has made them "someone" in particular. In Genesis 12:1–3, God's Word is the divine action. To Abram, representative of a people, the Word of God declares that the people will become a great nation, a nation that will be a blessing to all. God acted, and it was so. In Psalm 8, the God who created the heavens created the human creature, giving the creature dignity (glory and honor) and giving the creature dominion over the very works of God. In Romans 6:1–5 God has acted in our baptism and we share in the death and resurrection of Jesus and are brought to newness of life. God acts to make us who we are.

Bridge: In our discussion of "Who tells me who I am?" we have considered the assertion that other persons do "make" us who we are. Their actions upon us, including their words, do tell us who we are, and can "make" us who we are. For example, if another person acts upon us in love, that person makes us lovable. Or, if another person calls us "friend," he or she has made us a friend. We want to study and discuss three biblical passages, Genesis 12:1–3, Psalm 8 and Romans 6:1–5 which focus on an activity of God. These passages claim that God by divine action makes us who we are.

■   *Divide the group into three small groups. Each small group is to study and discuss one of the passages. Although working with different passages, each group is to work with the same set of questions:*

"According to the passage, what is the activity of God? What does God do?"

"What is the result of God's activity? What is the declaration that God's activity makes about the human creature? What does God's activity say about a people?"

"What is a people or human creature to do as the result of God's activity? What is expected of the people?"

"What are your reactions to the claims of the passages? Are those claims important to you? If so, in what ways? Do these passages tell anything about who you are?"

• *Genesis 12:1–3.* God's activity shown here is the Word, God's address to Abram. God's activity, God's Word does bless the people and does make of them a great nation. The people are to be a blessing to all others.

• *Psalm 8.* God's activity is that of creation. In the act of creation, God has made the human creature a little less than God. God's act of creation has therefore given dignity to the human creature, a creature crowned with glory and honor. That which God has made belongs to God. The human creature is to have dominion over all the works of God. (Relating this passage to Genesis 12:1–3, one might suggest that to have dominion is to be a blessing.)

• *Romans 6:1–5.* Baptism is God's activity. Those baptized are baptized into the death and resurrection of Jesus. They are no longer the slaves of sin. Sin does not have the last word about them. Those who are baptized are to walk in newness of life.

■   *Invite the small groups to share their discussions and conclusions with the total group. Each is to begin by reading aloud its assigned passage so that all may have some acquaintance with it. On the chalkboard or newsprint list the contributions of each group as it responds to the three sets of questions previously assigned. To-*

*gether, the groups will produce a more inclusive or broader re-
sponse than was possible by a single group. Give opportunity for
the participants to ask questions of each other, to seek for clarifications, and to express their concerns and understandings.*

Bridge: As we have produced the composite list, we have identified
some of the biblical claims concerning God's activity. There are
results flowing from God's action. In the passages studied there is
the claim that God's activity declares and makes a people who they
are. God expects the people of God to be and do who they are. For
us Christians the Bible is our book, telling stories of us. So let us
engage in translating these stories in terms of our own lives, asking what they tell us about ourselves and what they call us to do.

■ *Discussion of the following questions can be done within the total
group. Participants should be given ample opportunity for questioning each other, for probing each other's statements, for both
agreements and disagreements, and for testing out responses.*

"Where has God been active or where is God active in our lives?
How would we describe God's action upon us?" [*We hear the Word
of God preached—God's Word is God's action toward us. The Word
of God says that we are loved by God—it claims that we are forgiven. Our creation is God's action. And we are baptized; the sacraments speak God's Word to us. In the church, we hear God's Word,
telling what God has done and will yet do.*]

"If God has acted and continues to act in these ways, what does
God's activity declare about us?" [*We are loved and made lovable.
We are forgiven. We belong to God. We are God's people.*]

"According to the biblical stories God has declared who we are—
God's people. God expects that we will live as that people. How
might we be a blessing to others?" [*To speak words of love and
forgiveness. To proclaim God's love to all. To comfort, to support,
and to protect others.*]

"What is it for us to have dominion over the works of God?" [*To
care for and protect the creation. To use the environment rightly
and carefully. To protect the environment from misuse and destruction. To work that all may enjoy the fruits of the environment.*]

"What is it for us to walk in newness of life?" [*To live knowing that
we are loved by God. To know that we are forgiven and will be
forgiven. To live in love and kindness.*]

■ *Arrange three small groups. Each is to produce a collage, depicting
one of the following: God's Activity in Our Lives; God's Declaration
About Us; What God Expects of Us. These can be discussed in the
larger group.*

7. Exodus 19:3–6; Deuteronomy 7:6–11; 1 Peter 2:9 and 10. As we encounter these passages in the Bible, all three are words spoken to a people at the beginning of a relationship with God. Exodus 19:3–6, set within the wilderness of Sinai shortly after the Hebrews' deliverance, are words that Moses is to speak to Israel. The words declare who Israel is and set forth God's expectation. Deuteronomy 7:6–11, a writing calling for reform, reminds a people of who they are and calls them to be and do who they already are. 1 Peter 2:9 and 10, addressed to those who are baptized, declares who they are and God's expectation of them. In all three, we hear first a word which declares who a people are. It is only after the declaration do we hear words of expectations. God desires that the people should be and do who they are.

Bridge: We have discussed the question, "Who tells me who I am?" We have recognized that many voices *attempt* to tell us who we are, to describe and to define us. We have recognized that others *do* tell us who we are, and in a sense, these others make us who we are. We do not determine who we are all by ourselves. We want to study and discuss three biblical passages, Exodus 19:3–6, Deuteronomy 7:6–11, and 1 Peter 2:9 and 10, which make some claims about who we are. All three are words addressed on behalf of God to a people, claiming to tell them who they are.

■ *Divide the group into three small groups. Each small group is to study and discuss one of three passages. Although working with different passages, each group is to work with the same set of questions:*

"According to this passage, how does God regard the people? Who does God tell them they are?"

"Who are the people who are being told who they are?"

"After God declares who they are, what is expected of the people?"

• *Exodus 19:3–6.* They are a people brought near to God by divine leading. They are already God's possession. God delivered them, redeemed them from their bondage, brought them out of Egypt. By this act of deliverance God made them the people and possession of God. As God's people, they are to obey the voice of God, keep the covenant of God, and be a kingdom of priests and a holy nation.

• *Deuteronomy 7:6–11.* The declaration is clear. They are a holy people, chosen by God, possessed by God, and loved by God. The God who declared them and who made them a chosen people is one who keeps promises. And who was this people to whom the declaration was made? It is a people who had been brought and redeemed from the house of bondage in Egypt by the mighty hand of God. The holy people are to be careful to do the commandments, statutes, and ordinances of God.

• *1 Peter 2:9 and 10.* This epistle is written to Christians, those who have been baptized (see 3:21) and thus have membership in God's holy and elect people (see 2:4–10). Those who have been baptized are given particular names, "a chosen race," "a royal priesthood," "a holy nation," and "God's own people." Those who were no people at all are now God's people. God has declared it so. And that people are to declare "the marvelous deeds" of God.

■ *Invite the small groups to share their discussions and conclusions with the total group. Each is to begin by reading aloud its assigned passage so that all may have some acquaintance with it. On the chalkboard or newsprint, list the contributions of each group as it responds to the three questions previously assigned. Together the groups will produce a more inclusive or broader response than was possible by a single group. Give opportunity for the participants to ask questions of each other, to seek for clarifications and to express concerns and understandings.*

Bridge: As we have produced the composite list, we have identified some of the biblical claims concerning God's regard for the people of God. In the passages studied it is God who brings a people near to God, who delivers and redeems them. They have no claim on God. God has a claim on them. The biblical stories tell our stories also. So let us engage in translating these stories in terms of our own lives.

■ *Discussion of the following questions can be done within the total group. Participants should be given ample opportunity for questioning each other, for probing each other's statements, for listening to both agreements and disagreements, and for testing out responses.*

"How does God regard us? In what ways does the biblical material describe how God sees us?" [*Chosen. God's possession. A redeemed people. A holy people. A royal priesthood.*]

"Who are we that we should be regarded as such? Do we have any claims on God? Does God owe us anything that calls for such high regard?" [*God has called us. God declares us the people of God. We are baptized.*]

"As a people declared by God to be 'chosen,' 'holy,' 'redeemed,' and 'the possession of God,' what is expected of us?"

■ *Invite the group to make one large collage with the title, "How God Regards and Sees Us." The collage could be displayed prominently within the church building, and thus be shared with the congregation.*

□ *Instead of a collage, select a large bulletin board at a prominent place in the church. Using the title suggested earlier, invite the young people to create their response to the title.*

·8

Whose body is it, anyway?

A quick glance at magazine advertisements or a brief exposure to television commercials focuses our attention on the human body. We are bombarded with images of the beautiful or handsome body. We are urged to buy a variety of products: oils and lotions to keep our skin soft and young; shampoos to make our hair lovely to touch; soaps to pamper ourselves in the bath; toothpaste to give us sex appeal; solutions to erase that tale-telling gray hair; creams to eradicate those unattractive brown spots; and clothes to clad our bodies, making us attractive to the opposite sex. Advertising bombards us with images of the ideal female body or the ideal male body.

From the same sources we hear how to use our bodies so as to attract and keep the attention of the opposite sex. We receive powerful clues in how to use our bodies so as to be popular. We receive instruction in the use of sex for "recreation" and its use to gain what we want. Even activities clearly known to be abusive of the body are given approval.

In the presence of an obsession with the human body come serious and demanding questions that require considered and powerful responses. How ought we to regard our bodies? Is there an ideal female body or an ideal male body? How ought we to use our bodies and for what purpose? Ought we permit others to use our bodies for their purposes? What is it to abuse our bodies?

These questions are not answered once-and-for-all-time. How do we come to terms with the changes occurring in our bodies over time? Throughout the life span we experience physical changes. Wrinkles appear. We become gray or bald. Aches and pains push to the foreground. Senses may become blunted. Energy decreases. Illness or accident may alter certain uses of the body. Yet your body is yours, and it is the only way by which you live in this world. My body is mine, and it is the only way by which I live in this world. Time and time again we must come to new terms with our bodies.

How we regard our bodies is profoundly related to how we regard ourselves as persons. How we come to terms with our bodies informs and gives shape to the quality of our lives. How we use our bodies or permit others to use them also gives shape to the quality of our lives. How we use our body, how we regard it, and how we appreciate it is the way that we use ourselves, regard ourselves, and how we appreciate ourselves. Your body is "you." My body is "me."

Adolescents Responding to Their Bodies

The period of adolescence is marked by rapid, observable body changes. The changes create enormous confusion, uncertainty, and anxiety for many adolescents. In the midst of change, adolescents devote an extraordinary amount of attention and energy to their bodies. Not all adolescents experience the same body changes at the same rate and in the same proportions. Comparisons are made. Is my body changing too fast or too slow? Am I too short or too tall? Am I too big or too small in certain areas? Is my body attractive or ugly? The body can be a source of deep anguish for the adolescent.

How adolescents come to regard their bodies contributes significantly to their regard for themselves. There is a correlation between one's understanding of his or her body and the understanding of self, between one's appreciation of the body and appreciation of one's self as a person. A body perceived as unattractive can easily be translated into an unattractive person. It is not uncommon for an adolescent to focus on one part of his or her body, judging it to be ugly, unattractive, out of proportion, and even abnormal. Moreover, there is the easy assumption that everyone else makes the same judgment about that part of the body. Ears of slightly different sizes, a nose perceived as too big, slightly uneven teeth, and even big feet can be regarded as an utter disaster. The "flaw" is regarded as *the* barrier to attractiveness and popularity. Adult platitudes or "scoldings" accomplish very little.

The extreme attention, time, and energy which adolescents devote to their bodies are, in part, their attempts to come to terms with their bodies. Searching the body for pimples or blemishes, experimenting to find just the right make-up or hair style, frequent baths, constant grooming before the mirror and frequent changes of clothes—all, while creating exasperated parents, are attempts to come to terms with the body. The nature of attention given to the body differs from one segment of society to another. A particular segment may give focus to a specific part of the body or to specific body builds or to specific notions of what is feminine or masculine. In any case, adolescents must come to terms with their bodies, determining how they will be regarded and used.

Vast portions of our society encourage adolescents in narcissistic obsession with their bodies. Large industries, intent upon selling their products, give the promise of attractiveness, beautifulness, handsomeness, and popularity. As image-makers, they describe the "truly" beautiful female or the "truly" handsome male. The image-makers are powerful, calling forth the attention and devotion of adolescents.

Our anger and attacks against the purveyors of such ideas should not be reserved for the image-makers alone. Unwittingly perhaps, parents, teachers, and other significant persons often join forces with industry image-makers. We praise the athletic male, often giving preference to him. We rage over the shapely, attractive females in beauty contests. We applaud the husky, robust male and petite female. Our language betrays our notions of the ideal masculine or feminine body.

The truth of the matter is most simple and distressing for some. A great host of adolescents do not and cannot, regardless of what they do, "measure up" to popular, ideal images. The more they try, the more they fail. Disappointment increases. Anxiety and confusion mount. But at the same time, it is not necessarily the case that those adolescents who approximate the popular images automatically achieve an appropriate and adequate regard for their bodies. Popular images of the "ideal" body are heavy burdens for all adolescents to carry.

Adolescents, in achieving an adequate regard for their bodies, confront the task of learning how to use their bodies and for what purposes. They will frequently use their bodies in frantic efforts to attract the attention of others. Sexual activity, and the use of drugs, alcohol, and tobacco, may be efforts to attract others, or to prove that they are adults and independent, or to prove that they are masculine or feminine. In such activities, they may well abuse their bodies with destructive results, without realizing or anticipating the ends of their efforts. And yet, large segments of the society cheer them on. There is also the easy temptation for adolescents to permit others to abuse or misuse their bodies. They may not recognize the abuse or misuse for after all, how else is one to be popular, to be "included," and to be sought after?

Body changes can create bewilderment, anxiousness, and distress for adolescents. Often they do not know how to respond to or make sense of the occurring changes. Neither do they know how to express their concerns and to ask useful questions. Taken in by popular images, they may be uncomfortable with their bodies, even ashamed of them. It is critical that we assist them to frame and articulate their questions and to describe their thinking and feelings. We can sensitively and carefully assist adolescents to move through their bewilderment and uncertainty and to reject the popular images. We can assist them to appreciate, to rejoice in, and to celebrate their bodies.

As we offer assistance there is a critical issue which demands adolescents' serious consideration and which can radically shift their focus concerning the body. That issue can best be expressed in a series of statements. In a most profound sense we can say, "My body is me. How you regard my body is how you regard me. What you say about my body is what you say about me. What you do to my body is what you do to me." And more can be said, "What I do to my body is what I do to myself. If I abuse my body, I abuse myself. If I let you abuse my body, I have let you misuse me." And there still is more to be said, "I have the right and the responsibility to care for my body, to respect it, and to honor it. In so doing, I care for, respect, and honor myself. I have the right and the responsibility also to prevent you from misusing my body for any purpose. And in so doing, I respect both myself and you." The issue is that of recognizing, in a most profound way, that my body is me and that my regard for and use of my body is my regard and use of myself. And also, how I regard, use, and respect your body is how I regard, use, and respect you.

Adolescents Engaging the Question

In this section several exercises and activities, designed to engage adolescents in the question, "Whose body is it, anyway?" are offered. They encourage the participants to reflect upon and to articulate their understandings of and concerns with their bodies. They assist the adolescents to examine popular ideal images of the body and to question the adequacy of those images. They can assist the participants to describe the regard which they have for their bodies and to ask how one uses his or her body. And they encourage the adolescents to consider that "My body is me."

1. Body Images. Adolescents are often uncomfortable or unhappy with their body builds and shapes. They compare their bodies with others, at times wishing that they had different body builds and shapes. They may easily conclude that a different body build and shape would assure attractiveness and popularity. Fantasies about a different body can interfere in the adolescent's ability to come to terms with his or her body.

■ *Prepare two sets of pictures, one of males and the other of females. The pictures, numbered and mounted on the same color of paper, should depict a variety of body builds and shapes. Invite the participants, using the numbers, to rank the pictures in order from "the one I would most want to be like" to "the one I would least want to be like." Invite the group to discuss the rankings.*

"What factors influenced your ranking?"

"Why would you want to be like the one you ranked first?"

"In what ways do you think your life would be different if you were like your first choice?"

"Of all the pictures in your particular set, which one best depicts you?"

"Assuming that you will not or cannot look like your first choice, does that fact make you 'less than a person'?"

"Think of three of your relatives or friends. Do they all fit your number one choice? How much does their body shape and build influence your love and affection for them?"

"Do you think it is right that others should judge you as a person or describe you primarily on the basis of your body build and shape? Why? Why not? Are you happy and satisfied that others should judge or describe you primarily on the basis of your body build and shape?"

"How often do you judge another person primarily on the basis of his or her body build or shape? Is it right and appropriate to do that? Why? Why not?"

"Recognizing that we may tend to judge people on the basis of their body build and shape, why do we behave in such a way? Should we behave in such a way? How much attention should we give to magazine advertisements and TV commercials?"

2. Body Images. Adolescents function with images of the "ideal male body" and the "ideal female body." They compare their bodies with the "ideal." Convinced that body characteristics determine one's popularity and even worth, many strive to meet the "ideal." In reality, few adolescents approximate the ideal. Adolescents need to examine the sources and value of "ideal images." Moreover, they need to move to a high regard and appreciation of their bodies.

■ *Make available an abundant supply of magazines and other materials for making collages. Have each participant produce two collages, one depicting his or her image of the ideal male body and the other of the ideal female body. Invite and encourage the participants to share and discuss their collages. (A variation: arrange small groups and have each group produce the two collages. Working in small groups the participants will challenge and be challenged by each other.)*

"What body characteristics make up your ideal image of male/female?"

"What importance do those characteristics have for you? Why do you give importance to them?"

"How many of your close friends or relatives have those body characteristics? If they don't have those characteristics, does that lack make them 'less' than persons? If not, then what is the importance of them?"

"Who or what influences your image of the 'ideal' body?"

"For what purpose does advertisement push its ideal images on us? How worthwhile are the images offered by advertisement? How much attention do you pay to advertisement?"

☐ *Engage the participants in a comparison of the collages of the males with those of the females.*

"Do both females and males depict similar images of the 'ideal' male body? Of the female body?"

"If there are differences, how do you account for those differences? If there are no differences, are all of you listening to the same 'image makers'? If so, why do you listen to them?"

☐ *Engage the females (males) in responding to and discussing the collages of the males (females).*

"What do you think of the images portrayed in the collages? Are you happy or comfortable or annoyed by images which tell you how your body 'ought to look'?"

"Is it right or fair that you should be judged as a person on the basis of such images? Do you judge yourself as a person by those images? Do you judge others as persons on the basis of such images?"

"If we do judge others as persons on the basis of such images, why do we do that?"

"When we laugh at another's body or make jokes about it or avoid someone simply because of bodily characteristics, what are we saying not only about the other person, but about ourselves?"

☐ *Engage the adolescents in an individual and introspective exercise. Some may be willing to share their responses in the group, but the participants should not be compelled to do so.*

"Each of you has produced a collage depicting the ideal body for your sex. On an imaginary scale of one (lowest) to ten (highest) place yourself, thus describing how well you fulfill your ideal image. Privately, consider these questions."

"Just how well do you measure up to the ideal?"

"If you did not rank yourself high, are you any less a male or female than those who do rank themselves high?"

"Would you want others to judge you as a person on the basis of the ideal image you depicted in your collage? Is it fair, right, and just that you should judge others on the basis of such images?"

"Regardless of how you ranked yourself, how important is your body to you? For what purposes?"

"How do you feel if someone laughs or makes jokes about your body? How do you think others feel when you laugh at or make jokes about their bodies?"

"What ought we to do when we hear others ridiculing or laughing at another's body?"

3. Body Images. In dating relationships adolescents are much aware of their bodies as well as those of their companions. Moreover, they are sensitive to others' comments about the bodies of their dates. In another dimension, adolescents need to grow not only in appreciation and respect for their own bodies but for the bodies of others. One's respect and esteem for his or her body as well as the bodies of others may well prevent abuse of the human body.

■   *In small groups, provide the adolescents a series of questions for discussion.*

Would you date:

—a male shorter (a female taller) than you? Why? Why not? If you would, would you be comfortable? Would you be concerned about what others might think? Why? Why not?

—a person who must rely upon crutches for mobility? Why? Why not? If you did, would you be concerned about what others might think? Why?

—a person whom your friends considered ugly? Why? Why not?

—a dwarf? Why? Why not? If you did, would you be concerned about what others might think? Why?

—a person with an artificial limb? Why? Why not?

□   *In the total group, invite the adolescents to share the conversation of the small group, encouraging them to challenge and ask questions of each other. Additional questions may be posed.*

"How often do we let our friends determine our choice of a date? If so, why?"

"How often have we avoided another person because of some body characteristic? Can you think of a specific instance when you have avoided another person simply because of a body characteristic? Why did you do that?"

"When we shun or avoid a person because of some body characteristic, what are we saying about that person?"

"Do body characteristics determine the worth, value and humanness of another? If not, why do we put so much emphasis on body characteristics?"

"How can we help ourselves and others in ceasing to make judgments of others on the basis of body characteristics?"

4. Body Images. Adolescents are often uncomfortable in the presence of those with "physical handicaps." They are frequently embarrassed and do not know what to say in the presence of persons with physical disabilities. Popular images of the ideal body contribute to the uneasiness. At times, persons with disabilities may be regarded as "deficient." But persons with special needs can assist adolescents in achieving new understandings of the human body and in coming to terms with their own bodies.

■ *Invite a person with physical disabilities to share one or two sessions with the adolescents. The guest should be apprised beforehand of what will take place in the session(s). Rather than the guest beginning with a "talk," encourage and assist the adolescents to ask direct and significant questions of him or her. Some adult modeling may be desirable. Some initial information-gathering questions may be helpful. How long have you had your disability? Under what circumstances did it occur? More penetrating questions will be necessary:*

"What were your reactions when you realized that you had the disability? Were you discouraged? Angry?"

"In what ways do you consider your disability to be a handicap?"

"Do you regard yourself any 'less' a person because of your disability?"

"Have you ever experienced persons avoiding you because of your physical disability?"

"How do you react to persons who avoid you because of your physical disability?"

"How do you react to persons who are uncomfortable in your presence because of your handicap?"

"How do you regard your body? Do you regard it as imperfect? How have you come to terms with your body?"

□   *Some participants may have relatives or friends with physical dis-
     abilities. Invite the group members to describe the disability and
     engage them in a series of questions for discussion.*

"How do you feel when you are in the presence of that person? Can
you describe why you feel that way?"

"Do you ever think of that person as being 'less' than a person or
as 'imperfect'?"

"Do you enjoy being with that person?"

"Do you ever feel that you are 'more perfect' than that person?"

"How do you judge that the person regards his or her body?"

"How would you react to someone who did not want to be in the
presence of that person simply because of the handicap?"

5. Respect and Care for My Body. Adolescents are frequently unhappy
with their bodies. They can experience great distress when they regard
their bodies as unattractive, as having "flaws" or as failing to meet
societal ideal images of the body. They will do things to their bodies,
use their bodies, and let them be used in efforts to attract others, to be
acceptable to others, and to prove that they are adults. Adolescents
need to achieve a love and respect for their bodies as that means by
which they live in the world. They need to learn to care for their bodies.

■   *Prepare the following material in written form so that each partic-
     ipant has a copy. Each is to indicate his or her agreement with each
     statement, using a scale of one to five with five indicating "high
     agreement."*

On a scale of one to five indicate your agreement with the following statements. One represents "no agreement" and five represents "high agreement."
  1. My body is "me." ____
  2. No one has a right to use my body for any purpose. ____
  3. The only way that I can live in the world is in my body. ____
  4. What I do to my body I do to myself. ____
  5. I have a right to expect and demand that others should treat
       my body with care and respect. ____
  6. If I abuse my body, I abuse myself. ____
  7. I have no right to use my body in any way just to attract
       others or to be acceptable to others. ____
  8. I must protect my body from all possible harm. ____
  9. I have a right to do with my body whatever I choose. ____
  10. I should give proper care to my body. ____

☐ *Invite the adolescents to share and discuss their responses with each other. Explore with them their understandings of the statements and the implications of the statements. Encourage them to identify and discuss what ideas or persons influence their responses.*

■ *Prepare the following materials in written form so that each participant has a copy.*

Each of us must care for his or her body. Nevertheless, there are times when we misuse or abuse our bodies. There are times when we let others use or abuse our bodies for their purposes. It is important that we develop some understanding of what is abuse or misuse and to consider our own actions in the matter. To assist us in the effort, let's consider and respond to the following material.

1. What do you understand abuse or misuse of the body to be?

2. What abuses or misuses have you observed persons doing to others' bodies? Why would you consider those actions to be abuses or misuses? What have been the results of those actions?

3. What abuses or misuses have you observed persons doing to their own bodies? Why would you consider those actions to be abuses or misuses? What have been the results of those actions?

4. How might we abuse our bodies or permit them to be used by others with reference to the following?
   a. Body hygiene:
   b. Sexual activity:
   c. Following the suggestions of advertisements:
   d. Overeating:
   e. Clothes:
   f. Alcohol, drug, and tobacco use:
   g. Overdieting:

5. Why would we permit someone to use or abuse our bodies for their purposes?

At the same time, we must ask, "What is it to love, respect, and care for our bodies?" How might we respond to this question with reference to the following?
   1. Overeating:
   2. Body hygiene:
   3. Sexual activity:
   4. Clothes:
   5. Alcohol, drug, and tobacco use:
   6. Reckless adventure:

□ *Invite the adolescents to share their responses as they are willing.*
   Give opportunity for discussion, questions, and challenge. Encour-
   age them to identify and describe those things or persons which
   have influenced their understandings.

Engaging and Interpreting the Bible

The following biblical passages, with the accompanying exercises,
focus on the human body. They challenge adolescents to ask questions—questions of worth, regard, care, use, misuse, and abuse of their
own bodies. At the same time, the passages and exercises ask how we
are to regard, respect, care for, and treat the bodies of others. The last
passage and exercise in this section declares that the ministry and
mission of Jesus, and thus his people, is directed towards the human
body and its needs.

In succeeding chapters, concerns for the human body will emerge
from time to time. Such will be especially so in the chapters, "What Is
Required of Me?" and "Am I My Neighbor's Keeper?" Materials in those
chapters can assist in further exploration of the question, "Whose body
is it, anyway?"

1. 1 Corinthians 6:12–20; 1 Corinthians 3:16–17. These two passages
make a profound and significant response to the question, "Whose body
is it, anyway?" Each, in its own way, declares that our bodies are not
our own possessions to do with as we choose. Our bodies belong to God
who has created us. The first passage, focusing on the individual's body,
begins with a statement on Christian freedom. The Christian is not
bound by sheer rules and regulations. Yet, Christian freedom can be
abused. To act as if we can do whatever we wish in any way and at any
time we wish is to abuse freedom. The Apostle Paul asserts that the
body is not meant for immorality but for the Lord. He gives emphasis
to a particular sexual immorality to which one can be enslaved. In the
second passage, Paul writes of God's temple, a temple composed of many
"temples" and of many bodies. What happens to one body happens to
God's temple and is done to God.

Bridge: The question, "Whose body is it, anyway?" is an important one
   for us. Our bodies are "us." It is with our bodies only that we can
   live in the world. What we do to our bodies, what we permit to be
   done to them and how we use them determines who we are and
   the quality of our lives. Two biblical passages, 1 Corinthians 6:12–
   20 and 1 Corinthians 3:16–17, make certain claims about to whom

our bodies belong and about how we are to regard and use our bodies. We want to study and discuss the passages' claims asking "If these claims are true, what do they say about our bodies and how we are to treat our bodies?"

■ *Before moving directly to the passages, invite the adolescents to share and discuss their present understandings of what the Bible and the faith have to say about the human body. Encourage them to identify the information, persons, or ideas that have influenced those understandings.*

☐ *Arrange small groups. Make available the following material to guide study and discussion as they engage 1 Corinthians 6:12–20. Do not copy bracketed material.*

In vs. 12, Paul asserts that all things are lawful for the Christian, but not all things are helpful. What do you understand his intention to be? [*No set of rules and regulations can be imposed upon Christians or can describe how they should live. The Christian is free to be God's person. Yet, Christians can permit actions, things, persons, or desires to make slaves of them, preventing them from living as God's people.*]

What do you understand to be Paul's intention in the last part of vs. 13? [*No immorality is to be imposed on the body. Our bodies, however they may be described, come from God. By them, we are able to live in the world.*]

What do you understand Paul's intention to be in the first part of vs. 15? [*As Christians, our bodies belong to Christ. Our God has chosen to be bound to our bodies.*]

In the later part of vs. 15 and in vs. 16, Paul focuses upon a particular sexual activity. Why does he judge that activity as being evil? [*The immorality that one imposes upon his or her body causes the person to become exactly that "thing." The activities in which we engage make us who we are. How we use our bodies is also what we are.*]

In vs. 18, Paul asserts that the immoral person sins against his or her own body. Including sexual immorality, how would you describe ways by which we sin against our bodies?

According to this passage, to whom do our bodies belong? How do you understand the passage's claim?

How do you think that an individual glorifies God in his or her body? [*Regardless of how my body is described, shaped, or looks to others, I am to care for it and to protect it from harm and abuse.*]

☐ *In the total group, invite the participants to share their discussions, conclusions, and reactions. Afford opportunity for questions, clarification, and further discussion. Encourage and assist the participants to develop statements or a list of items which they can generally agree to be reflections of the passage.*

☐ *Return to the small groups. Assign 1 Corinthians 3:16–17. Note here that God's temple refers to the church, the community of God's people. In the previous passage, the individual's body is called the temple of the Holy Spirit.*

"What is God's temple? Who composes God's temple?" [*The community of God's people, people with bodies. God's temple consists of many temples, of many bodies.*]

"How might one destroy God's temple?" [*Misuse or abuse of one's own body. Misuse or abuse of another's body.*]

"Are our bodies our possessions to do with them as we please?" [*What is done to one body is done to the community of God's people.*]

■ *Prepare the material on the facing page so that each participant will have a copy.*

☐ *Invite the participants to share and discuss, as they are able, their responses with each other.*

2. Luke 10:25–37. This passage includes the familiar story of the Good Samaritan. The story is Jesus' response to a religious lawyer who asks what he might do to inherit eternal life. The lawyer, quoting Scripture, even answers his own question: Love God and love your neighbor as yourself. Yet, he asks another question, "Who is my neighbor?" Jesus responds, telling the story of a man who had been physically attacked, beaten, and left half-dead. It is the story of a man whose body had been violated and that needed care. The definition of "my neighbor" is related to my neighbor's body.

Bridge: We have been exploring the question, "Whose body is it, anyway?" We have discussed both the care and the abuse of our bodies and the bodies of others. We have suggested that your body is "you" and my body is "me." It is only by means of our bodies that we can live in this world. How we use our bodies, what happens to our bodies, and what others do to our bodies do help determine what shall be the content of our lives. Who we are is intimately bound up with our bodies. We want to study a biblical passage, Luke 10:25–37, which may give us some assistance as we respond to the question. The passage contains the familiar story of the Good Samaritan. As we study this passage, we should remember that Sa-

In the two passages we have studied a number of claims and declarations have been made. If those claims and declarations are true and appropriate, what do they say to us about our regard and use of our bodies? Concerning the various items below, how might these passages respond?

A. How might we sin against our own bodies in the following areas?
   1. Sexual activity:
   2. Overeating:
   3. Overdieting:
   4. Alcohol, drugs, tobacco:
   5. Clothing:
   6. Shame concerning our bodies:
   7. Letting others use our bodies:
   8. Can you think of other areas in which we may sin against our bodies?

B. How might we sin against the bodies of others in the following areas?
   1. Sexual activity:
   2. Use of alcohol, drugs, and tobacco:
   3. Ridicule of another's body:
   4. Use of another's body:
   5. Can you think of other areas in which we may sin against the bodies of others?

C. How might we glorify God in our bodies?
   1. Care of the body (hygiene):
   2. What we put in our bodies:
   3. Sexual activity:
   4. Protecting our body from harm and abuse:
   5. Protecting the bodies of others from harm and abuse:

D. Why would we be willing to sin against our own bodies? What do we expect to accomplish when we sin against our bodies? What are the results?

E. Why would we be willing to sin against the bodies of others? What do we expect to accomplish when we sin against the bodies of others? What are the results?

F. How would you describe what it is to love, care for, and properly use our bodies?
   How would you describe what it is to love, care for, and respect the bodies of others?

See exercise on facing page.

maritans were religious and social outcasts as far as the Jews of
Jesus' day were concerned. Samaritans were considered "nobod-
ies" by the popular religious and social norms of the day.

■   *Before moving directly to the passage, invite the adolescents to share
    their present understandings and impressions of the Good Samari-
    tan story. They will be working from their memory and may articu-
    late very sketchy understandings or impressions. In any event, list
    the various contributions on the chalkboard or on newsprint. The
    list can be used in later discussion.*

□   *Arrange small groups. Prepare the following questions in a written
    form so that all participants will have copies. Do not copy bracketed
    material.*

How would you describe what it is to love your neighbor as
yourself? How does Jesus describe it in this story? [*Jesus' description is related to the care given to another's body.*]

Is there a distinction between loving God and loving a neighbor
as self? [*No distinction is made in this story.*]

What is the response of the religious leaders, the priest and the
Levite, to a human body, to a body that had been beaten? Why
might they have responded as they did?

What were they saying through their responses about that
beaten man? [*Refusing to care for the man's body, they refused
to care for the person. They passed by their neighbor.*]

The Samaritan tended the man's body, and thus the person himself. Would you regard what the Samaritan did as a religious
act? Why? Why not? [*What the Samaritan did was a profound
religious act. He cared for the man as he cared for himself. He
did acts of love, and in so doing he loved God. The very act of
caring for another's body is defined as loving God. The failure to
care for another's body was a failure in love toward that person
and God.*]

What was required of the Samaritan? [*He interrupted his journey. His act cost money. He made promises to continue to care.*]

Is the caring, tending, and protecting of another's body a part
of fulfilling the commandment to love God and to love our
neighbor as ourselves?

□   *Invite the small groups to share their discussions and conclusions
    with the total group. Encourage them to reflect upon their first re-
    sponses to the passage, asking if they are saying something different
    after their study of the passage. Invite them to develop a set of state-
    ments concerning what the passage says about the human body.*

"In describing what it is to love one's neighbor, the story focuses upon care and regard for a person's body. Assuming that the story is one addressed to us also, how would you describe what it is for us today to care for, to tend, and to rightly regard another's body?" [*We will not abuse or misuse another's body for our purposes, for example, in sexual activity. We will not ignore others' behaviors as they abuse or misuse their own bodies through alcohol or drugs. We will not encourage others to abuse or misuse their bodies. We will call into judgment one who abuses or misuses another's body. We will do all that we can to protect the body of another from hurt, harm, and misuse. We may join with others in efforts to feed the hungry and to supply the necessities of the body. We may join with those who struggle against war.*]

"Can you describe some very specific ways that we do fail to care, tend and properly regard the body of another?" [*Ridicule. Driving while drinking. Sexual abuse.*]

"The great commandment as cited by the lawyer in the passage asserts that we are to love our neighbor as ourselves. If loving the neighbor involves caring for, tending, and having a proper regard for his or her body, what does the commandment say about us, concerning our bodies?" [*We are to care for, tend, protect, and have proper regard for our bodies. As we do this, we care for, tend, protect, and have proper regard for ourselves, all which are a part of loving God.*]

"In very specific ways, how would you describe what it is for us today to care for, tend, protect, and have proper regard for our bodies?" [*We must protect ourselves against others' attempts to use us or misuse us. We will not put into our bodies things that may hurt or harm us. We will not use our bodies, attempting to get others to do what we want.*]

"According to the passage, whose body is it, anyway?"

3. Matthew 25:31–46. This passage is a parable of the last judgment. It is startling and sharp, making clear distinctions and announcing unambiguous decisions. It assumes that Jesus is the king who makes the judgments. Some may think it strange that we choose a parable of the last judgment as an appropriate biblical passage with which to explore the question, "Whose body is it, anyway?" The passage, however, makes a profound and powerful statement about the body, particularly about our regard for and treatment of another's body. Though our engagement with the passage will not focus on the "details" of the last judgment, we will not ignore the larger context in which our question is considered. The details of the story sharpen our concern for the body.

Bridge: As we have explored the question, "Whose body is it, anyway?" we have discussed our behaviors toward the bodies of others. We have talked of ways that we may abuse other people's bodies and ways that our bodies may be abused by others. We want to study a parable of the last judgment. We are not concerned here with the "details" of the last judgment. We want to ask if this passage makes statements and claims concerning the body. As you read and study, keep in mind that the parable assumes that Jesus is the king spoken of in the parable.

■ *Have the adolescents work in pairs. They will share their findings, conclusions, and questions with the total group. Several questions will serve to focus attention and give direction.*

"On what basis were the judgments made, or what factors determined the judgments?"

"Who are the 'brothers'?"

"Were any of the characters in the story surprised? If so, why?"

"How does the story respond to the question, 'Whose body is it, anyway?'"

□ *In the total group, have the participants share their findings, conclusions, and questions. Encourage them to ask questions of each other, to challenge and to probe each others' responses. Encourage the group as a whole to make statements of the story with which all can generally agree.*

"Were the characters of the story surprised? If so, why were they surprised?" [*Both groups of persons were surprised. They were surprised about where they "ended up." They did not know how they got to where they were.*]

"What was the king's response to the surprise?" [*When I was in prison. . . . When I was hungry. . . . When I was naked. . . .*]

"Did the king's response remove the surprise?" [*No. They asked, "When did we feed, clothe . . . you?"*]

"What is the criterion for the judgments?" [*What they had done or not done to the "least" they had done or not done to the king, to Jesus himself. And the things that were done or not done were related to the body.*]

"Why did the king respond as he did? What are the implications of what was said?" [*Jesus, God, has so bound himself to the flesh and blood of human life that, whatever we do to the body of another person, we do that to Jesus, to God himself.*]

"Now if the claim is true—if it is true that whatever we do to another's body we do to Jesus, to God—what does it say about us:

When we want to use another's body for our purposes? When we abuse another's body? When we ridicule another's body? When we shun another because of his or her body? When we encourage another to misuse or abuse his or her body? When we do not protect the body of another? When we ignore others' need for food and clothing?"

There is another "twist" that can be given to our focus. Without suggesting in the slightest that we are God, we can say that Jesus, God, has bound himself to our flesh and blood. Thus, what we do to our bodies, what we permit to be done to our bodies, and what others do to our bodies are also done to Jesus, God himself. We have a right and responsibility to care for our bodies, not to misuse or abuse them. We have a right and a responsibility to demand that no one misuse or abuse our bodies.

4. Matthew 12:1–8; Luke 4:16–21. Both passages illustrate particular concerns of Jesus for the human body and its needs. In the Matthew passage, Jesus' regard and concern for the body and its needs sets him in sharp conflict with popular and well established religious norms and understandings. To work on the sabbath was regarded as unlawful. The action of the disciples was interpreted as the labor of harvesting. (Incidentally, their action as such was not one of stealing.) In his response to the religious leaders, according to the passage, Jesus declares that the human body and its needs take precedence over established religious norms. Before sacrifices, a concern for the temple, and religious practices, Jesus desires mercy—mercy directed to the human body and its needs.

In the Luke passage we read a description of the ministry and mission of Jesus. Not only is the ministry and mission to proclaim the gospel, but it includes direct ministry to the human body and its needs. Both concerns are "part and parcel" of Jesus' ministry and mission.

Bridge: We have been exploring the question, "Whose body is it, anyway?" We have discussed our regard and care for our own bodies. We have talked about what it is to respect and care for the body of another. We want to study and discuss two biblical passages, Matthew 12:1–8 and Luke 4:16–21, which illustrate Jesus' concern and regard for the human body and its needs. We want to ask, "If the claims of these two passages are true and appropriate, what do they say to us? What directions do they offer?"

■ *Arrange small groups. The groups will work with both passages.*

To assist the participants in their engagement with the text, make available the following material in a written form. Do not copy bracketed material.

Jesus finds himself in conflict with religious leaders and the established religious norms of the day. What is the conflict about? [*The disciples were doing the work of harvesting, which was considered an unlawful work on the sabbath. Jesus did not prevent his disciples from doing what was unlawful.*]

Jesus had to make a decision. What was his decision? What was his answer to the religious leaders?

What were the criteria used by Jesus in framing his response? [*The disciples were meeting legitimate bodily needs. They were not stealing. Legitimate body needs may take precedence over religious norms and practices.*]

The passage declares that something more than concerns for the temple, sacrifices, and religious practices is involved. What is the critical element according to the passage? [*Mercy, which is to minister to the human body and its needs.*]

In the passage, there is the suggestion that one may faithfully keep all the religious rules and engage in the prescribed religious practices, and yet be unfaithful. How do you respond to that suggestion? [*There is the expectation that attention and direct care will be given to the human body and its needs.*]

In the light of this passage, how would you define what it is to be religious? [*In part at least, to be religious is to direct acts of mercy toward the bodies of others and their physical needs.*]

In the second passage, Luke has Jesus reading from the book of the prophet Isaiah. The One of whom Jesus reads is to perform a mission and ministry. What are the contents, the parts of that mission and ministry? What is the anointed One to do? [*The anointed One is to do what we normally consider religious acts. The anointed One will preach good news to the poor; be concerned about captives; give sight to the blind; and work on behalf of the oppressed.*]

What do you understand to be the concern for the human body and its needs as expressed in the passage? [*Not only so-called religious acts but also acts of concern for the human body are part and parcel of the mission and ministry described.*]

The church, and we as members of the church, are to continue the ministry and mission of Jesus. Can we perform the ministry and mission of Jesus if we busy ourselves only with expected and established religious practices and norms? Why? Why not?

☐ *Invite the small groups to share their discussions and responses with each other. Encourage and assist the adolescents to develop some generally agreed upon statements which reflect the passages' concerns for the human body.*

☐ *In the total group, engage the participants in discussion, encouraging them to translate the concerns of the passages into contemporary situations.*

"Assuming that the claims of the passages are true and assuming that as Christian people we are to carry out the mission and ministry of Jesus, what might these passages expect of us with reference to the following concerns?"
1. Economic injustice and inequality.
2. World hunger.
3. The poor among us.
4. Political and physical oppression.
5. Adequate health care for all.
6. Build-up of a "war machine."

"Can you think of any ways in which the claims of the passages might set us in conflict with and opposition to contemporary social norms and practices?"

"How do you think the passages would respond to the following statements?"
1. All prisoners ought to be severely punished and denied all human rights. We should not be concerned about their physical needs.
2. Public welfare is a "rip-off." I should not be expected to spend my money on welfare people.
3. We must have a strong defense so that "they" will not get us first.
4. People who did not prepare for their retirement should not expect handouts.
5. It is not my concern if parents abuse their children.
6. What people do to their bodies is none of my business.

"In what ways do you think these passages should inform and shape the work and mission of the church?"

■ *Luke 4:19 may well refer to the Year of Jubilee described in Leviticus 25:8-55. There is no evidence that the jubilee year was ever strictly practiced. Nevertheless, it announces profound values which give attention to the human body and its needs. You may wish to use the Leviticus passage in conjunction with Luke 4:19.*

·9

What is it to be male or female?

Much of our society is struggling with the question, "What is it to be male or female?" In years past, clear and precise answers were offered, and both males and females accepted them as right and appropriate. They are still accepted as such by significant numbers of men and women. But for another significant number, those answers are not satisfying, sufficient, or appropriate. Moreover, many of those answers appear to demean both males and females.

The notions of innate female or male characteristics have been severely challenged. Assumptions about female submissiveness and male dominance or about emotive females and rational males have not held up well under attack. Stereotypic sex roles have also been challenged. Sex roles once assigned to women are now performed most efficiently and effectively by males, and vice versa.

To ask, "What is it to be male or female?" is to ask the larger question of human sexuality. Simplistically, human sexuality has been equated with sex gender and sexual activity. Sex gender is biologically determined but, in and of itself, is not sufficient for a broad and significant understanding of sexuality. Sexual activity, in and of itself, is not sexuality. Sexual activity tells or "proves" very little. An individual's sexuality is not some innate quality or quantity given at birth to unfold in time. An individual's sexuality is a knowledge and understanding constructed by the individual for and about himself or herself as male or female. One's sexuality is a way of being and doing as male or female in the world of persons.

There are many voices—fashion designers, cosmetic manufacturers, magazines, television programs, popular music, and movies—which seek to define maleness or femaleness in terms of sex and sexual activity. Such voices must be challenged. Any significant consideration of sex must be done within the larger context of human sexuality, asking what it is to be male or female in the world of persons. Sexual activity reflects and gives expressions of the persons involved. Sexual activity may be an expression of love, care, and affection; it may be an expression of unconcern, selfishness, and even fear. Much sexual experimentation among adolescents is an attempt to come to terms with their bodies, to achieve an identity as male or female and to prove that "I am a man" or "I am a woman." The experimentation may have disastrous effects. When sex and sexual activity are regarded as the primary criteria of maleness and femaleness, distortions of sexuality result. Sex and sexual activity, although critical and powerful elements, must be regarded as but two elements which contribute to the response of being and doing male or female in the world of persons.

Adolescents Constructing Sexuality

A significant task confronting the adolescent is that of determining what it is to be male or female, of constructing his or her sexuality. Sexuality is not something which emerges for the first time during adolescence. It has been in the making throughout childhood. Children construct for themselves some understanding of what it is to be boys or girls. Parents, adults, and society present powerful clues to be used in the construction. Clothes and toys, statements of what little girls or little boys do or do not do, games they are permitted to play, media portrayals, and parental actions and expressed attitudes are among the data and experiences children use as they construct their sexuality.

In the presence of rapid body changes, new sexual feelings, the push to achieve identity, and increased social relationships and interaction, adolescents must begin to respond anew to the question, "What is it for me to be male or female?" Responses achieved in childhood are not adequate.

Adolescents are caught in a most confusing and bewildering situation. An enormous supply of information is available to them, describing what it is to be male or female. That data, however, is marked by conflicting and contradictory claims and answers. Some segments of society insist that there are innate sex roles, roles that belong to a male or female simply because of sex gender. At the same time, there is insistence that there are certain behaviors which belong to males exclusively and others to females exclusively. All such understandings are being challenged. We are in danger of posing the wrong question, "What do males do? What do females do?" We need to engage adolescents in a more exciting question which can lead to rich, varied, and abundant responses: "What roles in society do I as a male or female wish to perform and fulfill?"

As stereotypic sex roles have been severely challenged so have assumptions concerning feminine and masculine characteristics. Not all the evidence is in yet on this matter, but there is sufficient cause for us to question some of the popular assumptions. The notions of submissive female and aggressive male, emotional female and rational male, tender female and rugged male, dainty female and robust male, weak female and strong male—all are insufficient and inadequate in determining femaleness and maleness. As adolescents endeavor to construct their sexuality, we do them a disservice if we lead them in a search for specific male or female characteristics. We can engage them in an exciting adventure, encouraging them to identify and claim for themselves those characteristics that should mark them as human beings, whether male or female.

Adolescents are surrounded by the so-called sexual revolution. They know that changes have occurred in attitudes concerning sexual activity, and they know that a wide range of sexual practices exist. They know that any sexual practice, in fact, will have the approval of some segment of society. But over all, loud and strong voices of the society equate sexual activity with what it is to be male or female. Along with the easy temptation to isolate sexual activity from such concerns as respect, care, and esteem for others, there is always the temptation to use sex "to prove" that one is male or female. In the face of all this, adolescents must determine what they will do with their sexual abilities.

As we engage young people in discussions of sex, it is not first a set of rules that they want from us. Adolescents want clear statements concerning our sexuality. They want to hear from us our values and understandings. They want us to share with them what has informed and shaped our sexuality. They want to hear how and why we have constructed our sexuality in a particular fashion. In such a discussion we may be asked pointed questions about our own sexual activity, not out of impudence but from a desire for clues for guidance.

Adolescents have a major work of beginning to respond anew to the question, "What is it to be male or female?" They must create anew their understanding of their sexuality. Their responses will influence greatly their regard for themselves as persons and their regard and use of their bodies. Their responses will influence the possibilities open to them as responsible persons in society. Their responses will influence greatly their regard for persons of the opposite sex and their regard for another's body. They have a major and profound decision to make, determining for themselves what it will be for them to be male or female in the world of persons.

Engaging Adolescents in the Question

In this section several exercises or activities are offered. They are designed to engage adolescents in the question "What is it to be male or female?" They encourage the participants to reflect upon and to describe their present understandings of maleness and femaleness. The exercises assist the adolescents to share their descriptions with each other. In the group activities adolescents can challenge each other and work for new descriptions.

1. Male and Female Roles: The Popular Statements. Understandings of maleness or femaleness are expressed in popular statements, which often are accepted with a mindlessness. Adolescents need to examine such statements.

■ *With chalk, draw a long line on the floor, dividing it into five segments labeled: agree, somewhat agree, don't know, somewhat disagree, and disagree. Indicate to the adolescents that you will read a series of statements related to male and female roles and that after each is read they should stand at the position on the line that describes their reactions to the statement. (The adult leader should be the last to take a position.) Statements which can be used are:*

"A woman's place is in the home."

"If a woman works, it's O.K. for the husband to stay home and care for the children and house."

"If a husband and wife both drive, the man should always drive when they go out together."

"Men make better politicians than women."

"If a husband and wife work, the husband's work is more important than the wife's."

"The major decisions in the family should be made finally by the wife."

"A female should not ask a male for a date."

"If she wishes, a female should be an automobile mechanic."

"A woman truck driver is not an attractive female to men."

"A male hairdresser is an odd-ball."

□ *After each statement and when the participants are positioned, invite each to discuss his or her reaction.*

"Why did you place yourself at that position?"

"What influences your agreement or disagreement?"

"Why did you take the position 'don't know'?"

□ *After the discussion of each statement, invite those who wish to do so to change positions on the line. If some make changes, invite them to discuss the factors which prompted the change.*

"What influenced you to make the change?"

■ *Following the exercise with the line, engage the participants in further conversation.*

"How would you account for the differing and conflicting responses present in the group?"

"How would your parents respond to the various statements?"

"How do you determine what are male or female roles? What influences your thinking?"

"Should we attempt to determine a set of roles which belong to males only and a set which belong to females only? Why? Why not?"

"In the line exercise, did you note any differences between male and female responses? How would you account for the differences?"

2. Male and Female Roles: The Occupations. Maleness or femaleness is often expressed in terms of occupation. There is an easy assumption at times that certain occupations are for men; others, for women.

■ *Give the following instructions to the group. "For its stability and continuance a society requires that many occupations should be fulfilled. Increasingly, both males and females are fulfilling many of the same occupations. I will read a list of 'real people.' On a piece of paper, I want you to write down your first reaction to each and read it." The list could include the following:*

Female doctor	Female politician	Female football player
Male secretary	Female minister	Male kindergarten teacher
Male nurse	Male hairdresser	Male telephone operator
House husband	Female astronaut	Female truck driver
Female lawyer	Male housecleaner	Female auto mechanic
Female jockey	Male babysitter	Male leader of Girl Scouts

□ *Invite the participants to share and discuss their reactions.*

"Were there some items to which you had negative reactions? Why?"

"Were there some items you considered 'odd' or 'funny'? Why?"

"Are there some of the occupations which should be fulfilled only by males? By females? Why?"

"Which of these various occupations would you want to fulfill?"

"Can we determine which occupations belong to males or females?"

"Can males and females fulfill all those occupations equally well? Explain."

"Does the occupation that an individual fulfills make that person 'more or less' female or 'more or less' male?"

3. Male and Female Roles: The Dating Patterns. Dating patterns tend to assign certain roles to males and others to females. Complying with and following those patterns, individuals permit them to define their "maleness" or "femaleness." Moreover, adolescents frequently use the results of the dating patterns as a judge of their "worthwhileness" and value. Dating patterns can inform and shape one's understanding of "maleness" and "femaleness," an understanding which operates far beyond dating. An examination of dating patterns can raise significant questions concerning "femaleness" and "maleness."

■ *Divide the group by sexes. Give to each group a prepared set of questions which it is to discuss.*

For the females:
- Would you ask a male for a date? Why? Why not?
- What would you think of a female who asked a male for a date? Why?
- What would your friends think if you asked a male for a date?
- Would you rather stay at home than ask a male for a date?
- What do you think a male would think of you if you asked him for a date?
- Have you ever discussed this matter with female friends, male friends, or your parents? What have been their opinions?
- Should the male always cover the costs of a date? Under what circumstances would you consider covering the total cost of a date?

For the males:
- A female asks you for a date. What would be your first reaction?
- What factors would influence your reaction?
- What would you think of a female who asked a male for a date?
- What would your friends think of you if you dated a female who asked you for a date? What would your friends think of her? What would your parents think of her?
- Would you ever ask a female on a "Dutch-treat" date? Would you permit a female to cover the total cost of a date?

■ *In the total group, make available both sets of questions to all participants. Invite each group to share its discussion and responses to the questions. Invite the total group to participate in a discussion of dating patterns.*

"From where do we get our ideas about dating patterns?"

"Are dating patterns 'fair' or 'unfair'? To whom? In what ways?"

"Do accepted dating patterns 'favor' males or females? Explain."

"What do dating patterns claim to tell us about who males are, who females are, and what each is to do?"

"How would you want to change dating patterns? Why?"

4. Male and Female Roles: The Difficulties in Agreement. Many segments of society easily assume that there are certain roles which innately belong to males and others that belong to females. We may also assume that all others share our assumptions.

■ *Using the chalkboard or newsprint, invite the group to develop two lists of sex roles: one for males and the other for females. The group can respond to the question: "What roles do males have in the family and society simply because they are males, and what roles do females have simply because they are females?" List all of the contributions without comment and discussion.*

□ *Using the items compiled on the two lists, produce two more lists which will contain items with which **all** can agree. The directions would include, "We have two suggested lists of sex roles. We want to produce two more lists, but we will include only items with which everyone agrees. Do you think that there are certain items which are inappropriate or do not belong? Do you want to eliminate any items?" In the process, encourage each to discuss his or her reasons for wanting to retain or eliminate a particular item.*

□ *The process will produce one of two results. First, the group may agree on a relatively short list of sex roles. These are to be discussed.*

"Do you think that all people would agree with the lists that we have produced? Why? Why not?"

"Do all males or females you know fulfill the roles on the respective lists? If not, could you give some examples?"

"About those who do not fulfill respective roles, would you consider them 'less male' or 'less female' than those who do? Why? Why not?"

□ *Second, the group may be unable to agree on the inclusion of any item. There may be no lists at all. The discussion and conversation will be greatly different from that of the first possible result.*

"Why can we not produce lists with which we all can agree?"

"What factors contribute to our difficulties and disagreements?"

"If we cannot agree on a list, can we appropriately assert that there are definite roles for males or females?"

"Does our inability to produce the lists suggest that we have different understandings of what it is to be male or female?"

"Do our differences create difficulty in our relationships with each other? In what ways? How can we minimize that difficulty?"

■ *Return to the initial set of lists.*

"Of all the roles listed which two would you want most to fulfill? Which two, least? Why?"

"Would you be comfortable fulfilling a role culturally assigned to your opposite sex?"

"Who should determine which roles you will exercise?"

5. Masculine and Feminine: Assumed Characteristics. We often describe and define masculinity and femininity by sets of characteristics which have been assigned by tradition, society, advertisements, and significant others. Individuals use those characteristics to define themselves as "masculine" and "feminine," frequently without questioning the appropriateness of assignments. An uncritical acceptance of assigned masculine and feminine characteristics can have disastrous effects on adolescents. Frequently, the assigned characteristics are used to judge one's worth and value.

■ *Prepare a mimeographed sheet listing a number of popularly assigned masculine and feminine characteristics. Instruct the group in a marking procedure. If they judge a characteristic to be masculine or feminine, mark it with "M" or "F." If they judge a characteristic to apply equally to males and females, mark it "M/F." If they judge a characteristic to apply to neither, mark it "N."*

The prepared list can include the following:

Aggressive	Independent	Adventurous
Rugged	Cries easily	Business leader
Dependent	Competitive	Family-oriented
Sneaky	Gentle	Dominant
Blunt	Logical	Passive
Very religious	Submissive	Ambitious
Self-confident	Decisive	Easily excitable
Emotional	Critical	Objective

□ *Invite the participants to discuss their responses.*

"Are there any characteristics which belong to males or females simply because they are males or females? What informs and influences your opinions?"

"How can we determine what is a masculine or feminine characteristic?"

"Could some persons portray all the characteristics at some point in their lives?"

"From where do we get our understandings of what is masculine and feminine? Do our understandings need to be altered? How?"

"Do you as a male or female fulfill all the popularly assigned characteristics of masculinity or femininity? If not, what do you say about yourself?"

□ *Using the characteristics listed earlier, invite the participants to select those items which best describe them.*

"Do your selections for yourself as a male or female fall within the popular notions of masculine or feminine?"

"How seriously should we take the popular notions of masculine and feminine? Why? Why not?"

□ *Invite the participants to select those items which they would wish their friends to possess regardless of sex.*

"Does your selection include both popular notions of maleness and femaleness?"

"How wise is it to define ourselves by popular notions of maleness and femaleness? Why? Why not?"

"Are popular notions of masculine and feminine characteristics destructive to human relationships? If yes, in what ways?"

6. Masculine and Feminine Characteristics: Thinking It Through.
Adolescents need to make realistic appraisals of themselves against the background of assumed masculine and feminine characteristics. It is essential that they should be able to identify and describe for themselves popular notions of masculine and feminine characteristics. Will they permit those popular notions to define them?

■ *Using the chalkboard or newsprint, invite the group to develop two lists of characteristics, one masculine and the other feminine. The group can respond to the question, "What characteristics do males have simply because they are males, and what characteristics do females have simply because they are females? List all of the contributions without comment or discussion.*

"Would all persons agree with our list of male and female characteristics? Why? Why not?"

"Do **all** of your male friends possess **all** of the masculine characteristics listed? If not, are they 'less' masculine than those who do?"

"Do **all** of your female friends posess **all** of the feminine characteristics listed? If not, are they 'less' feminine than those who do?"

"Do you as a male (female) possess all the masculine (feminine) characteristics listed? If not, what do you say about yourself as masculine (feminine)?"

"How do you determine that these are masculine and feminine characteristics?"

"Why are there popular notions of masculine or feminine characteristics? Are we 'fair' to people when we describe them by those characteristics?"

"Should we pay much attention to the popular notions? Why and for what purposes? Why not?"

"In what ways is it appropriate that we should label persons as masculine or feminine?"

"Even if someone should label you as masculine (feminine), what has that person said significantly about you?"

□ *Return to the initial list. Engage the adolescents in an additional exercise which can assist them to reflect about themselves. In this exercise, do not attempt to compel the participants to share unless they are willing. Read the characteristics listed, asking each person to rank himself or herself on each with a scale of one (lowest) to five (highest).*

"How do you measure yourself as a male (female) against the assumed masculine (feminine) characteristics?"

"Using your rankings on the masculine (feminine) characteristics, how would you describe yourself?"

"Did you rank yourself 'high' with characteristics from both lists? If so, what does that ranking say about you?"

"If you ranked yourself 'high' on characteristics from both lists, then are our distinctions between 'masculine' and 'feminine' helpful or appropriate?"

"If we were concerned primarily with characteristics of 'personness,' what would happen to our distinctions between masculine and feminine? Would we need those distinctions? Why? Why not?"

"If you were asked to describe 'personness,' which characteristics would you use?"

Engaging and Interpreting the Bible

The following biblical passages, with the accompanying exercises, will encourage and assist adolescents to consider the question "What is it to be male or female?" This question should be considered within the larger context of "What is it to be a human being?" We believe that it is within the larger question of personhood that adolescents can best begin to shape their responses to what it is to be male or female. We have not included passages related to marriage. Marriage is a special and unique relationship between one man and one woman. We all live within a multitude of relationships with both men and women. How one understands those relationships and his or her place in them will inform and influence that person's marriage relationship.

1. Jesus and Women. Throughout the four Gospels we have but few teachings of Jesus which may be regarded as a response to "What is it to be male or female?" Nevertheless, the Gospels are plentiful in stories of Jesus' encounters, dealings, and conversations with women. In the stories, Jesus' words and actions stood as contradictions, judgments, and challenges to accepted social and religious norms. In a most profound sense, Jesus' ministry was directed to the oppressed and dispossessed of the society. These two words aptly describe the place of women in the society of Jesus' time. The stories of Jesus' relationships with women can assist us in framing a response of the four Gospels to our question.

Bridge: We have been discussing the question, "What is it to be male or female?" We want to consider how the four Gospels, containing stories of Jesus' ministry, might respond to the question. We are asking how the Gospels can inform our response to it. In the Gospels there are but few specific passages which we can regard as direct responses by Jesus to the question. There are, however, many stories of his encounters, conversations, and dealings with women. We will study and discuss a number of short passages which illustrate Jesus' concern. From these passages, we will attempt to frame the response of the Gospels to the question.

■ *Have the participants work in pairs. Assign to each pair several of the biblical passages below. It is desirable that more than one pair should engage the same passage. Two questions can guide the young people's consideration of the passages.*

"How does what Jesus is saying or doing reflect his regard and concern for women?"

"Can you think of ways in which Jesus' sayings and actions might be in contradiction to the expectations of his society?"

- Matthew 5:27–30 (and for contrast, Deuteronomy 21:10–14). [*A woman convicted of adultery received severe punishment. Not all men convicted of adultery received severe punishment. There was a "double standard" concerning sexual activity. In the Matthew passage, Jesus attacks the "double standard" and gives a "larger" definition of adultery.*]

- Matthew 5:31, 32 (and for contrast, Deuteronomy 24:1–4). [*In the Old Testament, the right to divorce was limited to the man. A man could easily declare himself divorced from his wife. A divorced woman had little place in the society. While the Matthew passage is designed, in part, to protect wives against capricious and unfair treatment by men, it declares that a man does not have the right to divorce his wife summarily. Again, a "double standard" is attacked.*]

- John 4:7–15, 27. [*Jesus talks with a woman at a well and requests a drink of water. The woman was surprised that Jesus would talk to her, especially as she was a Samaritan woman belonging to a group that Jews tended to shun. The disciples marveled that Jesus would talk to the woman. Such an activity was not acceptable. Jesus breaks accepted norms on two accounts. Also, he speaks good news to her.*]

- John 8:1–11. [*A group of religious leaders bring a woman caught in adultery. They want to entrap Jesus in his words and want to know what he has to say about her. Jesus turns the question around and makes it a question about the men. Jesus does not condone adultery, but he attacks the double standard that the men were using in their efforts to entrap him.*]

- Luke 7:36–50. [*Jesus rebukes the Pharisee for his attitude toward the woman. Jesus deals kindly with the woman and declares forgiveness to her.*]

- Mark 7:24–30. [*Jesus does not dismiss the woman, even though he did not want anyone to know where he was located at the moment. He listens to her, even argues with her, and responds to her need.*]

- Mark 1:30, 31; Luke 8:40–56; Luke 13:10–13. [*These several passages illustrate that Jesus' healing ministry included women.*]

- Mark 15:40, 41; Luke 8:1–3. [*These two passages demonstrate that women were a part of the company of persons which traveled with Jesus. Though the identification of "disciple" is not used for the women, the passages suggest that it would not be inappropriate to call them "disciples."*]

- ■ *Invite the participants to develop a statement which would be a possible response of Jesus to the male/female questions. Items which may be included: attack on the double standard; women and men are to be treated equally; Jesus "broke" some societal and religious expectations which were harmful to women; the company of disciples surrounding Jesus was inclusive, including both males and females.*

"If, in any way, these Gospel passages should inform our response to our question, what do they require of us?"

"Are there some norms and expectations of our day concerning male and female which we should attack and call into judgment? What are they, and what might we do?"

"Should we tolerate a 'double standard' concerning male and female? How are females harmed by a 'double standard'? How are males harmed?" [*A "double standard" is destructive to human relationships. It causes distrust and suspicion. It encourages some to feel and act superior to others. It contributes to unequal treatment and expectations.*]

2. Genesis 1:26–31. This passage is located near the close of the first creation story in Genesis. It makes a beautiful and profound statement about "humankind" which includes both male and female. The statement challenges popular notions of what it is to be male or female. It can inform both our understanding and behaviors concerning a critical area of human life. To encounter the major thrusts and fine distinctions of the passage we will need to give careful attention to certain words.

Bridge: We have been examining the question, "What is it to be male or female?" We are aware that our culture gives many different responses to the question. Many of those responses ascribe certain roles and characteristics to females and others to males. Among us we have varying opinions and understandings. We want to consider a biblical passage, Genesis 1:26–31, which speaks of male and female. We want to ask how it responds to our question.

■ *Arrange small groups. Without any additional introduction to the passage, invite the adolescents to study and discuss. One question is to be assigned: what does this passage say about what it is to be male or female? After an appropriate period of time, invite the small groups to share their findings and conclusions with the larger group. Encourage the participants to ask questions of each other and to challenge each other. On the chalkboard or newsprint, make a list of the findings, concerns, and questions of the participants. These can be used in the later discussion.*

■ *Have the participants return to their small groups. Again, the adolescents are to study and discuss the passage but with particular information about certain words.*

"As you consider the passage a second time, some information about several words can be of assistance. In the Hebrew there is the word *adam* which can be translated 'man.' In the passage the word does not refer to *a man* or *a group of men*. It is a generic word, which is a word that refers to a whole group or kind. The word *adam*, then, refers to 'humankind.' Notice that when God created *adam* ('man') he created them *(otham)*. And, *adam* ('humankind') is male *(zakar)* and female *(neqebhah)*."

■ *After an appropriate period of time, invite the small groups to share the results of their study and discussion.*

"In your second study, did you come to any new or different understandings of the passage? What are those? What influenced your thinking?"

"Are there any items on the first list developed that are not true to the passage? If so, why?"

□ *Further work with and reflection on the passage can be done within the total group guided by a series of questions.*

"According to vs. 27, who is created in the image of God?" [*It is* adam, *'humankind,' which is male and female. Both male and female, then, are created in the image of God. There is no distinction made between male and female in this matter.*]

"According to vs. 28, **who** is blessed and given command to be fruitful, to multiply, and to have dominion?" [*Again, it is* adam, *male and female. There is no distinction.*]

"According to vss. 29 and 30, to whom are the various gifts of creation given?" [*To them,* otham, *male and female. There is no distinction.*]

"According to vs. 31, what is declared 'good'?" [*The whole creation including humankind, male and female.*]

"Are there any differences between our last set of statements about the passage and those made earlier? What are they?"

■ *In the passage no distinctions are made between male and female. Male and female constitute humankind. The passage is not eradicating or ignoring the biological sex differences. Since males and females live in the world as one kind, they need to order their individual and corporate lives as one kind. Males working with males, and females working with females—all humankind needs to order life together.*

"If this passage does reflect God's intention in creation, is it appropriate for us to assert that there are innate roles that males are to fulfill and innate roles that females are to fulfill? Is it appropriate to say that there are feminine characteristics and masculine characteristics which are innate?"

"When sex roles are assigned, who most normally does the assigning? Males or females?"

"What might this passage say about the notion of dominant males and subservient females?"

"What are the implications of the command—to be fruitful, to multiply, and to subdue and have dominion—for males and females in our world today?"

"When males attempt to dominate females, or vice versa, what is being done to the 'image of God'?" [*We attempt to make another something less than God intended her or him to be.*]

■ *Adolescents may be assisted in further reflection on the passage through two exercises. First, invite the group to produce a composite collage depicting the images of male and female suggested by the passage. Second, prepare a list of statements reflecting popular notions of male-female roles and characteristics.*

> "What response might the passage give to the following statements?"
> 1. A woman's place is in the home.
> 2. Men are naturally better in the business or political world than women.
> 3. Women should pursue any careers they wish.
> 4. Men are more rational and objective than women.
> 5. Women are more sensitive and understanding than men.
> 6. Men should be paid higher salaries than women for the same work.

3. Genesis 2:4b–24; 3:16; 5:1 and 2. The second creation story in Genesis addresses many concerns of human life, including marriage. Here we will focus on the story's response to the question, "What is it to be male or female?" Unlike the first creation story in Genesis this story makes a critical statement about the domination of the male over the female (3:16). Male domination occurs after the Fall and is regarded as a consequence of sin. Thus, a continuation of male domination over the female can be regarded as a continuation of sin. Genesis 5:1 and 2, which is not a part of the second creation story, is a declaration that the human creature (man in the generic sense) created in the image of God is defined as both male and female.

Bridge: In previous activities we have explored the question, "What is it to be male or female?" Our society offers many responses to this question, and we have suggested some of our own responses. The biblical passages, Genesis 2:4b–24; 3:16; 5:1 and 2, are responses to the question and may offer us some clues as we shape our responses to it. These passages deal with a number of issues, but we want to focus on the male-female dimension.

■ *Arrange small groups. Assign Genesis 2:4b–24. The only direction or information to be given is the one question with which the groups are to respond. "What does this passage say about male and female?"*

☐ *After an appropriate period of time, invite the small groups to share their discussions and responses with each other. Using the chalkboard or newsprint, list the various responses. Work for a series of statements concerning the passage with which there is general agreement. Constantly urge the participants to identify the portion of the passage which informs their responses. Retain the list which can be used in later discussion.*

☐ *Return to small groups. Provide the following information. Using the information, the groups are assigned the question, "Does this information help you to understand the passage in new ways?"*

Within the passage, the word *adam* is not used as a proper noun until vs. 25. Previous to that verse, it is used in a more general way to identify a creation of God.

That creation, *adam*, is made from the dust of the earth. It is made a living being as God breathes into the form the breath of life.

In vs. 18, the living being is all alone, all by itself. There is the suggestion that to be "all by oneself" is not to be human.

The word "helper" can be translated as "companion" or "one who helps" but not as "servant." The word "helper" suggests cooperation.

The "helper" that God will make will be "corresponding to" or "equal to" *adam*. That which is "equal to" is "fit."

It is from a "rib" of *adam* that woman is created. Nevertheless, both male and female are "made of the same stuff," the dust of the earth.

Marriage is a special relationship between a man and woman.

☐ *After an appropriate period of time, invite the small groups to share again their discussion and responses. Use the previously developed list as the beginning for the discussion.*

"Are there any items or statements that you would want to remove from the list? Why? Add? Why?"

"In what ways has your understanding of the passage altered or changed? If some change, what influenced the change?"

"Did the order of creation within the story confer any special status or privilege?"

"How is humankind defined by this passage?" [*Male and female.*]

"How is the relationship of male and female defined in the passage?" [*Male and female living in mutual harmony, helpfulness, and cooperation. Marriage is a special relationship.*]

"What distinctions, if any, does the story make between male and female?"

□   *Direct the participants to 3:16. Note that the verse occurs after the story's account of the Fall.*

"How does this verse, taken in context of the total story, account for the domination of the male over the female?" [*Domination is the result of sin.*]

"If domination is the result of sin, is the male's attempt to dominate the female a continuing act of sin? Why? Why not?" [*Domination is an attempt to make persons unequal, to make persons subservient.*]

"In all areas of our lives, what are the results when we attempt to dominate others, both male and female? Would it be appropriate to call our attempts to dominate by the label 'sin'? Why? Why not?"

□   *Direct the participants to 5:1 and 2. Note that this passage does not belong to the second creation story but that it does make a statement about male and female.*

"What does this passage say about male and female? How does it define humankind? How does it, in part, define the 'image of God'?"

"What distinctions does it make between male and female?"

□   *Assist the participants to translate the concerns of the passages into contemporary dimensions.*

"What might these passages say about our notions of sex roles and sex characteristics?"

"Do the popular notions of sex roles and sex characteristics tend to make males dominant over or superior to females? If so, might we label them as 'sin'? Why? Why not?"

"Marriage is noted as a special relationship between a man and a woman. In the normal course of life, we have many other relationships with many males and females. According to the passages, what characteristics, behaviors, and understandings should shape those relationships?" [*Harmony. Cooperation. Equality. Helpfulness. Together we will work to give order to our lives together. Together we will decide what roles, actions, and tasks we will do for our life together.*]

4. Galatians 3:23–29. The Apostle Paul has been associated with the view of male dominance and female subservience. Many of his statements identify him with that view. No doubt he shared many of his society's opinions concerning male-female relationships. In this passage, the Apostle soars beyond any notions of dominance and subservience and beyond societal norms. His understanding of the gospel, of Christian freedom, and of Christian community compelled him. In the material previous to this passage, Paul has written concerning the purpose of the Law. Here he writes of Christ. To us faith has been given. We are the children of God. All distinctions, separating persons from person and including male-female distinctions, have no place in the concern of Christ and have no place among the children of God.

Bridge: In our discussion of the question, "What is it to be male or female?" we have asked if there are some roles and characteristics which belong specifically to males or belong specifically to females. We have shared a number of suggestions and opinions. We want now to consider a biblical passage (Galatians 3:23–29) that is one response to our question and that may assist us as we frame our own response.

■ *Divide the larger group into small groups. Noting that the passage was written to Christians and about Christians, provide questions to direct the study and discussion.*

"How does this passage describe Christians? What does it claim about Christians?" [*Justified by faith. Children of God. Baptized into Christ.*]

"What does this passage say about male and female? Why does it make that claim?" [*In Christ, no distinction.*]

"If that claim is true, what does it say to us today?"

"Is it suggesting that there is no such thing as male or female?"

☐ *In the larger group, invite the adolescents to share their findings and conclusions. Encourage them to work for a commonly agreed-upon statement of the passage. Assist them to translate the passage into the present.*

"We are Christian people. We are the children of God. What claim does this passage want to make on us?" [*The sexes remain. There remains male and female. Distinctions between male and female, and any other distinctions between persons, which cause divisiveness, destroy human relationships, are used for exploitation, or are used to gain dominance or superiority over another, have no place among the children of God. Equality, in all its dimensions, is to prevail among the children of God.*]

"In what ways does this passage say something about the relationships of dating, engagement, and marriage?" [*Such relationships are special. If, in these relationships, we attempt to use others for our purposes and pleasure, to exploit others in any fashion or to assert dominance or superiority over others, we destroy human relationships. If we let anyone do these things to us, we let them hurt themselves as well as ourselves. We are to regard each other as the children of God.*]

"What might this passage say to us regarding the following: The male who wants the female 'to prove' that she loves him by engaging in sexual activity. The female who engages in certain sexual activity for fear that she may 'lose' a boy friend. The female who always wants to be attractive so that she can attract the attention of males. The male who asserts that females should serve males. The mass media advertisements telling females how 'to catch' a male or telling males how 'to handle' females."

"There are numerous male-female relationships other than dating, engagement and marriage. How might this passage inform and guide our male-female relationships? What guidelines might the passage offer as we develop our male-female relationships?"

"How easy or difficult is it for you to have positive relationships with persons of the opposite sex when there are no 'romantic' concerns?"

"Does this passage stand in opposition or in contradiction to social expectations or your opinions concerning male-female relationships?"

"What changes would need to occur in society—or in your opinions—if we take seriously the implications of this passage?"

·10
What is required of me?

The morality and moral fiber of our society has been examined, discussed, and lamented. We are stunned and appalled by immorality in both high and low places. We struggle to separate good and evil. Good has been called evil, evil, good. In a society which extols honesty most highly, stealing, lying, and cheating in various guises are commonplace, at times even permissible. In a society which overtly praises marriage, sexual infidelity and divorce cause little surprise. In a society which proclaims human rights, the abuse of others—the poor, the oppressed, minorities, a spouse, children or an employee—is glossed over as an unfortunate reality of life. In a society which calls for the respect of the law, we are amused by the stories of those who have "beaten" the law without getting caught. A society crying out for peace moves to build greater weapons of destruction.

We may imagine a time past when a society was clear about right and wrong, when its people knew what was required of them, and when they fulfilled the necessary requirements. And even if our imaginations are not romantic excursions into the past, we know that our images are not reflections of these days. Complex societies, lacking simple and static moral codes, demand complex moral decisions which cannot be regarded as fixed and final. Moreover, pluralistic societies must contend with a number of competing moral codes and systems. Yet, in the presence of conflicting and competing moralities, individuals and communities must make decisions.

In responding to the question, "What is required of me?" and to its companion, "What is required of us together?" we possess few, if any, final answers. Yet, we are called to make decisions for right and good. We do not always know beforehand if a decision or proposed action for good will result in such. The judgment can be made only after the fact. And distressingly so, some of our decisions for good turn out to be for bad. In our decisions to act for the good and right we, at the same time, take the risk of deciding for bad and wrong. We cannot avoid the risk, and its consequences belong to us. And even if we miss the mark, we ask again, "What is required of me—and of us, together?"

Adolescents Facing New Demands

Adolescents, with new abilities and experiences and a widening range of relationships, must confront anew, *"What is required of me?"* They must create for themselves a moral posture and ways of making moral decisions to which they will commit themselves. They need to be conscious of and deliberate in their moral decision-making, recognizing and understanding those persons, ideas, and ideologies which inform and shape their decision-making. In so doing they make not only choices for the right but gain significant control of their lives as responsible decision makers.

Adolescents, unlike children, readily recognize the plethora of conflicting moralities. They know that all people do not operate in the same moral system. They recognize sharp differences of opinions concerning critical issues. They associate with persons whose moral codes and moralities differ greatly from that of their families. They know that several solutions are given to the same moral problem. Bothersome and unsettling questions emerge. Is one moral code or system "better" than another? Does one code or system produce "better" decisions and people than another? Does it really matter which code or system one follows? Who knows what is right and wrong or good and bad, anyway? Why should I be concerned about what others do as long as they don't bother me?

Such questions do belong to adolescents. The questions are honest and serious. They are a part of the adolescents' attempts to come to terms with the task of moral decision-making. Adults may seek to give answers to the questions, but ultimately the adolescents must give their own answers. Consider the questions of "better." They place the burden of moral decision-making on the code or the system. One is asked "to prove" that one code or system is "better" than another. We may well examine and compare moral codes or systems, but to indulge in an effort "to prove" one "better" than another is a futile exercise. Moreover, the questions miss a most crucial matter. Reliance upon a static and fixed moral code may remove us from the arena of responsible moral decision-making.

Adolescents often float in a state of relativism concerning good and bad, right and wrong. They find themselves unable to make deliberate decisions about wrong and right. The harsh reality may be that they do not know how to make such decisions. They need the practice of proposing, testing out, and evaluating their moral decisions. In the presence of adolescent uncertainty, almost anything goes; almost anything is permissible. Adolescents' refusal to make judgments of their peers' sexual activity, cheating on school exams, or use of drugs and alcohol may well reflect an inability to do so. With so much "up for grabs," many adolescents face difficulty in breaking out of the state of relativism.

But make decisions they will. Some readily adopt an already-established moral code, following it narrowly and rigidly and giving themselves to making harsh judgments on others. The burden of decision-making is given to the moral code. Some adolescents work with the inarticulated assumption that what they desire and want to do is good. They afford the same prerogative to others. But some youth, so intent upon pleasing significant persons, are not able to make independent decisions. They need and seek the prior approval of others. Then, some young persons work with the assumption that intention determines good or bad. "If my intention was good, I should not be chastised because things went badly. After all, I tried." And still others, willing to take the risk of moral decision-making, commit themselves to values which inform and shape their decisions. They accept the reality that not all will agree with them. Having made their commitments, they take the risk of moral decision-making, willing to accept the consequences as their own.

Clearly there is no one way of describing all adolescents concerning their ability and willingness to engage in moral decision-making. There is no one way to describe them all as they approach issues of good and bad, right and wrong. As has been asserted throughout this book, we will work with diversity. We dare not expect all to be at the same place at the same time. As adolescents engage the question, "What is required of me and of us?" as they meet the responses of faithful people in the biblical literature, as they engage Christian adults who share their struggles with the question, and as they struggle with each other in responding to the question, they will be assisted and challenged in a more critical thinking about their values and decision-making. They will be aided to respond with responsible moral decisions.

Two additional comments deserve our attention. First, adolescents can be devastated by the results of their decisions. So certain that they were doing *good* and *right*, they still reap *bad* and *wrong*. They are bewildered and stunned. Guilt and despair overtake them. Even with our best efforts we will not be able in all instances to preserve adolescents from the destructive results of their decisions. In part, they were unable to anticipate the possible consequences of their decisions and actions. They could not imagine the possibility of havoc. A word of judgment may need to be spoken when the unimagined does happen. But more important, adolescents need to hear the proclamation of forgiveness and need to come to terms with what it is to be a forgiven people.

Second, and it is related to the first, in a discussion of good and bad, right and wrong, the word "sin" will emerge. For many adolescents the word "sin" is a "purely religious word," unrelated to ongoing, daily life. When asked to describe their understanding of sin, many respond, "something you do against God." Responding to probes they add, "Like a big crime. Like killing someone or breaking a commandment." Some will add, but without specificity, "Something you do against other people." It is extremely difficult for many adolescents to articulate a broad and complex concept of sin. In their efforts to do so, they frequently relate sin to some moral code, a code difficult for them to describe. The point here is simple. A narrow understanding of sin, defined in terms of narrow and static rules and regulations, can be a strong barrier to a significant encounter with the question, "What is required of me and of us?"

Adolescents Engaging the Question

In this section exercises and activities designed to engage adolescents in the question, "What is required of me?" are provided. They encourage the participants to examine their own decision-making and the values which influence decisions, to be conscious of their decisions and working values, and to ask of the appropriateness and adequacy of their decisions and values. Also, the exercises and activities call upon the adolescents to claim their decisions as their own—with resulting consequences. And a significant question is raised, "What are we to do when our decisions, made for the good, reap the bad?"

1. On Decision Making. Adolescents do not always anticipate possible consequences of their decisions. They do not always recognize how their decisions may "disappoint" others or cause others to distrust them. Frequently, what they want at the moment appears right and good. They need practice in taking the concerns of others into consideration.

■ *Assign to small groups the following problem.*

"Your parents will be away over a weekend, and you will be home alone. Your friends, knowing this, urge you to have a party at your house, assuring you that your parents will not know. Discuss the following questions. What would you do? Why would you make that decision? If you decide to have the party, what are some possible consequences? If you decide not to have the party, what are some possible consequences?"

☐ *Have the small groups report on their conversation for discussion by the total group.*

"What values were a part of your conversations?"

☐ *In the total group, have a role-play with one participant having the role of an adolescent and another having the role of a parent. Assign the following problem.*

"You do have the party. There is no damage to the house, and it is in good order when your parents return. However, your parents learn of the party, and they are upset. What will be the conversation between the two of you?"

☐ *Invite the group to respond to the conversation of the role-play.*

"What issues and problems were involved? Which ones were the most important and interesting to you? Why?"

"What values were expressed? What values did the adolescent illustrate? What values did the parent illustrate? Were two sets of values in conflict?"

"Was there evidence by the participants of 'owning their own behaviors'? Did either one attempt to blame someone else?"

"Were there evidences of understanding and respect? If so, can you describe them? If not, what would be necessary to have understanding and respect?"

"Did both participants listen to each other?"

"How is the conflict between adolescent and parent to be resolved?"

2. Examining a Decision. Adolescents can develop guidelines by which to judge their own decisions and the decisions of others. They can formulate alternatives for responding and reacting to a specific situation or event. In the process of developing and formulating, they can assist each other to achieve greater awareness of values, decisions and possible alternatives.

■ *Invite the adolescents to describe in writing a problem or a situation in which they were involved and which demanded some decision or action on their part. Give direction to their efforts by the following questions.*

"How would you describe the problem or situation? What were the most important elements?"

"What kind of decision was required of you?"

"What was the range of possible decisions that could have been made?"

"What decision did you make? Were you happy with your decision? Why? Why not?"

"What values informed your decision?"

□ *Invite each to share the description of his/her problem or situation with the group. At this point, do not ask for the decision which the individual made. The group should discuss the problem or situation.*

"If this had been your problem or situation, what do you think you would have done? Why?"

"In your response what values are you expressing?"

"What influences have shaped the values that you have expressed? How important are those values to you?"

□ *There may be a variety of values expressed, and the variety should be explored.*

"How do you account for the variety of values which has been expressed?"

"How might differing values bring us into conflict with each other? If so, how might we resolve the conflict?"

"Are all values of equal appropriateness? How do we determine which values we will hold?"

□ *Invite the writer of the problem or situation, if he/she is willing, to react to the conversation of the group and to share his/her decision.*

"Did the group recognize the struggle that you had in making your decision? Were there some elements that the group did not take into consideration?"

"How do you react to the possible decisions suggested by the group?"

"What decision did you make? What values played a role in your decision?"

"If you had the decision to make again, would you make the same decision? If not, why not? What new things would you take into consideration?"

3. Responding to a Problem. As adolescents reflect upon and respond to another's problem or situation, they bring into play their own values. They need assistance in identifying, reflecting upon, and describing their values.

■ *Select a letter from such sources as Ann Landers, Dear Abby or the advice column of a magazine popular with adolescents. The letter should deal with an adolescent concern. Make available only the letter to the columnist. Reserve the columnist's response for later use.*

"If you were the columnist, how would you respond to this letter?"

"Why would you respond in that manner?"

"What are the critical issues for you in the letter?"

"Do you consider this issue to be of any importance to you and your friends?"

"What values inform your response?

How important are those values for you?"

□ *At times adolescents will be reluctant to offer "advice," asserting that they do not have enough information. If such should be the case, the discussion could move in a particular direction.*

"What additional information would you want? How would the information inform your response? Why?"

"What questions would you want to ask the writer of the letter? Supposing that the writer answered, '_____.' What would your response be? Why?"

"What values are reflected in your response?"

"There are times when we must make decisions about problems and situations without having all the information we might desire. What do we do in such cases?"

"What do we do when even our best decisions result in harm to ourselves or others?"

□ *After discussion of the letter, make available the columnist's response.*

"What is your reaction to the response?"

"Do you think it would be helpful to the letter writer? How?

Would it be helpful to you if you were in a similar circumstance? Why? Why not?"

"What values are reflected in the columnist's response? Do you agree with those values?"

"What values has the columnist overlooked or ignored?"

4. On Discerning Values. Learning to discern the values of another and the importance given to them can assist young persons in a critical examination of their own values and the importance they hold.

■   *Using the chalkboard or newsprint, ask each participant to identify one value which his/her parents strongly hold. The accumulated list serves as the basis for discussion.*

"How important do you judge this value to be for your parents?"

"In what ways do you see this value informing your parents' decisions and actions?"

"Why do you think they so strongly hold this value? What has influenced them in this matter?"

"Do you share this value with your parents? As strongly as they do? Why? Why not?"

☐   *Using the chalkboard or newsprint, invite each participant to identify a value which he or she holds.*

"Indicate one value that you hold, a value that you would do all you possibly could to maintain. How and in what ways is this value important to you?"

"Do you know of other persons who hold this same value? Who?"

"How does this value inform your decisions, actions, and relationships with other persons?"

"What has influenced your commitment to this value?"

☐   *The list may include contradictory and conflicting values. If so, that fact should be acknowledged and discussed.*

"How would you account for the diversity of values listed?"

"Must you 'give up' acting on the basis of your values because another disagrees with them?"

"If someone wanted you to 'give up' one of your values simply to please him or her, what would be your reaction?"

"Can values be altered? Under what circumstances would you consider altering your values?"

"In life there are many differing and even conflicting values. How do we decide to which ones we will commit ourselves?"

"As we go about our daily life, we may not remain faithful to our values at times. If, for whatever reasons, you fail to be faithful to your values, what does that say about you? About your values? What is required of you? Does it say that we 'give up'?"

"Can we always expect to be rewarded because we maintain our values?"

5. Values Informing Decisions. Adolescents make many decisions. They need to be assisted and challenged to identify and reflect upon the values which inform and influence their decisions. Adolescents can be assisted to be more conscious and deliberate in decision-making.

■ *Prepare the following material in printed form so that each will have a copy.*

Below are a number of situations which you may encounter. What do you think you would do in each situation? What value or values would inform your decision or action?		
Situation	Decision	Value(s)
You have an easy opportunity to cheat on test at school.		
You are urged by friends to use alcohol or other drugs.		
Someone dares you to shoplift.		
Your group or club excludes a person on the basis of race.		
Your friends expect you to be sexually active.		
It's time for draft registration.		
Friends urge you to defy your parents.		
Your friends, knowing your parents will be away, urge you to have a party at your house.		
You hear malicious gossip about another person.		
The cashier at a shop gives you too much change.		
It is easy to avoid responsibilities at home.		
There is an easy opportunity to get out of a restaurant without paying bill.		

□ *Invite the participants to share their responses as they are willing. Give opportunity for discussion and questions.*

"Who or what do you believe has the greatest influence on your values?"

Engaging and Interpreting the Bible

The biblical passages, with the accompanying exercises, in this section focus on the individual. They challenge adolescents to be conscious of and deliberate in their decision-making. Also, the passages and exercises call upon the young people to identify their values and to reflect upon their adequacy and appropriateness. And the passages and exercises challenge adolescents with the question, "What is required of you as members of the household of faith?" And once again, they respond to the questions, "Who am I? To whom do I belong?" "As one who belongs to God, what is it for me to be and do who I am?"

1. 1 Corinthians 13:1–13. This passage is most familiar to us. Easy familiarity with it may blunt our awareness of both its glowing beauty and high demands. Paul was writing to the Christians at Corinth, to a community of people belonging to God. An underlying concern throughout 1 Corinthians was the question, "How are we to live out our lives in the world as Christian people?" The question may be asked somewhat differently, "What is it for us as individuals and a community to be Christians in the church and the world?" He was not asking how we might satisfy or placate God, but rather was asking how we can live out our lives as Christians. It is to a "more excellent way," the way of love, that Paul points us. As Paul points to love, he is not speaking of some inner emotion, some "warm feeling," or a set of narrow rules. Rather, he points to action.

Bridge: We have been exploring the question, "What is required of me?" We have discussed values, commitments, and the necessity of making decisions and choices. We have considered the persons, events, and ideas which influence and guide our values and decisions. It is not always easy to know what is required of us. In 1 Corinthians 13 the Apostle Paul, writing to a congregation of Christians, gives guidance concerning how they are to live out their lives. He points to a "more excellent way" (12:31), the way of love.

■   *Invite the adolescents to share their present understandings and impressions of "love." How do they describe it? Many will describe love as "an emotion," some inner feeling, or some moving force. Some will discuss love as an "ideal." Many of the descriptions will be vague, having little focus. We can expect a wide variety of expressions.*

"How important to you is 'love' as you have described it?"

"How does 'love' as you have described it inform and guide your life? Where might one 'see' that love in your life?"

"Is 'love' as you have described it a realistic way of life? Why? Why not?"

☐ *Invite the total group to study and discuss 1 Corinthians 13:1–3 together. The task here is not to define "love" but to consider the primary place which Paul gives to "love" in the life of the Christians.*

"What is the importance that Paul gives to love in these verses?"

"In our relationships with each other, how might we become noisy gongs or clanging cymbals?"

"How might we 'move mountains' or give our bodies 'to be burned' and yet be 'nothing' or 'gain nothing'?"

☐ *Direct the attention of the group to 1 Corinthians 13:4–8. In preparation for the exercises to follow, it is desirable that we share some of our understandings of the passage. We give some illustrations of love in action.*

• Love will not be discouraged because others fail or because others are ungrateful, but it will encourage and assist others.

• Love is not jealous of the success of others, and it does not brag.

• Love does not insist that others must let me have my way or that things must be done in my way. It does not build up resentment against others.

• Love rejoices in the good things and the success that others have. It is never glad when things go wrong. It will believe the best of others that can be believed. It hopes for the best of others. It will bear and be patient with the hurt that others may inflict upon us or the hurt they may inflict upon themselves.

■ *Prepare the material on the following page so that each participant has a copy. The adolescents should work in pairs, studying and discussing together as each prepares his or her response to the exercise.*

☐ *Invite the adolescents to share their responses in the total group.*

"As we put love into action, what are the results in our relationships with others? What are the results in our own lives?"

"Does love in action preserve us from being hurt or disappointed?" [*Love will make demands upon us. Yes, we will continue to know hurt and disappointment. Not everything will always be "rosy." But we need not respond to hurt and disappointment in hate, anger, and resentfulness.*]

In 1 Corinthians 13:4–8, the Apostle Paul gives some descriptions of love. As he does so, he understands love to be active in the lives of persons. Love is expressed in "doing." Notice that Paul does not describe love as some emotion or feeling inside us but as actions between persons. Using Paul's description, how might we describe love in action in our relationships with parents, with each other in this group, and with others? In each block below, note briefly one way in which a particular description of love might be expressed in actions toward others.

	Parents	This Group	Others*
Patient and kind			
Not jealous or boastful			
Not arrogant or rude			
Does not insist on own way			
Not irritable or resentful			
Rejoices in the right			
Bears all things			
Believes all things			
Hopes all things			
Never ends			

*You may have a specific person or group of persons in mind as you respond.

See exercise on preceding page.

"We are Christian people. We are called by God to love one another. But do we always know in each instance what it is to act in love?" [*We do not always know what it is to love. 1 Corinthians 13:12 suggests that only "dimly" do we see what it is that God would have us do. And verse 11 suggests that we are always discovering what God would have us do.*]

"There are times that we want to be active in love and yet we fail. There are times when we believe that we have acted in love, but we discover that our actions have caused hurt to others. In such situations, what are we to do?" [*We are told that God forgives our failures, both intentional and unintentional. Our failures to be active in love God puts behind us. And even though we have failed in the past, as the people of Jesus we are called to continue to act in love and to discover anew each day what it is to love each other. We are always discovering anew and learning anew.*]

2. Galatians 5:13–24. The Letter to the Galatians as well as all the writings of the Apostle Paul were written to Christians. This passage is addressed to persons who are members of the household of faith and who belong to God. It is an appeal that they should be and do who they already are. Paul makes a distinction between the "works of the flesh" and "the fruits of the Spirit." The word "flesh" does not refer to the physical body. It refers to those who refuse to live in responsible relationships with God and others. The "works of the flesh" result as persons choose to live their lives in any fashion they wish and to do what they want to do whenever they want to do it and however they want to do it. To "walk by the Spirit" is to live as the people of God. Christians are a redeemed people belonging to God. They are free to live as God's people.

Bridge: We have been asking the question, "What is required of me?" We recognize that many demands and expectations are placed upon us. Many voices tell us what we ought to be and do. We must determine to which voices we will listen. We must determine what values will guide our lives. To focus on one response to our question, we want to study a biblical passage, Galatians 5:13–24. This passage, written by the Apostle Paul, was addressed to Christians. We are Christians, and so it is addressed to us. In working with this passage, we should note that the word "flesh" does not refer to the physical body. It refers to persons who want to be in complete charge of their own lives, doing whatever they want to do, whenever and in whatever way they wish.

■ *Arrange small groups. Provide the participants with the following questions. Do not copy bracketed material.*

What is the freedom to which Paul refers? [*God has made us chosen people. We are Christians. God in Christ has claimed us. We are who God intends us to be, chosen people. We are free to live as God's people.*]

Does freedom suggest that we can do whatever we wish whenever we wish? Why? Why not? [*The Christian is not bound by rules and regulations. The Christian does not follow rules and regulations so as to win God's love. Christians are free to live as God's people.*]

How does Paul describe **the Law** in which Christians are to live?

What is the result of a failure to live in that **Law?** [*Mutual destruction. We destroy each other.*]

What are the "works of the flesh"?

What are the "fruits of the Spirit"?

☐ *Invite the small groups to share their discussions and conclusions with each other. Give opportunity for participants to question and challenge each other. Various terms within the passage may require additional description. It is critically important that the adult leader be able to identify for himself or herself and to share with the group contemporary examples of the various "works" and "fruits."*

☐ *Prepare a copy of the material on the facing page for each participant.*

☐ *It is not necessary that the participants should complete every item in the exercise. After an appropriate period of time, return to group discussion.*

"In the passage Paul asserts that the 'works of the flesh' lead to mutual destruction, that by them we destroy each other. As you have considered what you have written, would you agree with Paul? Why? Why not?"

"If the 'works of the flesh' result in mutual destruction, it is suggested that the 'fruits of the Spirit' build up our own lives, the lives of others, and our life together. As you consider what you have written, would you agree with that suggestion? Why? Why not?"

"As you consider the 'works of the flesh' and the 'fruits of the Spirit,' what is the freedom of Christian people?"

3. Jeremiah 9:23 and 24; Amos 5:21–24; Micah 6:6–8; Philippians 4:8 and 9. These four passages are cast in lofty and soaring language. They declare in magnificent and majestic terms what it is to be and do as God's people in the world. Their language can excite and challenge human imagination. Yet, at the same time, the language is ambiguous and nonspecific. Even after we have read the passages we do not have definitions of what is "righteousness in the earth," "justice rolling down like waters," "to do justice," or "honorable . . . pure . . . gracious." The ambiguity is part of the beauty of the language and also points us to a most critical and profound understanding. For example, what it is "to do justice" can never be defined beforehand. The people of God never have a detailed description of justice which can be met with precision or which can be followed at all times and in all situations. As God's pilgrim people in new seasons and circumstances we must discover anew what it is to do justice. And even if we fail, the demand of our God remains the same.

Bridge: We have discussed and explored the question, "What is required of me?" That question is not always easy to answer. We are not always sure what it is that we should do. We have discussed values and our decision-making. We want to study and discuss

Below are listed the "works of the flesh" and "fruits of the Spirit" as noted in Galatians 5:13–24. For each, you are to give a contemporary example. You may draw the example from your own experience, from the experience of another, or from some societal situation. Also, note briefly what you think was the result of that "work" or "fruit." [*The adult leader may need to give some examples so as to assist the participants in their work.*]

Works of Flesh	Example	Result
Immorality Impurity Licentiousness Idolatry Sorcery Enmity Strife Jealousy Anger Selfishness Dissension Party spirit Envy Drunkenness Carousing		
Fruits of Spirit		
Love Joy Peace Patience Kindness Goodness Faithfulness Gentleness Self-control		

four biblical passages, Jeremiah 9:23 and 24; Amos 5:21–24; Micah 6:6–8; and Philippians 4:8 and 9, which are responses to our question. Our task will be to describe those responses and to ask how they might inform our values and decision-making.

■ *Arrange small groups. Prepare the following questions in written form for the groups' use. Do not copy bracketed material.*

In Jeremiah 9:23 and 24, in what should one glory, or take satisfaction, or rejoice? According to this passage, what is it to know and understand the Lord? [*To practice kindness, justice, and righteousness is to know and understand the Lord.*]

In Amos 5:21–24, what is discounted as important or significant? [*Your feasts. Solemn assemblies. Burnt offerings and cereal offerings. The noise of songs.*]

According to Amos 5:21–24, what is the task of God's people? [*Let justice and righteousness roll down.*]

In Micah 6:6–8, several questions are asked. They ask what it is that one should bring to the Lord as an offering. How does the passage respond? [*To do justice. To love kindness. To walk humbly with God.*]

In Philippians 4:8 and 9, to what is the Christian to give his or her attention? About what qualities is the Christian to be concerned? [*Honorable. Just. Pure.*]

According to the passage, where has the Christian seen and heard these things? [*From another Christian.*]

Is there any common theme which runs throughout the four passages? [*Justice.*]

□ *Invite the small groups to share their discussions and findings with each other. Encourage the participants to ask and decide if the various contributions and conclusions offered reflect the content of the various passages. On the chalkboard or newsprint, list the conclusions which have the general agreement of the group.*

□ *The composite list produced by the total group will contain the majestic yet nonspecific language of the several passages. In producing the composite list, the participants may have expressed some displeasure with what they have read. They may have suggested that the passages don't tell them anything. They may have said that the passages do not help them very much. Such statements are to be taken seriously and can serve as the catalysts for continued discussion. In any event, we move the discussion in new directions. The following questions can be used in the total group.*

"Do you find these passages helpful or useful as you attempt to shape your values or make your decisions? Why? Why not? If yes, in what ways?" [*Encourage and challenge the participants to be as specific as possible.*]

"On the basis of the four passages, do you know what justice is? What is kindness? What is righteousness? What is it to be honorable? What is worthy of praise? Why? Why not? If yes, in what ways?" [*Encourage and challenge the participants to be as specific as possible. In most instances, the adolescents will be unable to articulate specifics flowing from the passages.*]

"Why are the passages so nonspecific in describing justice, righteousness, kindness, and honorableness? Did the writers of the passages not know what they were talking about?"

"Why do you think it is important that we should pay attention to these passages? Are there any useful clues for us in these passages?" [*Justice, kindness, righteousness, and graciousness cannot be described in any final fashion. The people of God are always in the process of determining and doing these things in new times and new circumstances, calling forth new ways of acting that we have never even thought of before. Justice, kindness, and righteousness cannot be reduced to rules and regulations.*]

"If these passages are appropriate interpretations of us as Christians, what challenges or demands are placed upon us?" [*In our times and circumstances, we have the task of determining—and doing—justice, kindness, and righteousness. We must ask what it is for us to do these things today. In striving to be Christian people, we must be involved in making judgments about these things.*]

"How might we get clues about doing justice, kindness, and righteousness?" [*How is it that God deals with us? As God deals with us, we are to deal with each other. When we talk together as Christians, and when we consider the needs of everyone in the world, we will receive clues from each other for doing justice, kindness, and righteousness.*]

"We may attempt to be faithful as God's people. Yet, we may act in injustice and in unrighteousness. What is to be said about us then?" [*We can be sure that God will forgive our failures. Even as forgiveness is proclaimed, the demand continues: do justice, do kindness, do righteousness.*]

☐ *Return the participants to small groups.*

"Select and discuss one of the following problems and issues in our society: racial discrimination; the poor; world hunger; the aging; the unemployed; abused children; or the arms race. What might justice, kindness, and righteousness require of us?"

☐   *In the total group, encourage the participants to describe their decision-making and to identify the various values which were influential in the discussion of a problem or an issue.*

"Do your conclusions reflect anything of the four passages? In what ways?"

4. Luke 6:27–36. This passage makes liberal use of the word "love." As a response to the question, "What is required of me?" the passage declares that we are to love. We are to love others, including our enemies. Let us note carefully how the passage speaks of "love." Love is not defined as some sentiment, feeling, or ideal. It is defined in terms of actions and behaviors. The passage presents expressions of love in action, expressions that reflect the times and circumstances in which the passage was written. We are not to ape them slavishly. But instead we are to translate them into new expressions for our times and circumstances. Verse 36 requires our special attention. We have been touched by the mercy of God. God has dealt with us in merciful ways, and therefore we know something of mercy. Because God has been merciful to us, we are to act in ways that are merciful.

Bridge: When we ask the question, "What is required of me?" we are asking several questions. What are the values or persons which will influence our lives? Who or what will give direction to our lives? How will we live out our lives in the world? What will inform our behaviors or actions? The biblical passage, Luke 6:27–36, claims to be one response to the questions for Christians. It makes frequent use of the word "love." For some, the word "love" suggests joy and excitement. For others, it suggests demands, foolishness, and weakness. We want to explore how this passage understands love. And if this passage is an appropriate expression of love for its particular times and circumstances, what does it say to us in our particular times and circumstances?

■   *Before moving directly to the passage, invite the young people to share and discuss their understandings of love. Give opportunity for them to ask questions of and discuss with each other.*

"How would you describe 'love'?"

"How important is 'love' in your life? Where and in what ways?"

"Do you think that 'love' is realistic expectation for our lives? Why? Why not?"

"Where and in what ways does 'love' influence and guide your life?"

■   *Arrange for small groups. Make available the following questions for the groups' use. Do not copy bracketed material.*

How does the passage in its entirety define "love"? [*Love is described in terms of action or behavior. Love is not described as a sentiment or feeling. Love is action, striving for the good of all.*]

Though the passage does not use the word "neighbor," how does it define that word? [*My neighbor includes my enemy—those who hate, curse, and abuse me. They need actions of love.*]

In vss. 27 and 28, why the insistence on loving enemies, doing good to those who hate us, and praying for those who abuse us? [*We are to seek the good of all people. We are to build up the lives of others. If we respond in hate and abuse, we will only add to destruction and meanness. We will destroy our own lives.*]

In vs. 29, the possibility of insult, hurt and injury are recognized. What is the expected response? [*Turn the cheek. Give your coat. Respond in practical expressions of love.*]

How would you describe the response of love in vss. 30 and 31? [*To respond in practical actions to those in need.*]

In vss. 32–35, there is a very specific concern addressed. Should love be exercised on the basis that we expect some reward from others by virtue of our loving actions? [*Love, if it is to be love, cannot expect or demand reward.*]

☐ *In the larger group, invite the participants to share their conclusions about the passage as well as their reactions to it. Give ample opportunity for discussion and challenge.*

"What are your reactions to the claims of the passage?"

"What problems do you have with the passage?"

"Are the expectations realistic? Unreasonable? Why? Why not?"

"Does this passage suggest that we are to be submissive to whatever anyone wishes to do to us? Do we have to put up with whatever others demand of us?" [*We are not to respond to hate with hate, to injury with injury, to insult with insult, or to need with unconcern. We are to act beyond those ways, seeking for practical expressions of love.*]

☐ *Attention of the participants should be focused on vs. 36.*

"In vs. 36, there is the declaration that we are to be merciful even as God is merciful to us. How would you describe God's mercy?" [*In Christ, God has called us to be the chosen people. Even though we sin, God loves us. Even though we may fail miserably as God's people, God does not retaliate. God does not strike out against us. God forgives us, continuing to call us the chosen people. God's loving action toward us does not cease.*]

■ *Prepare the following material so that each participant has a copy.*
  You may wish to add items.

At times the expectation of love seems to require too much of us.
At times we are afraid to risk actions of love. We often confine
our actions of love to a very narrow circle of persons, knowing
that they will reward us with what we consider their actions of
love. There are times when we are not certain about what love
expects of us. Below is a series of incomplete sentences which
you are to complete. As you do so, try to recall and respond to
specific instances in your experience, and try to be specific in
your responses.

1. When I have returned hate for hate the result has been
   _____.

2. When I have returned anger for anger the result has been
   _____.

3. When I have returned insult for insult the result has been
   _____.

4. When I have returned meanness for meanness the result has
   been _____.

5. When I have refused or failed to respond to the needs of others the result has been _____.

6. Some possible responses of love in the following situations
   might be:

   a. The build-up of weapons of war. _____
   _____

   b. The plight of the poor. _____
   _____

   c. Political and economic injustice. _____
   _____

   d. The victim of malicious gossip. _____
   _____

☐ *Invite the participants, as they are willing, to share and discuss*
  their responses with each other. Encourage them to identify and
  describe the values and understandings which inform and shape
  their responses. Encourage them to ask if their responses reflect the
  concerns of the passage.

·11
Am I my neighbor's keeper?

In the Genesis stories God asked Cain that haunting, accusing question, "Where is Abel your brother?" Strangely, it haunts and accuses us also. The continuing and arduous struggle for civil rights, the efforts to achieve appropriate social welfare programs, the protests against nuclear weapons, the struggle for women's rights, the human destruction resulting from widespread hunger, the efforts to protect and preserve the environment, the specter of the poor and homeless among us, and the tragedy of child abuse—all cry out to us, "Where are your brothers and sisters?"

Cain's response remains our question, "Am I my brother's keeper?" (Gen. 4:9). In subtle, acceptable, polite ways, our response is often a clear "No." Why should I support people who are too lazy to work? Why do people have children if they cannot support them? Should we not be prepared to wipe out our enemies before they wipe us out? Why should I get involved in other people's problems? If I don't look out for me and mine first, who will? Who am I to make judgments? Didn't Jesus say that the poor would always be with us?

There are those who cry out, "Yes. I am my neighbor's keeper!" With compassion they take for their own the burdens, sorrows, and tragedies of others. They dare to suffer with and for others. With whatever resources available they work for justice and the resolution of conflicts in the social order. How they are to proceed is not always clear. They dare take the risk of making errors in their struggles for others. The personal cost can be enormous. Yet, they live and work with a profound understanding that their lives are intimately bound up with the lives of their sisters and brothers, most of whom they do not even know.

God's question and Cain's response confronts us with a most perplexing human task. How do we take responsibility for ourselves, fulfilling it faithfully, while at the same time we take responsibility for our brothers and sisters, fulfilling it faithfully? We may live in a global village, but we are still learning to be that village. Responding to Cain's question we live between the "yes" and the "no." We are still learning to say "yes."

Developing Concern for Others

Adolescents have the possibility of developing a broad, deep concern for others. This is not to say that children have no such concern. The concern for others during childhood is necessarily limited by cognitive, affective, and social abilities. Adolescents have the opportunity for developing and achieving a more expansive, inclusive, and profound care for others than is possible for children. The opportunity does not fulfill itself automatically. It must be acknowledged, accepted, and engaged. And in so doing, adolescents encounter two major tasks.

First, adolescents need to develop continually the ability to take account of other people's thinking and feelings and to learn to assess, at least somewhat accurately, the thoughts and feelings of others. They need to sharpen the ability to differentiate with clarity between what they think and feel and what others think and feel. They must move beyond reliance on stereotypic images of others, images which are not only insufficient but are destructive of human relationships. Adolescents must ask and achieve answers to several questions. What is the thinking and the feelings of the other person? Why does that person think and feel in a particular way? What things have influenced that person's thinking and feeling? In what ways is that thinking and feeling important to the person? Working with such questions, adolescents can achieve a new understanding of others. Understanding does not require agreement, but it does enable one to respond to another in useful, helpful, caring ways.

Adolescents are frequently bound by a peculiar problem, "adolescent egocentrism." They often play to "an imaginary audience," an audience composed of all those others. Adolescents can easily assume that the imaginary audience is concerned about what they are concerned. They can easily assume that the audience is as concerned about their appearance, clothes, and problems as they are. They tend to believe that what they think and feel about themselves is what the audience thinks and feels about them. Bound in such a situation, adolescents can become "wrapped up" in themselves and extraordinarily concerned about their behaviors, feelings, ideas, wants, ideals, and thinking. Their ability to respond in care and concern for others is greatly blunted. Until movement out of that egocentrism is achieved, they are greatly restricted in their ability to act significantly in concern for others.

Second, and related to the first, adolescents need to increase their ability to imagine, to discern the plight or circumstances of another's life. The task requires that one be able to set himself or herself in the life of another, to see life from the other's perspective, to imagine how another puts life together, and to enter into the joys, expectations, disappointments, and burdens of another. It requires the same activity with reference to groups and segments of society. One may try to imagine, but it takes a sensitive and sharp imagination to locate oneself in the life of another. Imagination can offer, at least, glimpses of human life in its complexity and multiplicity. And it is in adolescence that imagination can be called forth in excitement and adventure. At the same time, adolescents need to learn the art of comparing the plight or situation of another with theirs, asking about the instruction and demands that the comparison gives to them.

Lectures on altruism and emotional appeals for doing good to others may result in some desired results temporarily. By attempting to create guilt we can con others into doing "good deeds" for others. But if we hope for a people who live and work with a deep and abiding love and concern for others, such efforts will not suffice. Adolescents need those experiences which will assist them to imagine, explore, and discern the thinking and feelings of others, to appreciate the life-perspective of others, and to enter into the lives of others. And so they may discover for themselves what it is to live in the human community, a community in which the lives of all its inhabitants are intimately bound together and a community in which all carry responsibility for each other.

Adolescents Responding to the Question

In this section exercises and activities, designed to engage adolescents in the question "Am I my neighbor's keeper?" are offered. They encourage the participants to imagine or discern the thinking and feelings of others and to imagine the circumstances of others. Also, they ask adolescents to put themselves "in the place" of another and to look at life from the perspective of another. The exercises and activities also ask the participants to consider their responsibility for the concern and care of others.

1. Caring for Friends. Learning to respond in care and compassion for others may well begin with those most immediate to us. If we cannot or will not act in love and concern for those most near us, it is doubtful that we will act in significant concern for those removed from us.

■ *Prepare the following chart in a printed form. You may wish to make additions or deletions.*

If you discover that one of your friends was engaging in one of the following behaviors, what would you do? Indicate your responses on the chart.

	Nothing	*Inform a teacher*	*Inform his/her parents*	*Talk with my parents*	*Talk with friend*	*Other?*
Cheating on tests						
Smoking cigarettes						
Shoplifting						
Lying about someone						
Using drugs						
Sexually active						
Selling drugs						
Getting drunk						
Reckless driving						
Lying to parents						

□ *To get a composite picture of the group's responses, replicate the chart on the chalkboard and tabulate each participant's responses in the appropriate blocks. A diversity of responses can be expected, and that diversity can be the occasion for discussion between the participants. Encourage them to ask questions of each other, to challenge each other, and to discuss more fully their responses.*

☐ *Focusing on one behavior at a time, invite the participants to discuss their responses.*

"Some of you have indicated that you would do nothing. Why?" [*Responses may be varied: "It's none of my business." "What he/she is doing is not all that bad." "I don't see any reason to get upset about that. Everybody's doing it." "If there is any harm, he/she is only hurting himself/herself."*]

"How might the behavior be harmful to your friend? If you would do nothing, does your 'nothing' say that you don't care? Why? Why not?"

"If you do nothing, do you add to the hurt of your friend?"

"How would you show concern and care for your friend?"

"Would your 'nothing' be harmful to your friend? How does your friend's behavior cause you to feel? Why do you think your friend engages in that behavior?"

"Some of you indicated that you would talk to your friend. What would you say?"

"What would you want your friend to do? Why?"

"Would you talk to your friend even if you thought he/she would become angry? At the risk of losing the friendship? Why?"

"Why would you inform a teacher? His/her parents? Talk to your parents?"

"Some of you indicate *other*. What would you do? Why?"

☐ *In such an exercise, the participants may want to argue the relative degree of "wrongness" of each behavior. The degree of "wrongness" is not the concern of the exercise.*

"Regardless of the degree of 'wrongness' which you attribute to the behaviors, do you have the responsibility to protect your friend from the harm his/her behavior may cause?"

"Do you have a right to make judgments of a friend's behaviors? Why? Why not?"

"If you do not make judgments and do not challenge his/her behavior, are you contributing to the possible hurt or harm of your friend?"

2. Endangering Others. Adolescents can recognize some clear possibilities by which they may endanger the physical welfare of others. Yet, there is the need to recognize that increasing harm may not always be limited to the physical. To be a brother's or sister's keeper in regard to the physical involves much more.

■ *Using the chalkboard or newsprint, invite the group to make a list of ways that we may endanger the lives of others. Normally the list will include obvious dangers to the physical well-being of others. Use the list for an initial discussion.*

"Has your life ever been endangered in any of these ways? If so, what were your feelings and reactions? What actions have you taken to protect yourself from persons who would endanger you?"

"How did you regard the person(s) who endangered your life?"

"Do we have a right to endanger the lives of others? Why? Why not?"

■ *For the second part of the activity, prepare printed copies of the following material.*

Here is a list of ways by which we may endanger the lives of others. Using the chart below, indicate how serious you consider each to be.

	Very much	Much	A little	Not at all
Encouraging a person to use drugs				
Child abuse				
Spreading rumors about a person				
Teenagers engaging in sex				
Racial slurs				
Denying food stamps to a needy family				
Driving under the influence of alcohol				
Ridiculing another's clothes				
Snubbing another person				
Defying parents' wishes				
Laughing at a person's body				

These items include but move beyond dangers to physical well-being. They include ways in which we may endanger the feelings of others and their sense of worth and value. They include ways in which we may endanger another's reputation. The exercise can assist adolescents to achieve a larger understanding of what it is to endanger another person.

☐ *Encourage the participants to discuss their rankings and the factors contributing to the rankings.*

"Have you ever been hurt or harmed by such actions on the part of others? How did you regard or feel about those persons who acted in such ways?"

"If we behave toward people in these ways, what are we saying about them? About our regard for them? About our concern for them?"

"What are we saying about ourselves?"

"What happens to our relationship with a person whom we have hurt or endangered?"

"Do we have a right to hurt or endanger anyone in any fashion? Why? Why not?"

"For what reasons would we hurt someone knowingly? How do we feel and think of ourselves when we have hurt or endangered someone unknowingly?"

"When we have hurt or endangered someone, what are we to do?"

"Who suffers when we hurt or endanger another? Do we? In what ways?"

3. For Myself and for Others. The Jewish scholar Hillel once wrote, "If I am not for myself, then who is for me? If I am only for myself, what am I? If not now, when?"[1]

■ *Have the participants, in small groups, discuss the quote.*

"What do you understand Hillel to be saying about self? Others? For Hillel, what do you think is the result of being 'only for myself'?"

☐ *Following the small group discussion, invite each participant to make a collage or finger paint which would give some expression to his or her understanding of the quote. Encourage each to discuss his or her collage or finger paint.*

"In what ways must you be for yourself? Can you be for yourself without being selfish? In what ways are you, and you alone, responsible for yourself?"

"If one is only for himself/herself, is that person human? Why? Why not?"

"What is it to be both 'for myself' and 'for others'? How can that be?"

4. A Visit with a Member of MADD (Mothers Against Drunk Driving).
Acting in care and concern for others is not always an individual matter. Frequently, concerned persons must join together so as to act lov-
ingly and responsibly. There are many organizations in most
communities which do act in a positive response to the question, "Am
I my brother's or sister's keeper?" Big Brother or Big Sister organizations, Alcoholics Anonymous, groups concerned for the aging, advocate
groups are but a few. Representatives from such groups could assist in
increasing the sensitivity of adolescents to the question under
consideration.

■   *Invite a member of the MADD organization to a session with the
    adolescents. The guest would describe the work of the organization.
    Help the adolescents to move beyond information about the orga-
    nization so as to explore the concerns and values motivating the
    guest. A number of questions can be put to the guest.*

    "What first sparked your interest in the MADD organization?"

    "You are concerned for the persons who may be hurt or killed by
    drunk drivers, but do you have any concern for drunk drivers?"

    "What has your participation in the organization cost you in terms
    of money, time, and energy? How do you 'justify' that cost?"

    "Have you experienced ridicule or sneers because of your partici-
    pation? If so, what has been your reaction?"

    "Aren't you trying to change the lives of other people? What right
    do you have to do that?"

5. Responding to Others. Adolescents have opportunity to respond in
care, respect, and assistance toward others. They need assistance in
identifying in specific terms what it might be to be their neighbor's
keeper.

■   *Prepare the material on the following page in a printed form so that
    each participant has a copy.*

☐   *Invite the participants to share their responses as they are willing.
    Give opportunity for questions and discussion.*

    "Are there risks in being the 'keeper'? Are the risks worthwhile?
    Why? Why not?"

    "If we refuse or fail to take the risk of being the 'keeper,' who have
    we become?"

Assuming that we are our neighbors' keepers, what might the following situations expect of us? How do we be and do as that keeper?	
Situation	What might it be to act as the "keeper"?
You hear malicious gossip about another.	
A friend who gets drunk at a party wants to drive his/her car home.	
Your friends make racial slurs.	
An elderly neighbor is no longer able to take care of his/her yard, chores, etc.	
An individual is unable to attend a school function because of the lack of money.	
You know of neighbors who abuse their child.	
A parent of your friend is an alcoholic.	
There is a classmate who is physically unattractive and without friends.	
You have a friend who refuses to register for the draft.	
You have a friend who cheats at school.	
A person who is not your friend cheats in school.	
Your friend lies to his/her parents about what he/she does and about where he/she has been.	

See exercise on facing page.

1. Genesis 4:1–16 and 1 John 3:11–18; 4:20 and 21. These three passages are significant responses to the question, "Am I my brother's/sister's keeper?" The first passage, the familiar story of Cain and Abel, contains a number of elements which could command attention. Do Cain and Abel represent two different societies? Why was not Cain's offering acceptable to God? Who were those people of whom Cain was afraid? In any event, we want to give attention to the story's response to the question. The first passage from 1 John uses the Cain and Abel story and gives an interpretation of it. At the same time, the passage gives two specific responses to the question before us. The third passage makes a most profound response. It intimately binds together "love of God" and "love of others," declaring that to love God is to love others also.

Bridge: As we have explored the question, "Am I my brother's/sister's keeper?" we have recognized that many different responses can be given to it. When we deal with this question, there is a major problem that we encounter. Assuming that the answer to the question is "Yes," how do we be the "keeper"? What is required of us? What is involved in being our neighbor's keeper? We want to consider three biblical passages (Genesis 4:1–16 and 1 John 3:11–18; 4:20 and 21) which offer a response to the first question and may offer some clues as we attempt to solve the problem.

■ *Arrange for small groups. Each group will work with the three passages and will share findings in the total group setting. As the adolescents will be working with the three passages, the set of questions for guiding study and discussion should be prepared in a written form.*

"In Genesis 4:1–16, what is the relationship between the two brothers?" [*Cain is angry. Cain's offering was not "regarded" by God. There is the suggestion that Cain had not "done well." Cain's anger is directed toward his brother.*]

"God asks Cain, 'Where is Abel your brother?' What is Cain's response?" [*Cain claims that he does not know. He lied. He asked God a question.*]

"What is God's answer to Cain's question?" [*The story does not answer, "Yes, you are." Cain's action of killing his brother and of lying is called into judgment. The consequences of the actions constitute the response. The land will not yield well for Cain. Cain becomes a fugitive and a wanderer. He is driven from the land, from his home.*]

"Cain was not his brother's keeper. Rather, he killed his brother. What did Cain lose?" [*Cain loses something of his own life. When he took the life of his brother, he "killed" something of his own life.*

He killed the one who could enrich his own life. Failing to be his brother's keeper, he failed to be his own keeper.]

"In 1 John 3:11–18, what is the immediate response to the question, 'Am I my brother's/sister's keeper?'"

"How does the writer of 1 John describe Cain's action? Does 1 John add anything to the Cain and Abel story?" [*We should love one another. Cain was of "the evil one," and he killed his brother because his actions were evil and his brother's were good.*]

"How does this passage define 'murder'? What is the importance of the definition?" [*In vs. 15 "murder" is defined as "hate." "Hate" is a way of killing someone. There is the suggestion that hate robs "the hater" of life.*]

"The passage takes an interesting twist, declaring that as Jesus laid down his life we are to lay down our lives for others. What do you understand this declaration to be asking?"

"What distinction is being made between 'love in word or speech' and 'love in deed and truth'? What is the significance of that distinction?" [*We may speak a word of love. We may declare love for another. Yet, love is to be expressed in deeds, in action.*]

"In 1 John 4:20 and 21, what is the response to the question, 'Am I my sister's/brother's keeper?'" [*We are to love our sisters and brothers. It is in loving that we are "keepers."*]

"Very blunt language is used in the passage. The label 'liar' is used. Why is the writer able to use such language?"

"In what way is the 'love of God' and 'the love of others' the same? Are they the same?" [*God has so chosen to be bound to the lives of persons so that what we do to others we do to God.*]

☐ *Invite the small groups to share their findings in the total group. Work for a set of statements concerning the passages and with which the group generally agrees to be reflective of the passages. Assist the group to "translate" the passages and findings into contemporary terms.*

"In 1 John 3:11–19, the writer defines 'murder' as 'hate.' 'Hate' is killing someone. What are some other ways that we might define 'murder'? What ways might we 'take away' another person's life?" [*Ridicule. Malicious remarks. Ignoring and belittling others. Unconcern. Abusing another's body. Failing to respond to the needs of another. Failing to call destructive behaviors into judgment. Urging or encouraging others to do things which may be harmful.*]

"What would it be to love 'in deed and truth'?" [*To speak well of another. To call into judgment those who ridicule or belittle others. To protect others' bodies against abuse. To share in the sorrow of others. To join groups which are working to demonstrate love and' concern for others. To give of our time, energy, and other resources to people in need. To protect another's name and reputation.*]

"When we love 'in deed and truth' what are we giving to others?" [*We share ourselves. We share our lives. We enrich the lives of others. We "give" them life.*]

"When we do not love 'in deed and truth' what happens to us? What happened to Cain?" [*We lose something of our own lives. We do not receive the life that others share with us. We become concerned about ourselves only.*]

"Do you agree that we cannot love God if we do not love others? Why? Why not?"

"Can we be 'human' if we do not love others? Why? Why not?" [*God has created us to live in relationships with others. We can only be "human" as we live in relationships with others. At best, part of what it is to be "human" is to act in love and concern for others, to be their "keepers." When we are concerned only about ourselves, we are not human.*]

2. Matthew 18:5 and 6, 15–17, 21 and 22, 23–35. These four passages are set within the context of Jesus' reply to a question of the disciples, "Who is the greatest in the kingdom of heaven?" (The parallel passage of Luke 9:46 suggests that the disciples had been arguing among themselves about the answer to the question.) Jesus, in the response, did not name persons but spoke of service and care for others. "The greatest" were described in terms of servanthood and caring.

Bridge: In our discussion of "Am I my brother's/sister's keeper?" we have heard a number of responses given to the question: the unqualified yes; the yes, but . . . ; and the unqualified no. In the passages that we will study (Matthew 18:5–6, 15–17, 21–22, 23–35) we will encounter several responses to the question. These responses are part of a larger response which Matthew has Jesus making to the question, "Who is the greatest in the kingdom of heaven?" Some of us may not be interested in the disciples' question. Nevertheless, as you study and discuss the passage, note how Jesus defines "greatness," and ask if the definitions are responses to our question.

■ *Have the participants divide into two groups. To one assign Matthew 18:5–6, and 15–17; to the other, Matthew 18:21–22, and 23–35. Questions will focus attention and give directions.*

"As you study and discuss ask, 'How do these passages define "greatness"?'"

Engaging and Interpreting the Bible

The biblical passages in this section, with the accompanying exercises, constantly ask the question, "Am I my brother's/sister's keeper?" The response of the biblical passages to this question is cast in terms of who we are, God's people, and in terms of what it is to love God. In this material emphasis is given to life in community. There is a subtle question present throughout: can I be human if I refuse to be my sister's or brother's keeper?

"Is there a common theme for the two passages?"

"Are these passages responses to our question about being my brother's/sister's keeper?"

"In what ways do you see the concerns of these passages being expressed in your life?"

□ *In the total group, have each smaller group read aloud its assigned passages and then share the results of its study and discussions. The findings should be noted on the chalkboard or newsprint. Using the findings, the group should be encouraged to develop a collective statement concerning the passage as it responds to the question, "Am I my brother's/sister's keeper?"*

"How do you judge these passages to respond to the question? What about the passages would lead you to make the judgment?"

"Is there a common theme or underlying theme connecting these passages?" [*All four discuss person's actions toward others. All four describe actions of caring and serving.*]

"What is the claim or demand of Matthew 18:5 and 6?" [*We are not to cause anyone to do something which may cause him/her to sin. We are not to do anything to entice or encourage anyone to sin.*]

"What is the claim or demand of Matthew 18:15–17?" [*We are to call our brothers and sisters into judgment.*] "We may not like to make judgments on others. But if we do not make a judgment when it is clearly necessary, what is the result of our failure?" [*We are not caring for them. We encourage them in their actions.*]

"What is the claim or demand of Matthew 18:21 and 22?" [*Forgiveness cannot be limited. We are to forgive and proclaim forgiveness without counting the number of times. Forgiveness restores relationships.*]

"What is the claim or demand of Matthew 18:23–35?" [*We have been forgiven. As God has declared full forgiveness to us, we are to declare our forgiveness to each other.*]

"Now, what is the response of these passages to the question, 'Am I my brother's/sister's keeper?'"

☐   *Encourage the adolescents to translate the responses of the passages and their own responses to them to their ordinary life.*

"Can you describe some ways by which we may encourage others, either deliberately or unintentionally, to sin?" [*Encourage another to use drugs or other harmful substances. Ask others to do certain things to prove that they like or love us. Ask others to do something they believe to be wrong or inappropriate. Encourage others by praising their breaking of rules and laws and "getting away with it." Encourage anything that may harm the body or the person.*]

"When we encourage such things, can we say that we are caring for others? Does our encouragement suggest that we do not care? Do we care for each other when we encourage such things? Why? Why not?"

"Are you willing to call others into judgment not only when they hurt you but when they hurt others? Why? Why not?"

"Have you ever called a friend into judgment? What were the results?"

"If we do not call another into judgment, can that person assume that we approve of his/her actions? If we say, 'Well, he/she is only hurting himself/herself,' what does that say about our care?"

"Can you describe various positions or parts of our society which we should call into judgment?" [*Concerns for the poor and oppressed. Build-up of war materials. Educational system. Treatment of minorities.*]

"Can we describe situations in which we have refused to be forgiving? Why do we act in unforgiving ways?"

"Are there limits to our forgiveness? If so, who sets those limits?"

"What is the result of our refusals to forgive?" [*We remain angry. Our relationship with others is destroyed.*]

"If the claims or demands of these passages are true, then what do they claim or demand of us?" [*We are God's people. We are our brother's/sister's keepers.*] "Can you describe from within your own life how those claims and demands can be expressed in our lives?"

3. Ephesians 4:25–5:2. The answer to the question, "Am I my neighbor's keeper?" is largely dependent upon who we are. This passage is addressed to Christians, to a community of God's people. It is a community of God's people whose lives are bound to each other and who are responsible to and for each other. This passage is not telling the Ephesians how to earn God's love or how to gain eternal life. Those are gifts that God gives. The passage is not concerned only with individual morality. It gives clues to Christians as they live in both the church and world communities. It calls Christians to *do* who they *are*. It calls them to live in community, community in which each is responsible to and for each other.

Bridge: We have been exploring the question, "Am I my brother's/sister's keeper?" It can be a bothersome question. The response "yes" can appear to make heavy demands upon us. What happens to concern and regard for ourselves? Can others make any demands upon us that they wish? Even when we say, "Yes," we are not always certain what it is to be that "keeper." We want to study and discuss a biblical passage, Ephesians 4:25—5:2, which is one response to our question. It was addressed to Christians—to us.

■ *Have the participants work in pairs. Three questions will guide their study and discussion.*

"What is the passage's response to the question, 'Am I my brother's/sister's keeper?'"

"What are the details of that response?"

"Why would the writer of the passage make special mention of these details? In what ways are they critical or important for the writer?" [*On the one hand, the writer points to actions which destroy life together, thus destroying an individual's life as well as the life of others. On the other hand, the writer points to actions which build up life together, thus enriching one's own life and the life of others.*]

☐ *After a period of study and discussion, invite each pair-group to share its responses with the total group. Using the chalkboard or newsprint, list the contributions. Give opportunity for participants to discuss, ask questions, and challenge. Do the responses reflect the passage appropriately?*

• Do not lie; speak the truth to each other.

• Be angry; don't let anger be an occasion for sin.

• Do not steal; do honest labor; contribute to those in need.

• No evil talk; speak what will be helpful to others.

• No bitterness; wrath, slander, or malice; be kind, tenderhearted, and forgiving.

• Imitate God; walk in love.

Bridge: We identified critical elements in the passage. We have asked why the writer of the passage gives importance to the various items. Now, let us translate the concerns of the passage into our contemporary life situation, asking how those concerns are related to the question, "Am I my brother's/sister's keeper?" Are those concerns of particular importance for us?

■   *The following concerns and questions can be discussed in the total group or in small groups. If small groups are used, assign two or three issues to each for consideration. Small groups should report to the total group, in which additional discussion will take place.*

"Why do you think that the passage gives attention to lying?" [*In life together, we must depend upon each other. We must be able to depend upon and trust the words of each other. Lying destroys trust. Lying destroys life together.*]

"When we lie to our parents, friends, or to the person closest to us in a love relationship, what are the results?" [*We are persons who cannot be trusted. When we lie we destroy our relationships with others. We misguide them. We leave them under wrong impressions. We harm the people to whom we lie. Whatever the relationship, it is built on falsehood. We have abused the other person.*]

"Is cheating on an examination a form of lying?"

"We may tell lies to another, and he or she will never know the difference. What's so bad about that?" [*Even if another never discovers our lies, we are still liars. We know that the relationship is built on a lie. We abuse the other person.*]

"Is it ever appropriate to be angry? How might anger harm both us and others?" [*There are times when we ought to be angry and to give expression to that anger. Injustice, meanness, and ridicule should cause anger. If we harbor anger toward another, we become hostile and vengeful. We become uncooperative and create strife. We can become mean people. Our anger can prompt us to do mean things toward others. It destroys our life together.*]

"When you harbor anger toward your parents or friends, what happens to you? What happens to your relationship with them?"

"How would you define 'stealing'? Could we define 'stealing' in ways other than referring to physical objects?"

"What are the results of 'evil talk' about others? What are the results when we ridicule and slander another?" [*We are destroying them. Using rather severe language, we can say that we are "murdering" them. We attempt to take away their life.*]

"Why the warning concerning bitterness and malice?" [*Bitterness and ill-feelings set us against one another. They disrupt our life together. They encourage meanness and strife.*]

"At the end of the passage, we are called to be imitators of God. What is it to be imitators of God?" [*We are to deal with each other as God deals with us. God in Christ is kind, tender-hearted, and forgiving—making us God's people in community and giving us life.*]

"While the passage points to actions and behaviors which destroy community and which harm others, it points us to behaviors which build community and enrich the lives of others. In very specific ways, how would you describe our opportunities for: speaking the truth with our neighbor; preventing our anger from becoming destructive to others; contributing to those in need; speaking helpful words to others; and being forgiving? What are the results of such behaviors?" [*Building up the community. Caring for others. Enriching the lives of others.*]

"Are these the behaviors and actions with which God has dealt with us?"

4. Leviticus 19:9–18. This passage is a resounding "yes" to the question, "Am I my neighbor's keeper?" In Leviticus 9:2, there is the declaration, "You shall be holy; for I the Lord your God am holy." Let us note carefully what the declaration is saying. It does not assert, "If you do this or that, then you will be holy." Rather, it declares, "Because I the Lord am holy, and you are my people, you will be holy." The passage for study contains several descriptions of what it is to be a holy people. Such is described in terms of actions that are done toward others. The descriptions reflect the times, circumstances, and situations in which the passage was written. It is appropriate that we should describe ourselves as a holy people. God in Christ has claimed us. We are God's people. And God's people in their particular times, circumstances, and situations are to discern what it is to be and do as a holy people, acting and behaving toward others.

Bridge: We have been exploring the question, "Am I my neighbor's keeper?" Even when we answer, "Yes," we have no rule books to which we can turn, rule books describing in detail what we are to do in every circumstance. In reality, sometimes we are not sure about what to do. We may have some general hints and understandings. Yet, in new circumstances and situations we must give shape to our actions and behaviors toward others. The passage that we will study and discuss, Leviticus 19:9–18, offers several responses to our question. We want to examine those responses.

■ *Arrange small groups. Make available the following questions. Do not copy bracketed material.*

What is the response of vss. 9 and 10 to our question?
[*Leave food for the poor and sojourner. Feed the hungry.*]

What is the response of vs. 11 to our question?
[*Do not steal. Do not deal falsely with others. Do not lie.*]

What is the response of vs. 13?
[*Do not oppress. Do not rob.*]

What is the response of vs. 14?
[*Do not curse the blind. Do not put a stumbling block for the blind. Do not curse or ridicule another's body.*]

What is the response of vs. 15?
[*No injustice in judgment. Treat all people equally.*]

What is the response of vs. 16?
[*Do not slander. Do not jeopardize another's life.*]

What is the response of vs. 17?
[*Do not hate another.*]

What is the response of vs. 18?
[*Take no vengeance. Hold no grudge. Love your neighbor as yourself.*]

Why do you think that the writer of this passage was so concerned about these matters?
[*Many of our actions and behaviors "rob" others of their life. Many of our actions and behaviors destroy our lives with others and our life together.*]

☐ *Using the chalkboard or newsprint, invite the group to produce the passage's responses to the question. Opportunity should be given for questions and discussion of the responses.*

"Look again at the passage and notice that at the end of each set of responses there is the statement, 'I am the Lord your God.' Why do you think that the statement is repeated several times?"

"Consider Leviticus 19:2. What do you understand that verse to be saying?" [*It does not say that if we do such and such, then we will be holy. It claims that our God is holy. We are God's people, and we will be holy. We will do as a holy people. Leviticus 19:9–18 is one expression of what it is to be and do "holy." That expression declares that we are our brother's and sister's keeper, to protect and to enrich their lives.*]

■ *Prepare the following material so that each participant has a copy.*

The following is a statement that can be made of Christians. "We are a holy people. We are not holy because we are 'better' than others or 'more good' than others or because we have done 'more good things' than others. We are God's people. We belong to the holy God. God calls us hcly, and we are to be holy. Being God's holy people, we are to live and do as God's holy people. To do as that holy people we will have active concern for others." If this is an appropriate statement concerning you and me, how might we translate the concerns of our passage into contemporary actions and behaviors? What might be some contemporary responses of God's holy people? The passage gave a number of responses in the negative. Attempt to give your responses in terms of positive actions and behaviors. Be as specific as possible.

Responses of the passage	*My contemporary responses*
Leave food for the poor	
Do not steal	
Do not deal falsely with others	
Do not lie	
Do not oppress	
Do not curse the blind	
Treat the poor and great alike	
Do not slander	
Do not stand against the life of your neighbor	
Do not hate	
Take no vengeance	
Hold no grudge	
Love your neighbor as yourself	

□ *Invite the participants to share and discuss their responses with each other.*

5. Romans 13:8–10; Exodus 20:2–17. These two passages are direct responses to the question, "Am I my neighbor's keeper?" In the Romans passage the Apostle Paul asserts that we do "owe" something to others. He begins to define love by citing several of the Ten Commandments and finally sums up all commandments with the sentence, "You shall love your neighbor as yourself." He adds that love does no wrong to another. The Exodus passage is one account of the Ten Commandments. The material in vss. 12–17 is one description of how persons are to deal with each other. Concerning both passages it is important to note to whom they were addressed. The first was written to Christians at Rome. The second was addressed to a people who had been brought out of the land of Egypt, out of the house of bondage. Both were addressed to God's people. Note carefully the direction of these passages. They do not claim, "If you do not do this or that, then you will be my people." Rather, they declare, "Because you are my people and I am your God, you will not do these things. You will not wrong your neighbor."

Bridge: We have been discussing the question, "Am I my neighbor's keeper?" There are other questions related to this one. "If I fail or refuse to be that keeper, what are the results? Whose life do we harm?" "What is it for us to be that keeper?" "How can we enrich the lives of others and our lives together?" "How are we to arrange our lives together so that we can support each other?" We want to study and discuss two passages which make a clear response to our first question and which also offer clues for responses to the other questions. These passages are Romans 13:8–10 and Exodus 20:2–17. If the claims set forth in these passages are true and appropriate, what do they say about us as we live with each other?

■ *Arrange small groups. Assign both passages. Provide the groups with the questions boxed on the next page. Do not copy bracketed material.*

☐ *Invite the participants to share and discuss their responses and conclusions with each other. Encourage them to ask questions of and to challenge each other. Many responses will be cast in terms of "negatives," in terms of what one is not to do. The "negatives," familiar to many adolescents, may not be regarded as "anything new." Some may encounter no difficulty with the "negatives," asserting that they do not do these things anyway.*

"Do you regard these various claims as very demanding? Why? Why not?"

To whom are the passages addressed?

In the Romans passage, what is it that God's people owe to others? How does Paul describe what is owed?

In Exodus 20:12–17, what is it that God's people owe to others? How does the passage describe what is owed?

Which of the following two statements do you think reflects best the claims of the passage? "If you do not do this or that, then God will love you." "Because you are my people and I am your God, you will not do these things." On what basis do you make your choice?

Is there a significant distinction between the two statements?

Why should we be concerned at all about others? [*We are created to live in community. We are human only as we live in community. The quality of our life together determines the quality of our individual lives. Those "others" are God's creation, loved by God. To love God is to love God's creation.*]

How would you express the various commandments in contemporary terms?

According to the passages, what do we owe to each other?

See exercise on facing page.

"Do you regard yourselves to be complying with or fulfilling these claims?"

"Have you gained any new insight or understanding from your study and discussion of the passages?"

Bridge: In these passages we are told primarily what not to do. The passages are expressed primarily in negative terms. We want to consider how we might express these claims or concerns in positive terms or positive actions. For example, if we are not to kill, can this be expressed in some positive way? There are many ways that we may "kill" others. We can do so by hatred, ridicule, ignoring another, and spreading rumor. If we are not to kill, to take away life, are we not called to give life, to enrich the lives of others? What can be done to enrich the lives of others? In the following exercise, we will attempt to translate actions stated in negative terms into positive actions, actions which will protect and add to the lives of others.

■ *Prepare the following material in some printed form so that each participant has a copy.*

The passages which we have studied cast many claims in negative terms. Here we want to translate these into positive terms and actions. For example, the demand is "You will not commit adultery." What positive actions might we take with reference to this concern? One response might be, "To protect another's body from sexual abuse."

If we are not to . . . ,	*We can act positively by . . .*
Kill	
Commit adultery	
Steal	
Bear false witness	
Covet	
Do wrong	

☐ *Invite the participants to share and discuss their responses. Afford opportunity for questions and challenges.*

"How do your responses answer the question, 'Am I my neighbor's keeper?'"

"Was this a difficult exercise? Why? Why not?" [*It is often easier to say what we are not to do, than it is to say what we should do.*]

epilogue

As we come to the end of this book we want to call attention to what we hope has been obvious throughout the presentation. No final answers are given to any of the issues or questions raised in the discussion. This is so because we are convinced that there are no final answers that can be given. The issues faced here are constantly with us and need constant attention.

Our concern throughout has been to take seriously the adolescents with whom we live, work, and serve. This involves taking them seriously as human beings with different abilities, skills, and needs. The adolescent is a vital and important person. At the same time we have endeavored to take seriously the Bible. We are convinced that the biblical tradition is an essential and vital ingredient in the Christian faith and life. The Bible can help illumine and interpret the lives of Christian people as they grow and mature in the faith. The process of interpretation has also been attended to with seriousness since it is an essential and necessary ingredient in the whole task of helping adolescents use the Bible.

Nowhere do we make the claim that what is proposed and explicated here is an easy task. Indeed, our experience leads us to the conviction that it is a demanding and difficult task. We are convinced that what we have set forth in this book is an important and vital process in helping adolescents grow and mature as Christian people and in helping our youth to gain skills and facility in interpreting the Scriptures and their lives in light of the Scriptures.

Our hope is that your engagement with adolescents in their using the Bible will be an exciting and stimulating opportunity for yourself and for them.

notes

CHAPTER 1
1. H. Edward Everding, Jr., "A Hermeneutical Approach to Educational Theory" in *Foundations for Christian Education in an Era of Change*, ed. Marvin J. Taylor (Nashville: Abingdon, 1976), p. 42.

CHAPTER 2
1. For another statement of the questions expressed here, see: Foster R. McCurley, Jr. and John Reumann, *Word and Witness: Understanding the Bible I* (Philadelphia: Division for Parish Services, Lutheran Church in America, 1980), pp. 55–57.

CHAPTER 3
1. Richard M. Lerner and Graham B. Spanier, *Adolescent Development: A Life-Span Perspective* (New York: McGraw-Hill, 1980), p. 41.
2. Jeanette M. Gallagher and Richard S. Mansfield, "Cognitive Development in Adolescence" in *Understanding Adolescence: Current Development in Adolescent Psychology* (4th edition), ed. J. F. Adams (Boston: Allyn and Bacon, Inc.), p. 136.
3. Edwin Arthur Peel, *The Nature of Adolescent Judgment* (New York: John Wiley and Sons, 1971), p. 35.
4. Ibid., p. 36.
5. James E. Marcia, "Identity Development in Adolescence," in *Handbook of Adolescent Psychology*, ed. Joseph Adelson (New York: John Wiley and Sons, 1980), pp. 159–187.
6. "Hedonistic Sex, Mutual Affection Sex and Bible Sex" (A Report), *Religious Education*, 65, 2 (March–April 1970), pp. 170f.
7. For a fuller discussion, see: Patricia Miller and William Simon, "The Development of Sexuality in Adolescence," in *Handbook of Adolescent Psychology*, ed. Joseph Adelson (New York: John Wiley and Sons, 1980), pp. 383–407.

8. Ann R. Held, "Formation of Conscience and Sexual Stereotypes," *The Living Light*, 15, 2 (Summer 1978), p. 218.
9. For a fuller discussion, see: Norman T. Feather, "Values in Adolescence" in *Handbook of Adolescent Psychology*, ed. Joseph Adelson (New York: John Wiley and Sons, 1980), pp. 247–294.
10. For a fuller discussion, see: Martin L. Hoffman, "Moral Development in Adolescence" in *Handbook of Adolescent Psychology*, ed. Joseph Adelson (New York: John Wiley and Sons, 1980), pp. 295–343.

CHAPTER 4
1. The perspective of developmental constructivism, reflecting the work of Jean Piaget, is described in: Irving E. Sigel and Rodney R. Cocking, *Cognitive Development from Childhood to Adolescence: A Constructivist Perspective* (New York: Holt, Rinehart and Winston, 1977).
2. This question echoes that of Westerhoff. John Westerhoff, "A Call to Catechesis." *The Living Light*, 14, 3 (Fall 1977), p. 357.

CHAPTER 5
1. The material in this section is influenced by: Thomas H. Groome, *Christian Religious Education: Sharing Our Story and Vision* (San Francisco: Harper and Row, 1980), pp. 184–201.

CHAPTER 11
1. Quoted from: Diana Baumrind, "A Dialectical Materialist's Perspective on Knowing Social Reality" in *Moral Development*, ed. William Damon (San Francisco: Jossey-Bass, Inc., 1978), p. 64.

bibliography

ACHTEMEIER, PAUL J. *The Inspiration of Scripture*. Philadelphia: The Westminster Press, 1980.

BAUMRIND, DIANA. "A Dialectical Materialist's Perspective on Knowing Social Reality." In *Moral Development*, edited by William Damon. San Francisco: Jossey-Bass, Inc., (1978): pp. 61–82.

BOYS, MARY C. AND GROOME, THOMAS H. "Principles and Pedagogy in Biblical Study." *Religious Education*, 77, 5 (September–October 1982): pp. 486–507.

CHANDLER, MICHAEL J. "Relativism and the Problem of Epistemological Loneliness." *Human Development* 18 (1975): pp. 171–180.

EVERDING, H. EDWARD, JR. "A Hermeneutical Approach to Educational Theory." In *Foundations for Christian Education in an Era of Change*, edited by Marvin J. Taylor, pp. 41–53. Nashville: Abingdon, 1976.

FEATHER, NORMAN T. "Values in Adolescence." In *Handbook of Adolescent Psychology*, edited by Joseph Adelson, pp. 247–294. New York: John Wiley and Sons, 1980.

———. *Values in Education and Society*. New York: Free Press, 1975.

FOWLER, JAMES W. *Stages of Faith: The Psychology of Human Development and the Quest for Meaning*. San Francisco: Harper and Row, 1981.

GALLAGHER, JEANETTE M. AND MANSFIELD, RICHARD S. "Cognitive Development in Adolescence." In *Understanding Adolescence: Current Developments in Adolescent Psychology* (4th edition), edited by J. F. Adams, pp. 135–163. Boston: Allyn and Bacon, Inc., 1980.

GOBBEL, A. ROGER. "Catechetical Instruction: An Invitation to Thinking." *Bulletin* (Lutheran Theological Seminary at Gettysburg) 60, 1 (February 1980): pp. 32–42.

GOBBEL, A. ROGER AND GOBBEL, GERTRUDE G. "Constructing Sexuality." *Dialog* 18, 3 (Summer 1979): pp. 186–191.

GROOME, THOMAS H. *Christian Religious Education: Sharing Our Story and Vision.* San Francisco: Harper and Row, 1980.

"Hedonistic Sex, Mutual Affection Sex and Bible Sex" (A Report). *Religious Education,* 65, 2 (March–April 1970): pp. 170–176.

HELD, ANN R. "Formation of Conscience and Sexual Stereotypes." *The Living Light* 15, 2 (Summer 1978): pp. 218–230.

HOFFMAN, MARTIN L. "Empathy, Its Development and Prosocial Implications." In *Nebraska Symposium on Motivation (Vol. 25)* edited by C. Keasey, pp. 169–218. Lincoln: University of Nebraska Press, 1977.

————. "Moral Development in Adolescence." In *Handbook of Adolescent Psychology,* edited by Joseph Adelson, pp. 295–343. New York: John Wiley and Sons, 1980.

JANCOSKI, LORETTA. "Developmental Theories and Decision Making: Focus on Youth." *The Living Light* 18, 3 (Fall 1981): pp. 242–252.

JEWETT, PAUL K. *Man as Male and Female.* Grand Rapids: William B. Eerdmans Publishing Company, 1975.

LERNER, RICHARD M. AND SPANIER, GRAHAM B. *Adolescent Development: A Life-Span Perspective.* New York: McGraw-Hill, 1980.

MARCIA, JAMES E. "Identity Development in Adolescence." In *Handbook of Adolescent Psychology,* edited by Joseph Adelson, pp. 159–187. New York: John Wiley and Sons, 1980.

MCCURLEY, FOSTER R., JR. AND REUMANN, JOHN. *Word and Witness: Understanding the Bible I.* Philadelphia: Division for Parish Services, Lutheran Church in America, 1980.

MILLER, PATRICIA AND SIMON, WILLIAM. "The Development of Sexuality in Adolescence." In *Handbook of Adolescent Psychology,* edited by Joseph Adelson, pp. 383 407. New York: John Wiley and Sons, 1980.

PEEL, E. A. *The Nature of Adolescent Judgment.* New York: John Wiley and Sons, 1971.

RIDENHOUR, THOMAS E. "Exploring the Bible." In *Renewing: God's People Called to Mission,* edited by John S. Kerr, pp. 8–16. Philadelphia: Division for Parish Services, Lutheran Church in America, 1982.

————. "Exploring the Bible." In *Renewing: God's People Gathered for Mission,* edited by John S. Kerr, pp. 8–17. Philadelphia: Division for Parish Services, Lutheran Church in America, 1983.

RUSSELL, LETTY M., ed. *The Liberating Word: A Guide to Nonsexist Interpretation of the Bible.* Philadelphia: The Westminster Press, 1976.

SIGEL, IRVING E. AND COCKING, RODNEY R. *Cognitive Development from Childhood to Adolescence: A Constructivist Perspective.* New York: Holt, Rinehart and Winston, 1977.

TRIBLE, PHYLLIS. *God and the Rhetoric of Sexuality.* Philadelphia: Fortress Press, 1978.

WESTERHOFF, JOHN. "A Call to Catechesis." *The Living Light,* 14, 3 (Fall 1977): pp. 354–358.